Computing Curricula 2001
Computer Science

Final Report

December 2001

Computing Curricula 2001
Computer Science

Final Report

December 2001

The Joint Task Force on Computing Curricula
IEEE Computer Society
Association for Computing Machinery

This material is based upon work supported by the National Science Foundation under Grant No. 0003263.

IEEE
COMPUTER
SOCIETY
http://computer.org

Los Alamitos, California

Washington • Brussels • Tokyo

IEEE Computer Society Order Number BP01499
ISBN 0-7695-1499-5
Library of Congress Number 2001099729

Additional copies may be ordered from:

IEEE Computer Society
Customer Service Center
10662 Los Vaqueros Circle
P.O. Box 3014
Los Alamitos, CA 90720-1314
Tel: + 1 800 272 6657
Fax: + 1 714 821 4641
http://computer.org/
csbooks@computer.org

IEEE Service Center
445 Hoes Lane
P.O. Box 1331
Piscataway, NJ 08855-1331
Tel: + 1 732 981 0060
Fax: + 1 732 981 9667
http://shop.ieee.org/store/
customer-service@ieee.org

IEEE Computer Society
Asia/Pacific Office
Watanabe Bldg., 1-4-2
Minami-Aoyama
Minato-ku, Tokyo 107-0062
JAPAN
Tel: + 81 3 3408 3118
Fax: + 81 3 3408 3553
tokyo.ofc@computer.org

Cover art production by Joe Daigle/Studio Productions
Printed in the United States of America by The Printing House

Composition of the Curriculum 2001 Joint Task Force

Vice-President, IEEE-CS Education Activities Board
    Carl K. Chang

Chair, ACM Education Board
    Peter J. Denning

IEEE-CS delegation
    James H. Cross II (co-chair)
    Gerald Engel (co-chair and editor)
    Robert Sloan (secretary)
    Doris Carver
    Richard Eckhouse
    Willis King
    Francis Lau
    Susan Mengel
    Pradip Srimani

ACM delegation
    Eric Roberts (co-chair and editor)
    Russell Shackelford (co-chair)
    Richard Austing
    C. Fay Cover
    Gordon Davies
    Andrew McGettrick
    G. Michael Schneider
    Ursula Wolz

Endorsed by the ACM Council, November 2001.
Endorsed by the IEEE-CS Board of Governors, December 2001.

Computing Curricula 2001: Computer Science
Table of Contents

Executive Summary

This document represents the final report of the Computing Curricula 2001 project (CC2001)—a joint undertaking of the Computer Society of the Institute for Electrical and Electronic Engineers (IEEE-CS) and the Association for Computing Machinery (ACM) to develop curricular guidelines for undergraduate programs in computing. The report continues a long tradition of recommendations for academic programs in computing-related fields dating back to 1965, as described in Chapter 2 of the report.

This volume of the report outlines a set of recommendations for undergraduate programs in computer science. As described in Chapter 1, the CC2001 report will eventually consist of several volumes containing separate recommendations for other computing disciplines, including computer engineering, software engineering, and information systems. Those reports are each under the control of separate committees and will be published as they are completed.

Highlights of this report include the following:

- *The CS body of knowledge.* We have identified a body of knowledge appropriate to undergraduate computer science programs. Drawing on the structure of earlier curriculum reports, we have arranged that body of knowledge hierarchically, subdividing the field into areas, which are then broken down further into units and individual topics. An overview of the body of knowledge appears in Chapter 5.

- *The CS undergraduate core.* From the 132 units in the body of knowledge, we have selected 64 that represent core material, accounting for approximately 280 hours of instruction. As noted in our statement of principles in Chapter 4, we defined the core as the set of units for which there is a broad consensus that the material is essential to an undergraduate degree in computer science. The philosophy behind the definition of the core is described in more detail in Chapter 5.

- *Learning objectives.* For each of the units in the body of knowledge, we have developed a set of learning objectives designed to assess student achievement. These learning objectives appear as part of the description of the body of knowledge in Appendix A. In addition to the individual learning objectives, Chapter 11 outlines a more general set of objectives that all computer science graduates should be able to meet.

- *Curriculum models.* The report identifies six approaches to introductory computer science that have proven successful in practice, as described in Chapter 7. Building on that foundation, Chapter 8 offers a set of four thematic approaches for presenting the core material in intermediate-level courses. The discussion of curricular models continues in Chapter 9, which offers several models for the curriculum as a whole.

- *Course descriptions.* Appendix B contains detailed course descriptions for 47 courses that are part of the various curricular models. In addition, we have identified over 80 additional advanced courses that would be appropriate for undergraduate programs.

The process of developing the report has been highly inclusive. More than 150 people have been directly involved in the focus groups established to contribute to the process. In addition, the report has been widely reviewed by academics and practitioners through a series of three public drafts. We have also held a series of feedback sessions at conferences and meetings, including the Special Interest Group on Computer Science Education symposium (SIGCSE), the Frontiers in Education conference (FIE), the World Congress on Computers and Education (WCCE), along with smaller meetings in Europe, Asia, and various parts of the United States. These meetings have provided us with critically important feedback, which we have used to shape the final report.

Introduction

In the fall of 1998, the Computer Society of the Institute for Electrical and Electronic Engineers (IEEE-CS) and the Association for Computing Machinery (ACM) established the Joint Task Force on Computing Curricula 2001 (CC2001) to undertake a major review of curriculum guidelines for undergraduate programs in computing. The charter of the task force was expressed as follows:

> To review the Joint ACM and IEEE/CS Computing Curricula 1991 and develop a revised and enhanced version for the year 2001 that will match the latest developments of computing technologies in the past decade and endure through the next decade.

As indicated in our charter, the goal of the CC2001 effort is to revise *Computing Curricula 1991* so that it incorporates the developments of the past decade. That task has proven to be much more daunting than we had originally realized. Computing has changed dramatically over that time in ways that have a profound effect on curriculum design and pedagogy. Moreover, the scope of what we call *computing* has broadened to the point that it is difficult to define it as a single discipline. Past curriculum reports have attempted to merge such disciplines as computer science, computer engineering, and software engineering into a single report about computing education. While such an approach may have seemed reasonable ten years ago, there is no question that computing in the 21st century encompasses many vital disciplines with their own integrity and pedagogical traditions.

1.1 Overall structure of the CC2001 series

In light of the broadening scope of computing—and because the feedback we received on our initial draft strongly encouraged us to move in this direction—we have chosen to divide the CC2001 report into several volumes. This volume focuses specifically on computer science. To encompass the other disciplines that are part of the overall scope of computing and information technology, however, IEEE-CS and ACM have created additional committees to undertake similar efforts in other areas, including computer engineering, software engineering, and information systems.

Once the individual reports have been completed, representatives from all the disciplines will come together to produce an overview volume that links the series. That overview volume will contain definitions of the various computing disciplines along with an assessment of the commonalities that exist in the curricular approaches. The structure of the series as a whole is illustrated in Figure 1-1.

1.2 Overview of the CC2001 process

Developing the recommendations in this volume is primarily the responsibility of the CC2001 Task Force, the members of which are listed at the beginning of this report. Given the scale and scope of the CC2001 project, it was necessary to secure the involvement of many people, representing a wide range of constituencies and areas of expertise. To ensure the broad participation necessary for success in a project of this kind, the task force established a total of 20 focus groups, divided into two categories: knowledge focus groups (KFGs) and pedagogy focus groups (PFGs).

Figure 1-1. Overall structure of the CC2001 report

The overview document will be produced by representatives of the various disciplines after the individual reports are complete. It will focus on computing education as a whole.

This report (which you are reading now in draft) will be published in 2001 by the CC2001 Task Force.

A separate committee has been established to prepare the volume on Computer Engineering.

These reports—perhaps with additional volumes for other disciplines—will be prepared in consultation with existing curriculum committees in these areas. In many cases, these committees have already published curriculum guidelines that can easily be incorporated into the CC2001 structure.

Computing Curricula 2001

Overview

The Joint Task Force on Computing Curricula

IEEE Computer Society
Association for Computing Machinery

Computing Curricula 2001

Computer Science

The Joint Task Force on Computing Curricula

IEEE Computer Society
Association for Computing Machinery

Computing Curricula 2001

Computer Engineering

The Joint Task Force on Computing Curricula

IEEE Computer Society
Association for Computing Machinery

Computing Curricula 2001

Software Engineering

The Joint Task Force on Software Engineering Education Project (SWEEP)

Computing Curricula 2001

Information Systems

Association for Computing Machinery
Association for Information Systems
Association of Information Technology Professionals

Note: This diagram represents our vision of the eventual structure of the CC2001 report. No official organizational endorsements have yet been obtained.

1.2.1 Knowledge focus groups (KFGs)

Early in its history, the CC2001 Task Force identified a set of 14 areas that together represented the body of knowledge for computer science at the undergraduate level, as shown in Figure 1-2. For each area, the task force appointed a *knowledge focus group* composed of people with expertise and teaching experience in that domain. Each KFG was charged to prepare a report on the area from which the task force could assemble the complete CS body of knowledge. Additional details on this aspect of the process appear in Chapter 5 and Appendix A.

1.2.2 Pedagogy focus groups

Although the KFGs are essential in terms of defining the body of knowledge in each subdiscipline, they are not in themselves sufficient. Because each group looks at the field of computer science through a lens that reflects a particular specialty area, the KFG structure does not encourage the development of a broad vision of the curriculum that focuses on crosscutting themes common throughout the discipline. To develop that more holistic perspective and to address a variety of questions that transcend the boundaries of the individual subdisciplines, the CC2001 Task Force established six *pedagogy focus groups* to consider curricular issues across computer science as a whole. These groups are listed, along with their specific charges, in Figure 1-3.

The PFGs were formed later in the process than the counterpart focus groups examining the knowledge areas. The work of the PFGs , moreover, proved more difficult to carry out solely through electronic communication. With the support of a grant from the National Science Foundation, the CC2001 Task Force was able to convene a face-to-face meeting of the PFGs in June 2000, which proved valuable in developing the final reports.

1.2.3 Two-Year College Task Force

Following the release in early 2001 of a draft version of CC2001, the ACM Two-Year College Education Committee formed a joint ACM/IEEE-CS task force whose purpose was to formulate a parallel curriculum report for the two-year college setting. This task force undertook a detailed examination of the draft CC2001 guidelines, focusing on the introductory computer science topics and associated learning objectives, the mathematics content, and electives at the introductory level. The CC2001 report was subsequently influenced by the work of the two-year college task force, and that work provided the basis for parallel introductory course sequences that foster greater compatibility between two-year and four-year curricula, thereby facilitating the transfer process.

1.3 Structure of the CC2001 computer science report

This volume of the CC2001 report looks specifically at computer science. The main body of the report consists of 13 chapters. Chapter 2 begins with a survey and analysis of past reports, focusing most closely on *Computing Curricula 1991*. Chapter 3 outlines the changes that have occurred in computer science since the publication of the CC1991 report and the implications that those changes have for curriculum design and pedagogy.

Figure 1-2. The 14 knowledge focus groups

Discrete Structures (DS)	Human-Computer Interaction (HC)
Programming Fundamentals (PF)	Graphics and Visual Computing (GV)
Algorithms and Complexity (AL)	Intelligent Systems (IS)
Architecture and Organization (AR)	Information Management (IM)
Operating Systems (OS)	Social and Professional Issues (SP)
Net-Centric Computing (NC)	Software Engineering (SE)
Programming Languages (PL)	Computational Science (CN)

Figure 1-3. The six pedagogy focus groups and their charges

PFG1. Introductory topics and courses
   a. Identify the goals of the first year of study.
   b. Report on the strengths and weaknesses of the traditional programming-first approach.
   c. Provide a short list of alternative approaches that have credibility in terms of meeting those goals.
   d. Identify and/or develop one or more introductory course sequences that address the problem of dissimilar preparation of incoming students, do not rely on terminal service courses to discriminate among the various needs and backgrounds of students who are just beginning their undergraduate careers, and introduce computer science as a mainstream discipline that forms part of the academic core for a broad population of undergraduate students.
   e. Present syllabi for a short list of options for the first year of computer science study that satisfy the goals in point (a) and that can serve as models for colleges and publishers.

PFG2. Supporting topics and courses
   a. Specify a set of educational goals outside of traditional computer science that support undergraduate computer science education, such as mathematics, engineering, science, technical writing, public speaking, economics, project management, and so forth.
   b. Identify a minimal list of supporting topics deemed essential to any undergraduate computer science curriculum regardless of the nature of the institution.
   c. Present suggestions for additional supporting topics beyond the minimum that may vary depending on the type of institution, the populations an institution serves, and the number of courses that the institution is allowed to include in a program.
   d. Develop specifications for one or more sets of non-CS courses that satisfy these goals.
   e. Develop one or more models for satisfying some or all of these goals by integrating them into computing courses.

PFG3. The computing core
   a. Given the specification of the CS core as input, develop a small number of curricular models that satisfy the core requirements. Each model should consist of a short list of courses (four or five courses beyond the introductory year of study), which would be required of every computer science graduate and which would be manageable by virtually every type of undergraduate program.
   b. Develop at least one curricular model that is an alternative to the traditional approach of organizing programs around artifacts (such as courses in compilers and operating systems). Such models will consist of cross-cutting courses focused on fundamental concepts, principles, and skills.
   c. Develop at least one curricular model that uses the Internet as its unifying theme.

PFG4. Professional practices
   a. Report on those aspects of professional practices that our graduates have (or should have) assimilated as a result of current curricula.
   b. Report on what we do and do not know about supporting effective education in those professional practices.
   c. Report on how these needs can be integrated into courses in the curriculum.
   d. Report on industrial and internship work and its relationship to the development of professional practices.
   e. Report on other aspects of professionalism (including ethical, social, legal, and moral issues) and their relationship to the computer science curriculum.

PFG5. Advanced study and undergraduate research
   a. Given the definition of the CS core, develop a specification of computer science education beyond the core that is necessary and sufficient for an undergraduate degree in computer science.
   b. Develop a specification of the characteristics of graduates who have earned a four-year undergraduate degree.
   c. Include a specification of courses in both traditional and nontraditional areas that may be important for modern undergraduate CS curricula.
   d. Report on undergraduate research, including an evaluation of various existing models.

PFG6. Computing across the curriculum
   a. Articulate "the core of the core" relevant to all citizens and to various families of academic disciplines.
   b. Plan a curriculum development effort that will address rigorously the challenge of computing curricula for non-CS majors, be appropriate to institutions other than traditional four-year universities (such as two-year community colleges in the United States), and appeal to those from other computing-related disciplines.
   c. Acknowledge that this is a crucial area but one for which we cannot unilaterally develop an adequate solution.
   d. Acknowledge that this group's job is not to solve the problem but rather to plan, develop, and initiate a process that can and will lead to a solution.

In Chapter 4, we articulate a set of principles that have guided the development of CC2001 as we build on the strengths of our predecessors while avoiding some of the problems observed in previous reports. Chapters 5 and 6 present overviews of the computer science body of knowledge and the curriculum recommendations that are examined in the appendices. Chapters 7 and 8 describe the courses and approaches we recommend at the introductory and intermediate levels of the curriculum, respectively. Because these courses alone do not constitute a complete undergraduate curriculum, Chapter 9 summarizes additional courses and topics that must be included as part of the academic program. One important aspect of the complete curriculum involves the study of professional practice, which is discussed in Chapter 10. In Chapter 11, we outline characteristics that define the successful computer science graduate. Chapter 12 looks at the problem of teaching computer science and computing-related skills to students in other disciplines. Finally, Chapter 13 offers strategic and tactical suggestions for addressing the institutional challenges that affect the implementation of this report.

The bulk of the material in the report appears in two appendices. Appendix A looks in detail at the body of knowledge for undergraduate computer science. Appendix B describes the recommended courses that comprise the sample curricula. We hope that providing both the body of knowledge and course descriptions will help departments to create effective curricula more easily than using either of these sources alone.

Chapter 2
Lessons from Past Reports

In developing this report, the CC2001 Task Force did not have to start from scratch. We have benefited from past curriculum studies, and we thank the authors of those studies for their dedicated efforts. As part of our early work on *Computing Curricula 2001,* we looked carefully at the most recent curriculum studies—particulary *Computing Curricula 1991*—to get a sense of how those studies have influenced computer science education. By identifying which aspects of the previous reports have been successful and which have not, we hoped to structure the CC2001 report to maximize its impact. This chapter offers an overview of the earlier reports and the lessons we have taken from them.

2.1 Historical background

Efforts to design model curricula for programs in computer science and computer engineering began in the 1960s, shortly after the first departments in these areas were established. In 1968, following on a series of earlier studies [ACM65, COSINE67, SAC67], the Association for Computing Machinery (ACM) published *Curriculum '68* [ACM68], which offered detailed recommendations for academic programs in computer science, along with a set of course descriptions and extensive bibliographies for each topic area.

Over the next decade, computer science developed rapidly, to the point that the recommendations in *Curriculum '68* became largely obsolete. During the 1970s, both the ACM and the Computer Society of the Institute of Electrical and Electronics Engineers (IEEE-CS) appointed committees to develop revised computer science curricula. In 1977, the Education Committee of the IEEE-CS published a report for programs in computer science and engineering [EC77]. The Computer Society's report was significant in that it took a broader view of the discipline, incorporating more engineering into the curriculum and bridging the gap between software- and hardware-oriented programs. Responding to the pressures generated by the rapidly developing field, the Computer Society updated its computer science and engineering curriculum in 1983 [EAB83]. The ACM *Curriculum '68* report was superseded by a more comprehensive *Curriculum '78,* which had a substantial impact on computer science education. Among its contributions, *Curriculum '78* proposed a standard syllabus for a set of courses that encompassed the core knowledge of computer science as a discipline.

In the late 1980s, the Computer Society and ACM joined forces to undertake a more ambitious curriculum review, which was published as *Computing Curricula 1991* [Tucker91], hereafter referred to as CC1991. The CC1991 report was more comprehensive than its predecessors, but took a different approach. Unlike *Curriculum '78* and the 1983 IEEE-CS report, each of which focused on identifying a standard syllabus for individual courses, CC1991 divided the body of knowledge associated with computer science into individual *knowledge units.* Each knowledge unit in CC1991 corresponds to a topic that must be covered at some point during the undergraduate curriculum, although individual institutions have considerable flexibility to assemble the knowledge units into course structures that fit their particular needs. The appendix of the CC1991 report included 11 sample implementations that show how the knowledge units can be combined to form courses and programs to serve a variety of needs.

2.2 Evaluation of previous curriculum efforts

The decision to produce a new curriculum report was driven primarily by the enormous changes that have occurred in computer science over the past decade. At the same time, there was also a perception among some computer science educators that CC1991 was not as influential as some of its predecessors. Although CC1991 is certainly more detailed, institutions have sometimes found it harder to adopt than *Curriculum '78* and the IEEE-CS model curriculum in computer science and engineering.

To understand both the strengths and the limitations of CC1991, the task force undertook an informal survey of computer science educators. We developed a short questionnaire, which we then mailed to the chairs of all computer science departments in the United States and Canada. We also made the questionnaire available more generally through the World Wide Web, although the vast majority of the responses still came from North America. A copy of the questionnaire appears in Figure 2-1.

More than 98 percent of the respondents—we received 124 responses through the Web and about 30 responses through regular mail—supported the concept of updating the CC1991 report. The survey responses also revealed the following general reactions:

- *Knowledge units are often not as useful as course or curriculum designs.* Although many respondents indicated that they liked the concept of knowledge units as a resource, there was strong sentiment for a greater emphasis on course design along with the knowledge units. Our survey indicated that many institutions continue to work with the curricular models outlined in *Curriculum '78,* largely because it included specific course designs.

- *There is strong support for a more concrete definition of a minimal core.* CC1991 argues that all undergraduate programs in computer science should incorporate the entire collection of knowledge units in the nine areas that comprise the common requirements. If the area encompassing Introduction to a Programming Language is included, the knowledge units in the common requirements account for 283 hours of classroom time. As our discipline evolves, it is tempting to add new material to the required set, thereby increasing the number of hours mandated by the curriculum. Our survey indicated considerable support for the idea of identifying a smaller set of core topics that would serve as a foundation for more advanced study. The areas and

Figure 2-1. Questionnaire to assess the impact of Computing Curricula 1991

1. Did you use CC1991 in any way in the past?
2. If you are a college or university teacher, do you know if your department ever looked at or used CC1991?
3. If you answered yes to either question, how was it used, and what features of it were helpful?
4. Do you think there is a need to create CC2001? Why?
5. CC1991 had 10 main content areas. Do you think any new areas should be added? Any existing area deleted? Any existing area updated?
6. Do you believe CC2001 should provide guidelines about a minimal core? If so, what would that core include?
7. Do you have any suggestions about the format? CC1991 was designed in terms of knowledge units along with possible model curricula in terms of those knowledge units.
8. Have you any other comments or suggestions for updating CC1991?

structure of the more advanced courses could vary markedly depending on the nature of the institution, the academic program, and the needs and interests of individual students.

- *Curriculum reports should pay greater attention to accreditation criteria for computer science programs.* Accreditation was an important issue for many survey respondents in the United States. It is important to note, however, that the structure of accreditation has changed markedly with the new criteria proposed by the Accreditation Board for Engineering and Technology (ABET) and the Computing Sciences Accreditation Board (CSAB) [ABET2000, CSAB2000]. Under the new guidelines, programs will be allowed much greater flexibility than they have enjoyed in the past, but each program must provide a coherent rationale for its curriculum and demonstrate that the curriculum meets the program's stated goals. This report is designed not only to help institutions design their computer science curriculum but also to assist them in the preparation of the underlying rationale they need to meet the new accreditation criteria. We also hope that this report will prove useful to accreditation bodies in other parts of the world.

Chapter 3
Changes in the Computer Science Discipline

As we enter the new millennium, computer science is an enormously vibrant field. From its inception just half a century ago, computing has become the defining technology of our age. Computers are integral to modern culture and are the primary engine behind much of the world's economic growth. The field, moreover, continues to evolve at an astonishing pace. New technologies are introduced continually, and existing ones become obsolete almost as soon as they appear.

The rapid evolution of the discipline has a profound effect on computer science education, affecting both content and pedagogy. When CC1991 was published, for example, networking was not seen as a major topic area, accounting for only six hours in the common requirements. The lack of emphasis on networking is not particularly surprising. After all, networking was not yet a mass-market phenomenon, and the World Wide Web was little more than an idea in the minds of its creators. Today, networking and the Web have become the underpinning for much of our economy. They have become critical foundations of computer science, and it is impossible to imagine that undergraduate programs would not devote significantly more time to this topic. At the same time, the existence of the Web has changed the nature of the educational process itself. Modern networking technology enhances everyone's ability to communicate and gives people throughout the world unprecedented access to information. In most academic programs today—not only in computer science but in other fields as well—networking technology has become an essential pedagogical tool.

The charter of the CC2001 Task Force requires us to "review the Joint ACM and IEEE/CS Computing Curricula 1991 and develop a revised and enhanced version for the year 2001 that will match the latest developments of computing technologies." To do so, we felt it was important to spend part of our effort getting a sense of what aspects of computer science had changed over the past decade. We believe that these changes fall into two categories—technical and cultural—each of which has a significant effect on computer science education.

3.1 Technical changes

Much of the change that affects computer science comes from advances in technology. Many of these advances are part of an ongoing evolutionary process that has continued for many years. Moore's Law—the 1965 prediction by Intel founder Gordon Moore that microprocessor chip density would double every 18 months—continues to hold true. As a result, we have seen exponential increases in available computing power that have made it possible to solve problems that would have been out of reach just a few years ago. Other changes in the discipline, such as the rapid growth of networking after the appearance of the World Wide Web, are more dramatic, suggesting that change also occurs in revolutionary steps. Both evolutionary and revolutionary change affects the body of knowledge required for computer science and the educational process.

Technical advances over the past decade has increased the importance of many curricular topics, such as the following:

- The World Wide Web and its applications
- Networking technologies, particularly those based on TCP/IP
- Graphics and multimedia

- Embedded systems
- Relational databases
- Interoperability
- Object-oriented programming
- Use of sophisticated application programmer interfaces (APIs)
- Human-computer interaction
- Software safety
- Security and cryptography
- Application domains

As these topics increase in prominence, it is tempting to include them as undergraduate requirements. Unfortunately, the restrictions of most degree programs make it difficult to add new topics without taking others away. It is often impossible to cover new areas without reducing the amount of time devoted to more traditional topics whose importance has arguably faded with time. The CC2001 Task Force has therefore sought to reduce the required level of coverage in most areas so as to make room for new areas. This point is discussed further in Chapter 4.

3.2 Cultural changes

Computing education is also affected by changes in the cultural and sociological context in which it occurs. The following changes, for example, have all had an influence on the nature of the educational process:

- *Changes in pedagogy enabled by new technologies.* The technical changes that have driven the recent expansion of computing have direct implications on the culture of education. Computer networks, for example, make distance education much more feasible, leading to enormous growth in this area. Those networks also make it much easier to share curricular resources among widely distributed institutions. Technology also affects the nature of pedagogy. Demonstration software, computer projection, and individual laboratory stations have made a significant difference in the way computer science is taught. The design of computer science curricula must take into account those changing technologies.

- *The dramatic growth of computing throughout the world.* Computing has expanded enormously over the past decade. For example, in 1990, few households—even in the United States—were connected to the Internet. A U.S. Department of Commerce study [NTIA99] reported that by 1999 over a third of all Americans had Internet access from some location. Similar growth patterns have occurred in other countries as well. The rapid expansion in the level of computer access brings with it many changes that affect education, including a general increase in the familiarity of students with computing and its applications along with a widening gap between the skill levels of those who have access and those who do not.

- *The growing economic influence of computing technology.* The dramatic excitement surrounding high-tech industry—so evident in the Internet startup fever of the late 1990s—has significant effects on education and its available resources. The enormous demand for computing expertise and the vision of large fortunes to be made have attracted more students to the field, including some who have little intrinsic interest in the material. At the same time, the demand from industry has made it harder for most institutions to attract and retain faculty, imposing significant limits on the capacity of those institutions to meet the demand.

- *Greater acceptance of computer science as an academic discipline.* In its early years, computer science—a new discipline without the historical foundations that support most academic fields—had to struggle for legitimacy in many institutions. To some extent, this problem persisted through the creation of CC1991, which was closely associated with the *Computing as a Discipline* report [Denning89]. Partly as a result of computing technology's emergence into the cultural and economic mainstream, the battle for legitimacy has largely been won. On many campuses, computer science has become one of the largest and most active disciplines. There is no longer any need to defend the inclusion of computer science education within the academy. The problem today is to find ways to meet the demand.

- *Broadening of the discipline.* As our discipline has grown and gained legitimacy, it has also broadened in scope. In its early years, computing was primarily focused on computer science. Over the years, an increasing number of fields have become part of a larger, more encompassing discipline of computing. Our CC2001 Task Force believes that a critical component of our work is to understand how those specialties fit together and how the broadening of the discipline affects computer science education.

Chapter 4
Principles

Based on our analysis of past curriculum reports and the changes in our discipline, the CC2001 Task Force has adopted the following principles to guide our work:

1. *Computing is a broad field that extends well beyond the boundaries of computer science.* A single report that covers only computer science cannot address the full range of issue that colleges and universities must consider as they seek to address their computing curricula. Additional reports in this series will be required to cover other computing disciplines.

2. *Computer science draws its foundations from a wide variety of disciplines.* Undergraduate study of computer science requires students to utilize concepts from many different fields. All computer science students must learn to integrate theory and practice, to recognize the importance of abstraction, and to appreciate the value of good engineering design.

3. *The rapid evolution of computer science requires an ongoing review of the corresponding curriculum.* Given the pace of change in our discipline, updating the curriculum once a decade has become unworkable. The professional associations in this discipline must establish an ongoing review process that allows individual components of the curriculum recommendations to be updated on a recurring basis.

4. *A computer science curriculum must be sensitive to changes in technology, new developments in pedagogy, and the importance of lifelong learning.* In a field that evolves as rapidly as computer science, educational institutions must adopt explicit strategies for responding to change. Institutions, for example, must recognize the importance of remaining abreast of progress in both technology and pedagogy, subject to the constraints of available resources. Computer science education, moreover, must seek to prepare students for lifelong learning that will enable them to move beyond today's technology to meet the challenges of the future.

5. *CC2001 must go beyond knowledge units to offer significant guidance in terms of individual course design.* Although the knowledge-unit structure used in CC1991 can serve as a useful framework, most institutions need more detailed guidance. For such institutions, CC2001 will be effective only to the extent that it defines a small set of alternative models—preferably between two and four—that assemble the knowledge units into reasonable, easily implemented courses. Specifying a set of well-defined models will make it easier for institutions to share pedagogical strategies and tools. It will also provide a framework for publishers who provide the textbooks and other materials for those courses.

6. *CC2001 should seek to identify the fundamental skills and knowledge that all computing students must possess.* Despite the enormous breadth of computer science, there are nonetheless concepts and skills that are common to computing as a whole. CC2001 must define the common themes of the discipline and make sure that all undergraduate programs include this material.

7. *The required body of knowledge must be made as small as possible.* As computer science has grown, the number of topics required in the undergraduate curriculum has grown as well. Over the last decade, computer science has expanded to such an extent that it is no longer possible simply to add new topics without taking others away. We believe that the best strategic approach is to *reduce* the number of topics in the required core so that it consists only of those topics for which there is a broad consensus that the topic is essential to undergraduate degrees. Coverage of the core

is not limited to introductory courses, but will extend throughout the curriculum. At the same time, it is important to recognize that this core does not constitute a complete undergraduate curriculum, but must be supplemented by additional courses that may vary by institution, degree program, or individual student.

8. *CC2001 must strive to be international in scope.* Despite the fact that curricular requirements differ from country to country, CC2001 is intended to be useful to computing educators throughout the world. Although it will be strongly influenced by educational practice in the United States, we will make every effort to ensure that the curriculum recommendations are sensitive to national and cultural differences so that they will be applicable throughout the world.

9. *The development of CC2001 must be broadly based.* To be successful, the process of creating the CC2001 recommendations must include participation from different constituencies including industry, government, and the full range of higher educational institutions involved in computer science education.

10. *CC2001 must include professional practice as an integral component of the undergraduate curriculum.* These practices encompass a wide range of activites including management, ethics and values, written and oral communication, working as part of a team, and remaining current in a rapidly changing discipline. We further endorse the position articulated in the CC1991 report that "mastery of the discipline includes not only an understanding of basic subject matter, but also an understanding of the applicability of the concepts to real-world problems."

11. *CC2001 must include discussions of strategies and tactics for implementation along with high-level recommendations.* Although it is important for Computing Curricula 2001 to articulate a broad vision of computing education, the success of any curriculum depends heavily on implementation details. CC2001 must provide institutions with advice on the practical concerns of setting up a curriculum by including sections on strategy and tactics along with technical descriptions of the curricular material.

As one would expect in any project of this scale, it is clear in retrospect that the CC2001 Task Force has been more successful in implementing some of these principles than we have in others. We have, for example, been less successful in terms of producing an international document than we had hoped. The structure of undergraduate degrees varies around the world, to the point that it is impossible to articulate a single set of recommendations that would work globally. Although we have included in Chapter 9 examples of curricular implementations designed for use in other countries, the structure of computing education in the United States has had a profound impact on the report. Similarly, we were unable to get as much feedback and involvement from industry as we would like. We do, however, see curriculum development as an ongoing process and hope that companies can become more engaged in the curriculum-development process with individual institutions.

At the same time, we believe that we have maintained our commitment to keep the core to a manageable size while ensuring that graduates have a solid foundation in the field. Moreover, we are confident that Appendix A and Appendix B will provide enough detail about the underlying material and the structure of appropriate courses to be of value to curriculum planners throughout the world.

Chapter 5
Overview of the CS Body of Knowledge

In developing an undergraduate curriculum in computer science, the first step is to identify and organize the material that would be appropriate for that level. As discussed in Chapter 1, the CC2001 Task Force sought to accomplish this goal by convening a set of knowledge focus groups, assigning to each one the responsibility of defining the body of knowledge associated with one of the following areas:

Discrete Structures (DS)
Programming Fundamentals (PF)
Algorithms and Complexity (AL)
Architecture and Organization (AR)
Operating Systems (OS)
Net-Centric Computing (NC)
Programming Languages (PL)
Human-Computer Interaction (HC)
Graphics and Visual Computing (GV)
Intelligent Systems (IS)
Information Management (IM)
Social and Professional Issues (SP)
Software Engineering (SE)
Computational Science and Numerical Methods (CN)

Each KFG submitted a report to the CC2001 Task Force, which reviewed those reports to determine whether the recommendations made by that group was appropriate in the context of the curriculum as a whole.

5.1 Structure of the body of knowledge

The CS body of knowledge is organized hierarchically into three levels. The **area**—the highest level of the hierarchy—represents a particular disciplinary subfield. Each area is identified by a two-letter abbreviation, such as OS (operating systems) or PL (programming languages). The areas are broken down into smaller divisions called **units,** which represent individual thematic modules within an area. Each unit is identified by adding a numeric suffix to the area name; as an example, OS3 is a unit on *concurrency*. Each unit is further subdivided into a set of **topics**—the hierarchy's lowest level.

5.1.1 Core and elective units

As discussed in Chapter 4, one of our goals in proposing curricular recommendations is to keep the required component of the body of knowledge as small as possible. To implement this principle, the CC2001 Task Force has defined a minimal **core** consisting of those units for which there is a broad consensus that the corresponding material is essential to anyone obtaining an undergraduate degree in this field. Units that are taught as part of an undergraduate program but which fall outside the core are considered to be **elective.**

In discussing the CC2001 recommendations during their development, we have found that it helps to emphasize the following points:

- *The core refers to those units required of all students in all computer science degree programs.* Several topics that are important in the education of many students are not included in the core. This lack of inclusion in the core does not imply a negative judgment about the value, importance, or relevance of those topics. Rather, it simply means that there was not a broad consensus that the topic should be required of *every* student in *every* computer science degree program.

- *The core is not a complete curriculum.* Because the core is defined as minimal, it does not, by itself, constitute a complete undergraduate curriculum.

- *The core must be supplemented by additional material.* Every undergraduate program must include additional elective topics from the body of knowledge. The CC2001 report does not define what those topics must be, as this additional work can and should vary based on institutional mission, the areas of concentration offered by a given institution, and individual student choice.

- *Core units are not necessarily those taken in a set of introductory courses early in the undergraduate curriculum.* Although many of the units defined as core are indeed introductory, there are also some core units that clearly must be covered only after students have developed significant background in the field. For example, the task force believes that all students must develop a significant application at some point during their undergraduate program. The material that is essential to successful management of projects at this scale is therefore part of the core, since it is required of all students. At the same time, the project course experience is very likely to come toward the end of a student's undergraduate program. Similarly, introductory courses may include elective units alongside the coverage of core material. The designation *core* simply means *required* and says nothing about the level of the course in which it appears.

5.1.2 Assessing the time required to cover a unit

To give readers a sense of the time required to cover a particular unit, the CC2001 report must define a metric that establishes a standard of measurement. Choosing such a metric has proven difficult, because no standard measure is recognized throughout the world. For consistency with the earlier curriculum reports, the task force has chosen to express time in **hours,** corresponding to the in-class time required to present the material in a traditional lecture-oriented format. To dispel any potential confusion, however, it is important to underscore the following observations about the use of lecture hours as a measure:

- *The task force does not seek to endorse the lecture format.* Even though we have used a metric with its roots in a classical, lecture-oriented form, the task force believes that there are other styles—particularly given recent improvements in educational technology—that can be at least as effective. For some of these styles, the notion of *hours* may be difficult to apply. Even so, the time specifications should at least serve as a comparative measure, in the sense that a 5-hour unit will presumably take roughly five times as much time to cover as a 1-hour unit, independent of the teaching style.

- *The hours specified do not include time spent outside of class.* The time assigned to a unit does not include the instructor's preparation time or the time students spend outside of class. As a general guideline, the amount of out-of-class work is approximately three times the in-class time. Thus, a unit that is listed as requiring 3 hours will typically entail a total of 12 hours (3 in class and 9 outside).

- *The hours listed for a unit represent a minumum level of coverage.* The time measurements we have assigned for each unit should be interpreted as the *minimum* amount of time necessary to enable a student to achieve the learning objectives for that unit. It is always appropriate to spend more time on a unit than the mandated minimum.

5.1.3 Packaging units into courses

The structure and format of courses vary significantly from institution to institution and from country to country. Even within the United States, some colleges and universities use a semester system while others follow a shorter quarter system. Under either system, there can be differences in the number of weeks in a semester, the number of lectures in a week, and the number of minutes in a lecture.

For the purposes of this report, we assume that a **course** meets three times a week over a 15-week semester and that the individual class meetings run somewhere between 50 minutes and an hour. This schedule is typical for a 3-credit semester course in the United States. Given that some of the available time will be taken up with examinations and other activities, we have assumed that 40 hours of lecture are available during the semester. In addition, students are expected to devote three hours of time outside of class for each in-class hour, which means that each student is expected to invest 160 hours in each course. Other countries use different metrics for expressing the expected level of work. In the United Kingdom, for example, a course described in this report would correspond to 15-16 points under the Credit Accumulation and Transfer Scheme (CATS).

5.2 Summary of the CS body of knowledge

A summary of the body of knowledge—showing the areas, units, which units are core, and the minimum time required for each—appears in Figure 5-1. The details of the body of knowledge appear in Appendix A.

Figure 5-1. Computer science body of knowledge with core topics underlined

DS. Discrete Structures (43 core hours)
DS1. Functions, relations, and sets (6)
DS2. Basic logic (10)
DS3. Proof techniques (12)
DS4. Basics of counting (5)
DS5. Graphs and trees (4)
DS6. Discrete probability (6)

PF. Programming Fundamentals (38 core hours)
PF1. Fundamental programming constructs (9)
PF2. Algorithms and problem solving (6)
PF3. Fundamental data structures (14)
PF4. Recursion (5)
PF5. Event-driven programming (4)

AL. Algorithms and Complexity (31 core hours)
AL1. Basic algorithmic analysis (4)
AL2. Algorithmic strategies (6)
AL3. Fundamental computing algorithms (12)
AL4. Distributed algorithms (3)
AL5. Basic computability (6)
AL6. The complexity classes P and NP
AL7. Automata theory
AL8. Advanced algorithmic analysis
AL9. Cryptographic algorithms
AL10. Geometric algorithms
AL11. Parallel algorithms

AR. Architecture and Organization (36 core hours)
AR1. Digital logic and digital systems (6)
AR2. Machine level representation of data (3)
AR3. Assembly level machine organization (9)
AR4. Memory system organization and architecture (5)
AR5. Interfacing and communication (3)
AR6. Functional organization (7)
AR7. Multiprocessing and alternative architectures (3)
AR8. Performance enhancements
AR9. Architecture for networks and distributed systems

OS. Operating Systems (18 core hours)
OS1. Overview of operating systems (2)
OS2. Operating-system principles (2)
OS3. Concurrency (6)
OS4. Scheduling and dispatch (3)
OS5. Memory management (5)
OS6. Device management
OS7. Security and protection
OS8. File systems
OS9. Real-time and embedded systems
OS10. Fault tolerance
OS11. System performance evaluation
OS12. Scripting

NC. Net-Centric Computing (15 core hours)
NC1. Introduction to net-centric computing (2)
NC2. Communication and networking (7)
NC3. Network security (3)
NC4. The Web as an example of client-server computing (3)
NC5. Building Web applications
NC6. Network management
NC7. Compression and decompression
NC8. Multimedia data technologies
NC9. Wireless and mobile computing

PL. Programming Languages (21 core hours)
PL1. Overview of programming languages (2)
PL2. Virtual machines (1)
PL3. Introduction to language translation (2)
PL4. Declarations and types (3)
PL5. Abstraction mechanisms (3)
PL6. Object-oriented programming (10)
PL7. Functional programming
PL8. Language translation systems
PL9. Type systems
PL10. Programming language semantics
PL11. Programming language design

Note: The numbers in parentheses represent the minimum number of hours required to cover this material in a lecture format. It is always appropriate to include mor

HC. Human-Computer Interaction (8 core hours)
HC1. Foundations of human-computer interaction (6)
HC2. Building a simple graphical user interface (2)
HC3. Human-centered software evaluation
HC4. Human-centered software development
HC5. Graphical user-interface design
HC6. Graphical user-interface programming
HC7. HCI aspects of multimedia systems
HC8. HCI aspects of collaboration and communication

GV. Graphics and Visual Computing (3 core hours)
GV1. Fundamental techniques in graphics (2)
GV2. Graphic systems (1)
GV3. Graphic communication
GV4. Geometric modeling
GV5. Basic rendering
GV6. Advanced rendering
GV7. Advanced techniques
GV8. Computer animation
GV9. Visualization
GV10. Virtual reality
GV11. Computer vision

IS. Intelligent Systems (10 core hours)
IS1. Fundamental issues in intelligent systems (1)
IS2. Search and constraint satisfaction (5)
IS3. Knowledge representation and reasoning (4)
IS4. Advanced search
IS5. Advanced knowledge representation and reasoning
IS6. Agents
IS7. Natural language processing
IS8. Machine learning and neural networks
IS9. AI planning systems
IS10. Robotics

IM. Information Management (10 core hours)
IM1. Information models and systems (3)
IM2. Database systems (3)
IM3. Data modeling (4)
IM4. Relational databases
IM5. Database query languages
IM6. Relational database design
IM7. Transaction processing
IM8. Distributed databases
IM9. Physical database design
IM10. Data mining
IM11. Information storage and retrieval
IM12. Hypertext and hypermedia
IM13. Multimedia information and systems
IM14. Digital libraries

SP. Social and Professional Issues (16 core hours)
SP1. History of computing (1)
SP2. Social context of computing (3)
SP3. Methods and tools of analysis (2)
SP4. Professional and ethical responsibilities (3)
SP5. Risks and liabilities of computer-based systems (2)
SP6. Intellectual property (3)
SP7. Privacy and civil liberties (2)
SP8. Computer crime
SP9. Economic issues in computing
SP10. Philosophical frameworks

SE. Software Engineering (31 core hours)
SE1. Software design (8)
SE2. Using APIs (5)
SE3. Software tools and environments (3)
SE4. Software processes (2)
SE5. Software requirements and specifications (4)
SE6. Software validation (3)
SE7. Software evolution (3)
SE8. Software project management (3)
SE9. Component-based computing
SE10. Formal methods
SE11. Software reliability
SE12. Specialized systems development

CN. Computational Science (no core hours)
CN1. Numerical analysis
CN2. Operations research
CN3. Modeling and simulation
CN4. High-performance computing

Chapter 6
Overview of the Curricular Models

The body of knowledge presented in Chapter 5 does not by itself constitute a curriculum. To be useful, the CC2001 report must also define detailed course implementations and strategies for assembling the individual courses into a complete undergraduate curriculum. This chapter presents a brief description of the overall philosophy behind the proposed curricular models. The course descriptions appear in Appendix B.

6.1 Overall structure of the model curricula

The courses described in this report are divided into three categories according to the level at which they occur in the curriculum. Courses designated as *introductory* are typically entry-level courses offered in the first or second year of a college or university curriculum. Courses listed as *intermediate* are usually second- or third-year courses and build a foundation for further study in the field. Courses designated as *advanced* are taken in later years and focus on those topics that require significant preparation in terms of earlier coursework.

While these distinctions are easy to understand in their own right, it is important to recognize that there is no necessary relationship between the level of the course and the notions of *core* and *elective,* which apply only to units in the body of knowledge. Although introductory and intermediate courses will certainly concentrate on core material, it is perfectly reasonable to include some elective material even in the earliest courses. Similarly, advanced courses will sometimes include some core material. These designations are independent and should not be confused.

6.2 Overview of the implementation strategies

The point of establishing the distinction among introductory, intermediate, and advanced courses is to provide natural boundaries for selecting implementation strategies. This report, for example, defines six distinct instantiations of the introductory curriculum and four thematic approaches to the intermediate courses. These implementations and their relationship in the structure of the curriculum as a whole are illustrated in Figure 6-1. The idea behind this structure is to offer greater flexibility by making it possible to start with any of the introductory approaches and then follow up that introduction with any of the intermediate approaches.

Figure 6-1. Course levels and implementation strategies

Introductory courses	Imperative first	Objects first	Functional first	Breadth first	Algorithms first	Hardware first
Intermediate courses	Topic-based approach		Compressed approach		Systems-based approach	Web-based approach
Advanced courses	Additional courses used to complete the undergraduate program					

6.3 Managing the transition between different strategies

Given that the implementation strategies adopt different approaches and cover different material, it is difficult to make the various tracks directly interchangeable. To offer institutions as much flexibility as possible, we have tried to eliminate significant transition problems by adopting the following policies:

- We have established a set of expectations for the introductory approaches in the form of a set of units and topics that each of those approaches must cover. The details of this coverage are outlined in Chapter 7. Given these guidelines for the introductory coverage, intermediate courses can always depend on a certain level of preparation for students emerging from any of the introductory tracks. This definition of a common background at the end of a student's introductory work should also make it easier for institutions to meet the needs of students transferring from other programs.

- We have tried to leave unscheduled time in each course syllabus, both to give instructors flexibility and to allow for the inclusion of transitional material.

- We have allowed the material covered at the various levels of the curriculum to overlap to a certain extent. If an intermediate or advanced course depends on material that is covered by some but not all of the introductory tracks, we have included explicit coverage of that material in the follow-on course to ensure that all possible combinations of strategies can be made to work.

6.4 Covering the core

As illustrated in Figure 6-1, a complete undergraduate curriculum consists of an introductory phase to establish basic foundations for further study, an intermediate phase to cover most of the core units in the body of knowledge, and additional advanced courses to round out the curriculum. Institutions that adopt the CC2001 model will typically begin by choosing an implementation for the introductory phase and an implementation for the intermediate phase. In most cases, institutions will then adapt each of these implementations to fit the particular characteristics of the institution, the preferences of the faculty, and the needs of the students. In doing so, it is important to ensure that the curriculum that results includes at least the minimum coverage specified in the core of the body of knowledge. If specific core units are not included in the introductory and intermediate phase, the institution must then ensure that students acquire this material in advanced courses and set the requirements for graduation accordingly. Beyond the coverage of the computer science core, institutions must ensure that students acquire the necessary background in other areas, as described in Chapter 9.

Figures 6-2 and 6-3 show two examples of how to combine the various strategies to cover the computer science core. The model in Figure 6-2 uses the imperative-first implementation for the introductory phase and a traditional topics-based model for the intermediate courses; the model in Figure 6-3 uses an objects-first introductory strategy and the compressed approach for the intermediate level. Other combinations will work as well. To help potential adopters determine whether a set of courses covers the core, the CC2001 Web site includes a curriculum worksheet implemented as a Java applet.

The tables shown in Figures 6-2 and 6-3 also illustrate the importance of redundant coverage in ensuring that the individual models are interchangeable. The final column in each table shows the number of additional hours allocated to the various units under that combination. The entry for PL3 (Introduction to language translation) in Figure 6-2, for example, indicates that the two core hours assigned to this unit are included in both CS111I and CS210T. Adopters choosing this pair of strategies could either leave the coverage out of one of the courses, thereby making time for additional topics, or include it in both to reinforce the students' understanding of the material.

Figure 6-2. Coverage of core units
Imperative-first introduction
Traditional topic-based approach

Topic	CS111. Intro to Programming	CS112. Data Abstraction	CS115. Discrete Structures	CS210. Algorithm Analysis	CS220. Computer Architecture	CS225. Operating Systems	CS230. Net-centric Computing	CS260. Artificial Intelligence	CS270. Databases	CS280. Social and Prof Issues	CS290. Software Development	CS490. Capstone Project	Total	Extra hours
DS1. Functions, relations, and sets			6										6	
DS2. Basic logic			10										10	
DS3. Proof techniques			9	3									12	
DS4. Basics of counting			5										5	
DS5. Graphs and trees		2		4									6	+2
DS6. Discrete probability			6										6	
PF1. Fundamental programming constructs	9												9	
PF2. Algorithms and problem-solving	3			3									6	
PF3. Fundamental data structures	6	6		3									15	+1
PF4. Recursion		5											5	
PF5. Event-driven programming							2				4		6	+2
AL1. Basic algorithmic analysis		2		2									4	
AL2. Algorithmic strategies				6									6	
AL3. Fundamental computing algorithms	2	4		6									12	
AL4. Distributed algorithms						3							3	
AL5. Basic computability	1			6									7	+1
AR1. Digital logic and digital systems			3		3								6	
AR2. Machine level representation of data	1				3								4	+1
AR3. Assembly level machine organization	2				9								11	+2
AR4. Memory system organization and architecture					5								5	
AR5. Interfacing and communication					3								3	
AR6. Functional organization					7								7	
AR7. Multiprocessing and alternative architectures					3								3	
OS1. Overview of operating systems						2							2	
OS2. Operating system principles						2							2	
OS3. Concurrency						6							6	
OS4. Scheduling and dispatch						3							3	
OS5. Memory management						5							5	
NC1. Introduction to net-centric computing							2						2	
NC2. Communication and networking							7						7	
NC3. Network security							3						3	
NC4. The Web as an example of client-server computing							3						3	
PL1. Overview of programming languages	1	1											2	
PL2. Virtual machines		1											1	
PL3. Introduction to language translation		2		2									4	+2
PL4. Declarations and types	1	2											3	
PL5. Abstraction mechanisms	2	1											3	
PL6. Object-oriented programming	3	7					2						12	+2
HC1. Foundations of human-computer interaction									2		6	2	10	+4
HC2. Building a simple graphical user interface											2		2	
GV1. Fundamental techniques in graphics	2										2		4	+2
GV2. Graphic systems											1		1	
IS1. Fundamental issues in intelligent systems								1					1	
IS2. Search and constraint satisfaction								5					5	
IS3. Knowledge representation and reasoning								4					4	
IM1. Information models and systems									3				3	
IM2. Database systems									3				3	
IM3. Data modeling									4				4	
SP1. History of computing	1										1		2	+1
SP2. Social context of computing										3			3	
SP3. Methods and tools of analysis										2			2	
SP4. Professional and ethical responsibilities										3			3	
SP5. Risks and liabilities of computer-based systems										2			2	
SP6. Intellectual property										3	3		6	+3
SP7. Privacy and civil liberties										2	2		4	+2
SE1. Software design	2	2									2	4	10	+2
SE2. Using APIs		2									3	3	8	+3
SE3. Software tools and environments	1	2									2	3	8	+5
SE4. Software processes												2	2	
SE5. Software requirements and specifications	1										2	2	5	+1
SE6. Software validation	1										1	3	5	+2
SE7. Software evolution											2	2	4	+1
SE8. Software project management											2	3	5	+2
Total	39	39	39	35	33	21	19	10	17	16	29	24		

Figure 6-3. Coverage of core units
Objects-first introduction
Compressed approach

	CS111 o. OO Programming	CS112 o. OO Design	CS115. Discrete Structures	CS210 c. Algorithm Analysis	CS220 c. Computer Architecture	CS226 c. OS and Networking	CS262 c. Info+Knowledge Mgmt	CS262 c. Software Dev and Practice	Total	Extra hours
DS1. Functions, relations, and sets			6						6	
DS2. Basic logic			10						10	
DS3. Proof techniques			9	3					12	
DS4. Basics of counting			5						5	
DS5. Graphs and trees				4					4	
DS6. Discrete probability			6						6	
PF1. Fundamental programming constructs	7	2							9	
PF2. Algorithms and problem-solving	2	2		3					7	+1
PF3. Fundamental data structures	3	8		3					14	
PF4. Recursion	2	3							5	
PF5. Event-driven programming		2				2		2	6	+2
AL1. Basic algorithmic analysis		2		2					4	
AL2. Algorithmic strategies		2		6					8	+2
AL3. Fundamental computing algorithms	3	3		6					12	
AL4. Distributed algorithms						3			3	
AL5. Basic computability	1			6					7	+1
AR1. Digital logic and digital systems			3		3				6	
AR2. Machine level representation of data					3				3	
AR3. Assembly level machine organization					9				9	
AR4. Memory system organization and architecture					5				5	
AR5. Interfacing and communication					3				3	
AR6. Functional organization					7				7	
AR7. Multiprocessing and alternative architectures					3				3	
OS1. Overview of operating systems						2			2	
OS2. Operating system principles						2			2	
OS3. Concurrency						6			6	
OS4. Scheduling and dispatch						3			3	
OS5. Memory management						5			5	
NC1. Introduction to net-centric computing						2			2	
NC2. Communication and networking						7			7	
NC3. Network security						3			3	
NC4. The Web as an example of client-server computing						3			3	
PL1. Overview of programming languages		2							2	
PL2. Virtual machines		1							1	
PL3. Introduction to language translation				2					2	
PL4. Declarations and types	2	1							3	
PL5. Abstraction mechanisms	1	2							3	
PL6. Object-oriented programming	8	4				2			14	+4
HC1. Foundations of human-computer interaction		1					4	2	7	+1
HC2. Building a simple graphical user interface								2	2	
GV1. Fundamental techniques in graphics	2							2	4	+2
GV2. Graphic systems								1	1	
IS1. Fundamental issues in intelligent systems							1		1	
IS2. Search and constraint satisfaction							5		5	
IS3. Knowledge representation and reasoning							4		4	
IM1. Information models and systems							3		3	
IM2. Database systems							3		3	
IM3. Data modeling							4		4	
SP1. History of computing	1								1	
SP2. Social context of computing								3	3	
SP3. Methods and tools of analysis								2	2	
SP4. Professional and ethical responsibilities								3	3	
SP5. Risks and liabilities of computer-based systems	1							2	3	+1
SP6. Intellectual property							3		3	
SP7. Privacy and civil liberties							2		2	
SE1. Software design	2	2						4	8	
SE2. Using APIs	1	1						3	5	
SE3. Software tools and environments	2							1	3	
SE4. Software processes								2	2	
SE5. Software requirements and specifications		1						3	4	
SE6. Software validation		1						2	3	
SE7. Software evolution								3	3	
SE8. Software project management								3	3	
Total core hours per course	38	40	39	35	33	40	29	40		

26

Chapter 7
Introductory Courses

This chapter looks at the introductory phase of the undergraduate curriculum, when students receive their first college-level exposure to computer science. Section 7.1 outlines our overall philosophy concerning the introductory curriculum. Sections 7.2, 7.3, and 7.4 then look at three topics that are central to the design of introductory courses: the role of programming, the length of the introductory sequence, and strategies for integrating discrete mathematics. Section 7.5 enumerates the set of concepts, knowledge, and skills that we believe should be part of an ideal introductory sequence. Finally, section 7.6 enumerates a set of six introductory strategies that have proven successful in practice. This section also provides critiques of each approach to help faculty make informed decisions about which alternatives best address the needs of their students, their department, their institution, and their community.

7.1 Overall philosophy

Throughout the history of computer science education, the structure of the introductory computer science course has been the subject of intense debate. Many strategies have been proposed over the years, most of which have strong proponents and equally strong detractors. Like the problem of selecting an implementation language, recommending a strategy for the introductory year of a computer science curriculum all too often takes on the character of a religious war that generates far more heat than light.

In the interest of promoting peace among the warring factions, the CC2001 Task Force has chosen not to recommend any single approach. The truth is that no ideal strategy has yet been found, and that every approach has strengths and weaknesses. Given the current state of the art in this area, we are convinced that no one-size-fits-all approach will succeed at all institutions. Because introductory programs differ so dramatically in their goals, structure, resources, and intended audience, we need a range of strategies that have been validated by practice. Moreover, we must encourage institutions and individual faculty members to continue experimentation in this area. Given a field that changes as rapidly as computer science, pedagogical innovation is necessary for continued success.

7.2 Where does programming fit in the introductory curriculum

One of the most hotly debated questions in computer science education is the role of programming in the introductory curriculum. Throughout the history of the discipline, most introductory computer science courses have focused primarily on the development of programming skills. The adoption of a programming-first introduction arises from a number of practical and historical factors, including the following:

- Programming is an essential skill that must be mastered by anyone studying computer science. Placing it early in the curriculum ensures that students have the necessary facility with programming when they enroll in intermediate and advanced courses.

- Computer science did not become an academic discipline until after most institutions had already developed a set of introductory programming courses to serve a much wider audience. By the time our predecessors began to develop computer science curricula, the antecedents of our introductory courses had already evolved explicitly as "skills courses" dating from a time in which programming was regarded primarily as a tool. Thus, computer science curricula were often built on top of existing programming courses, which never had the opportunity to evolve into a more broadly based introduction to computer science as a field.

- The programming-first model was implicitly endorsed by the early curriculum reports through the design of their recommended courses. Curriculum '68 [ACM68], for example, begins with a course entitled "Introduction to Computing" in which the overwhelming majority of the topics are programming-related. The centrality of programming in introductory courses was further reinforced by the definitions of CS1 and CS2 in Curriculum '78 [ACM78], which defined these courses as an "Introduction to Programming" sequence.

The programming-first approach, however, has several shortcomings. The most commonly cited objections to this approach are the following:

- Focusing on programming to the exclusion of other topics gives students a limited sense of the discipline, thereby reinforcing the common misperception that "computer science equals programming."

- Theoretical topics that would enhance the students' understanding of the practical material are deferred to later points in the curriculum, when they no longer have the same immediate relevance. This limitation has implications for both majors and nonmajors. Nonmajors who take only introductory courses are deprived of any exposure to the conceptual and intellectual foundations that underlie the revolutionary technological developments driving change throughout society. For majors, the fact that theory is not introduced in the early courses fuels the bias of many students who conclude that theory is irrelevant their educational and professional needs.

- Programming courses often focus on syntax and the particular characteristics of a programming language, leading students to concentrate on these relatively unimportant details rather than the underlying algorithmic skills. This focus on details means that many students fail to comprehend the essential algorithmic model that transcends particular programming languages. Moreover, concentrating on the mechanistic details of programming constructs often leaves students to figure out the essential character of programming through an *ad hoc* process of trial and error. Such courses thus risk leaving students who are at the very beginning of their academic careers to flounder on their own with respect to the complex activity of programming.

- Introductory programming courses often oversimplify the programming process to make it accessible to beginning students, giving too little weight to design, analysis, and testing relative to the conceptually simpler process of coding. Thus, the superficial impression students take from their mastery of programming skills masks fundamental shortcomings that will limit their ability to adapt to different kinds of problems and problem-solving contexts in the future.

- Programming-intensive courses disadvantage students who have no prior exposure to computers while giving the illusion to those who have previously used computers that they know more than they really do. As a result, students who are new to computing are often overwhelmed, while students who have a prior background often simply continue bad habits.

- Programming-first approaches can lead students to believe that writing a program is the only viable approach to solving problems using a computer. The power and versatility of application programs have increased substantially in recent years, and it is important for students to recognize that such applications can be extremely effective as a problem-solving tool without the need for classical programming. This concern is particularly relevant to nonmajors, whose problem-solving abilities and sense of empowerment can be significantly increased through a knowledge of modern applications.

Despite these shortcomings, however, the programming-first model has proven to be extraordinarily durable. Even though the Computing Curricula 1991 report argued strongly for a broader introduction to the discipline, the majority of institutions continue to focus on programming in their introductory sequence. It is important to recognize that the programming-first model has some strengths that have led to its longevity. Of these, the most important are the following:

- In most institutions (at least in the United States), the primary audience of the introductory computer science course consists of students outside of computer science who are seeking to acquire programming skills. Departments that adopt a programming-first strategy can use a single course for computer science majors and nonmajors alike. If an institution adopts an alternative strategy that serves only its majors—even if it is arguably superior pedagogically—that institution may then need to offer additional programming courses to satisfy the demand from other departments.

- Programming is a prerequisite for many advanced courses in computer science. Curricular strategies that delay mastery of fundamental programming skills make it harder for students to take as many advanced courses as they would like, since they do not have the necessary background until a later point in their studies.

- Students often like programming more than other aspects of the field. Programming-based courses therefore tend to attract more students to computer science.

- Programming courses offer skills and training that meets many of the needs expressed by students, their near-term employers, and non-CS faculty.

The members of the CC2001 Task Force believe that the programming-first model is likely to remain dominant for the foreseeable future. It is therefore incumbent on the task force to provide guidance as to how to make that approach work, even as we acknowledge its inherent problems. We therefore encourage continued innovation and experimentation with alternative models aimed at addressing these problems. Alternative approaches that seek to challenge the dominance of the programming-first model, however, must take into account the pragmatic demands for applicable computing skills.

In section 7.6, we offer three implementations of a programming-first model and three that adopt an alternative paradigm. The programming-first implementations are an imperative-first approach that uses the traditional imperative paradigm, an objects-first approach that emphasizes early use of objects and object-oriented design, and a functional-first approach that introduces algorithmic concepts in a language with a simple functional syntax, such as Scheme. In each case, we have sought to identify curricular models that minimize the weaknesses of the programming-first approach by focusing on algorithmic and problem-solving concepts rather than the vagaries of language syntax. The three alternative models are a breadth-first approach that begins with a general overview of the discipline, an algorithms-first strategy that focuses on algorithms over syntax, and a hardware-first model that begins with circuits and then builds up through increasingly sophisticated layers in the abstract machine hierarchy.

7.3 The length of the introductory sequence

Although the philosophy and structure of introductory courses have varied widely over the years, one aspect of the computer science curriculum has remained surprisingly constant: the length of the introductory sequence. For several decades, the vast majority of institutions have used a two-course sequence to introduce students to computer science. In the computer science education community, these two courses are generally known as CS1 and CS2, following the lead of Curriculum '78 [ACM78]. While the content of these courses has evolved over time in response to changes in technology and pedagogical approach, the length of the sequence has remained the same.

We believe the time is right to question this two-course assumption. The number and complexity of topics that entering students must understand have increased substantially, just as the problems we ask them to solve and the tools they must use have become more sophisticated. An increasing number of institutions are finding that a two-course sequence is no longer sufficient to cover the fundamental concepts of programming, particularly when those same courses seek to offer a broader vision of the field. Expanding the introductory sequence to three courses makes it far easier to cover the growing body of knowledge in a way that gives students adequate time to assimilate the material.

The CC2001 Task Force strongly endorses the concept of moving to a three-course introductory sequence and believes that this option will prove optimal for a relatively wide range of institutions. At the same time, the three-course approach will not be right for everyone. The fact that the traditional two-course approach fits into a single year of study at semester-based institutions often makes it easier to fit the introductory material into the whole of the curriculum without interfering with the scheduling of sophomore-level courses. Similarly, the task of assigning credit for courses taken at other institutions, including advanced placement programs in secondary schools, becomes more complicated if one institution follows a two-semester calendar while the other covers the introductory material in three.

To support both two- and three-course introductions, the CC2001 Task Force has developed both options for three of the introductory tracks—imperative-first, objects-first, and breadth-first—for which the three-course model seems to have the greatest advantages. Similar extensions could be developed for the other three approaches, but are not included in this report. For each of the tracks, the two- and three-course variants are distinguished using the course numbering system. The three-course sequences for each track use the numbers 101, 102, and 103; the two-course sequences use 111 and 112.

7.4 Integrating discrete mathematics into the introductory curriculum

As we discuss in Chapter 9, the CC2001 Task Force believes it is important for computer science students to study discrete mathematics early in their academic program, preferably in the first year. There are at least two workable strategies for accomplishing this goal:

1. Require computer science students to take courses in discrete mathematics concurrently with the introductory sequence. The course descriptions in Appendix B include two implementations of a discrete mathematics course: a one-term course (CS115) that covers the bulk of the material in the Discrete Structures (DS) area of the body of knowledge in an intensive way, and a two-term sequence (CS105 and CS106) that covers the required material, together with some useful elective topics, at a slower pace that encourages greater thoroughness of coverage.

2. Integrate at least part of the material on discrete mathematics directly into the introductory computer science sequence so that students can more easily appreciate how these mathematical tools apply in practical contexts. While it is certainly advantageous to adopt this approach for certain topics, it is important to ensure that students have sufficient exposure to discrete mathematics to provide the necessary mastery of the material. Given the size of the Discrete Structures (DS) area in the body of knowledge, it is impossible to incorporate all the required topics into the introductory sequence without adding an additional course to the introductory sequence. Typical implementations will therefore incorporate some material into the computer science sequence but retain a one-term course in discrete structures to

complete the coverage. The three-course implementation of the breadth-first approach (CS101B/102B/103B) adopts this model of integrating the mathematical material directly into the introductory courses.

7.5 Expectations of the introductory curriculum

Despite the ongoing debates over pedagogical approaches, there are many values that virtually all advocates of computer science education share. In this section, we outline what we believe constitutes a general consensus about a minimal set of goals for an introductory curriculum. Each individual strategy in section 7.6 seeks to accomplish more than what we describe here, but each will cover a common set of topics that can serve as a base for intermediate course structures.

In today's world, computers are ubiquitous. Because of the importance of computer systems and the wide applicability of computer-based skills, introductory computer science experience should certainly expose students to the design, construction, and application of computer systems and offer them training in skills that have demonstrated utility. At the same time, introductory computer science courses must also introduce students to some of the central intellectual aspects of the discipline. When we view computer science as a discipline, it is important to look beyond its popular conception as a tool to consider its conceptual foundations. Upon what principles does it stand? What new concepts does it bring to the realm of knowledge? What kinds of questions do computer scientists ask? What modes of thought and mental disciplines do they bring to bear on problems?

We believe it is possible to develop an introductory computer science experience that accomplishes each of the following goals:

- Introduces students to a set of fundamental computer science concepts
- Facilitates the development of cognitive models for these concepts
- Encourages students to develop the skills necessary to apply the conceptual knowledge
- Facilitates the transfer of students from two-year colleges into four-year programs by establishing clearly defined outcomes and content equivalencies

To this end, Figure 7-1 presents a set of concepts, knowledge, and skills that we believe should be a part of each introductory curriculum. While the order of presentation and level of emphasis will vary among individual computer science programs, we expect that all introductory programs will seek to meet these goals. Figure 7-2 expresses similar guidelines in terms of units and topics from the body of knowledge introduced in Chapter 5.

7.6 Implementation strategies for introductory computer science

This section describes six implementations of the introductory curriculum that the CC2001 Task Force feels have achieved a level of success that allows them to serve as models of best practices. Determining whether an approach has been successful, however, is more difficult than it might appear. Albert Shanker, the former president of the American Federation of Teachers, wrote that "educational experiments are doomed to succeed," in part because the energy their creators bring to the experiment creates an excitement that encourages success. Given enough enthusiasm, almost any pedagogical approach will succeed as long as its proponents remain committed to that vision. The real test is whether the initial success can be sustained when the approach is adopted by others.

Figure 7-1. Concepts covered in the introductory curriculum

Algorithmic thinking

Concept	Description	Associated activities
Algorithmic computation	Algorithms as models of computational processes; examples of important algorithms	Read and explain algorithms; reason about algorithmic correctness; use, apply, and adapt standard algorithms; write algorithms
Algorithmic efficiency and resource usage	Simple analysis of algorithmic complexity; evaluation of tradeoff considerations; techniques for estimation and measurement	Estimate time and space usage; conduct laboratory experiments to evaluate algorithmic efficiency

Programming fundamentals

Concept	Description	Associated activities
Data models	Standard structures for representing data; abstract (described by a model) and concrete (described by an implementation) descriptions	Read and explain values of program objects; create, implement, use, and modify programs that manipulate standard data structures
Control structures	Effects of applying operations to program objects; what an operation does (described by a model); how an operation does it (described by an implementation)	Read and explain the effects of operations; implement and describe operations; construct programs to implement a range of standard algorithms
Order of execution	Standard control structures: sequence, selection, iteration; function calls and parameter passing	Make appropriate use of control structures in the design of algorithms and then implement those structures in executable programs
Encapsulation	Indivisible bundling of related entities; client view based on abstraction and information-hiding; implementer view based on internal detail	Use existing encapsulated components in programs; design, implement, and document encapsulated components
Relationships among encapsulated components	The role of interfaces in mediating information exchange; responsibilities of encapsulated components to their clients; the value of inheritance	Explain and make use of inheritance and interface relationships; incorporate inheritance and interfaces into the design and implementation of programs
Testing and debugging	The importance of testing; debugging strategies	Design effective tests; identify and correct coding and logic errors

Computing environments

Concept	Description	Associated activities
Layers of abstraction	Computer systems as a hierarchy of virtual machines	Describe the roles of the various layers in the virtual machine hierarchy
Programming languages and paradigms	Role of programming languages; the translation process; the existence of multiple programming paradigms	Outline the program translation process; identify at least two programming paradigms and describe their differences
Basic hardware and data representation	Rudiments of machine organization; machine-level representation of data	Explain basic machine structure; show how different kinds of information can be represented using bits
Tools	Compilers, editors, debuggers, and other components of programming environments	Use tools successfully to develop software
Applications	Web browsers, word processors spreadsheets, data bases, e-mail systems	Make effective use of standard computing applications

Figure 7-2. Units covered by all six introductory tracks

> ## Units for which all topics must be covered:
>
> DS1. Functions, relations, and sets
> DS2. Basic logic
> DS4. Basics of counting
> DS6. Discrete probability
> PF1. Fundamental programming constructs
> PF4. Recursion
> PL1. Overview of programming languages
> PL2. Virtual machines
> PL4. Declarations and types
> PL5. Abstraction mechanisms
> SP1. History of computing
>
> ## Units for which only a subset of the topics must be covered:
>
> DS3. Proof techniques: The structure of formal proofs; proof techniques: direct, counterexample, contraposition, contradiction; mathematical induction
> PF2. Algorithms and problem solving: Problem-solving strategies; the role of algorithms in the problem-solving process; the concept and properties of algorithms; debugging strategies
> PF3. Fundamental data structures: Primitive types; arrays; records; strings and string processing; data representation in memory; static, stack, and heap allocation; runtime storage management; pointers and references; linked structures
> AL1. Basic algorithmic analysis: Big O notation; standard complexity classes; empirical measurements of performance; time and space tradeoffs in algorithms
> AL3. Fundamental computing algorithms: Simple numerical algorithms; sequential and binary search algorithms; quadratic and O(N log N) sorting algorithms; hashing; binary search trees
> AR1. Digital logic and digital systems: Logic gates; logic expressions
> PL6. Object-oriented programming: Object-oriented design; encapsulation and information-hiding; separation of behavior and implementation; classes, subclasses, and inheritance; polymorphism; class hierarchies
> SE1. Software design: Fundamental design concepts and principles; object-oriented analysis and design; design for reuse
> SE2. Using APIs: API programming; class browsers and related tools; programming by example; debugging in the API environment
> SE3. Software tools and environments: Programming environments; testing tools
> SE5. Software requirements and specifications: Importance of specification in the software process
> SE6. Software validation: Testing fundamentals; test-case generation

In choosing our set of models for the first year, we have insisted that each strategy be endorsed by people *other than the creator* who have used the approach successfully. By doing so, we hope to limit our attention to those strategies that already have a track record of successful adoption. The six models identified in the sections that follow have each met the criterion of having a successful track record when taught by faculty other than the original designer. At the same time, it is important to note that only the underlying approaches have been subjected to this level of validation and not the specific course designs included in Appendix B. In particular, we did not find existing models for the three-semester implementations we have proposed under the imperative-first, objects-first, and breadth-first approaches. The approaches themselves have proven successful in the more traditional two-semester packaging, and we believe that there is good reason to believe that the three-semester implementations will achieve similar levels of success.

7.6.1 Imperative-first

The imperative-first approach is the most traditional of the models we have included in this report. As noted in section 7.3, we have proposed two implementations of the imperative-first model, one that covers the material in three semesters and one that completes the presentation in two, as follows:

CS101ɪ. Programming Fundamentals
CS102ɪ. The Object-Oriented Paradigm
CS103ɪ. Data Structures and Algorithms

CS111ɪ. Introduction to Programming
CS112ɪ. Data Abstraction

The two-semester model is the traditional implementation. CS111ɪ offers an introduction to programming in an imperative style, using a structure similar to that in CS1 as defined in Curriculum '78 [ACM78, Koffman84]. CS112ɪ then extends this base by presenting much of the material from the traditional CS2 course [Koffman85], but with an explicit focus on programming in the object-oriented paradigm. The three-semester implementation (CS101ɪ/102ɪ/103ɪ) expands the coverage of most topics to ensure that students are able to master these fundamental concepts before moving on. These courses also offer space for additional topics that will give students a wider conception of the discipline.

It is important to note that first course in either sequence—CS101ɪ or CS111ɪ—may well use an object-oriented language for its programming examples and exercises. What distinguishes this approach from the objects-first model is the emphasis and ordering of the early topics. Even if it is taught using an object-oriented language, the first course focuses on the imperative aspects of that language: expressions, control structures, procedures and functions, and other central elements of the traditional procedural model. The techniques of object-oriented design are deferred to the follow-on course.

The imperative-first strategy is subject to the disadvantages—as well as the advantages—of any programming-first implementation, as outlined in section 7.2. In addition, adopting the imperative-first strategy means that students will get less exposure to the techniques of object-oriented programming than they would if the curriculum followed the objects-first model. Given the centrality of object-oriented programming in the curriculum requirements and the difficulty students have learning to program in an object-oriented style, the fact that the introduction of this material is delayed to the second course is clearly a weakness in this approach. At the same time, students do need exposure to the traditional imperative style of programming, which remains in widespread use and which is an integral part of any object-oriented languages. Opinion in the community is divided as to which model should be presented first. Some argue that students who have learned the imperative model first have more trouble adopting an object-oriented approach. Others counter that students who have grown used to working in an object-oriented language will chafe at the idea of learning to work without those features that makes object-oriented programming so powerful.

In any event, institutions adopting the imperative-first model will need to include additional coverage of object-oriented design principles at the intermediate level.

7.6.2 Objects-first

The objects-first model also focuses on programming, but emphasizes the principles of object-oriented programming and design from the beginning. As with the imperative model, we propose both a two- and three-semester implementation in this report, as follows:

> CS101o. Introduction to Object-Oriented Programming
> CS102o. Objects and Data Abstraction
> CS103o. Algorithms and Data Structures
>
> CS111o. Object-Oriented Programming
> CS112o. Object-Oriented Design and Methodology

The first course in either sequence begins immediately with the notions of objects and inheritance, giving students early exposure to these ideas. After experimenting with these ideas in the context of simple interactive programs, the course then goes on to introduce more traditional control structures, but always in the context of an overarching focus on object-oriented design. The follow-on courses then cover in more detail algorithms, fundamental data structures, and software engineering issues.

The principal advantage in the objects-first strategy is the early exposure to object-oriented programming, which has become increasingly important in both academia and industry. In December 2000, the College Board announced that they plan to introduce a more object-oriented approach in the Advanced Placement curriculum, underscoring the importance of this approach [AP2000]. At the same time, the objects-first model does not specifically address many of the disadvantages common to programming-first approaches, as described in section 7.2. In fact, the problems of the programming-first approach can be exacerbated in the objects-first model because many of the languages used for object-oriented programming in industry—particularly C++, but to a certain extent Java as well—are significantly more complex than classical languages. Unless instructors take special care to introduce the material in a way that limits this complexity, such details can easily overwhelm introductory students.

7.6.3 Functional-first

The functional-first style was pioneered at MIT in the 1980s [Abelson85] and is characterized by using a simple functional language, such as Scheme, in the first course. Compared with the other programming-first implementations, this approach has the following advantages:

- Using a language outside the professional mainstream reduces the effect of diversity in background, since relatively few students coming into college will already have experience programming in this paradigm.
- The minimalist syntax of functional languages means that courses can focus on more fundamental issues.
- Several important ideas—most notably recursion, linked data structures, and functions as first-class data objects—occur naturally in this domain and can be covered much earlier in the curriculum.

There are, however, some dangers in this approach. The first is that students may react skeptically to learning a language that they see as outside of the mainstream. For students who are already committed to computer science, it is possible to overcome this objection by exploiting the expressive power of these languages and showing how much students can accomplish using these tools. For students who are taking an introductory computer science course to test the waters before jumping in, and particularly for students who see the course as a way to learn some practical programming skills, functional languages are a much harder sell. The second danger is that this approach typically requires students to think more abstractly at an early stage than is true with more traditional programming languages. While forcing students to think in this way is certainly valuable and needs to be part of the curriculum at some point, placing it so early can discourage some students with less experience in that style of thought.

To cover the material that is essential in the first year, an introductory course that follows the functional-first strategy must be followed by an intensive course that covers object-oriented programming and design. The sample courses that implement this strategy are

CS111F. Introduction to Functional Programming
CS112F. Objects and Algorithms

7.6.4 Breadth-first

For many years, there has been concern in the computer science education community that the traditional "programming-oriented" introduction to computer science gives students a limited view of the discipline. Computer science, after all, is an ever-expanding field that includes many activities beyond programming. Courses that emphasize only this one aspect fail to let students experience the many other areas and styles of thought that are part of computer science as a whole.

To provide that more holistic view of the discipline, many computer science educators have argued for a "breadth-first" approach in which the first course considers a much broader range of topics. This approach was recommended strongly in both *Computing Curricula 1991* and the earlier "Computing as a Discipline" report, which envisioned a curriculum in which "the first courses in computer science would not only introduce programming, algorithms, and data structures, but introduce material from all the other subdisciplines as well," making sure that "mathematics and other theory would be well integrated into the lectures at appropriate points" [Denning89].

Developing a successful breadth-first implementation, however, has proven to be difficult. In our surveys, the most common implementation of the breadth-first idea was to create an introductory "breadth-first" course that introduces the field to majors and nonmajors alike. Such a course gives students exposure to a range of interesting and important topics rather than plunging them immediately into the details of one specific area. Students who are interested in learning more about the field can then begin a "regular" one-year introductory sequence. Thus, most existing models involve the addition of a single breadth-first introductory course as the entry point into the discipline for all students. Students who complete such a course can then move on to other introductory sequences with a stronger perspective on the field.

Offering the breadth-first model as a lead-in to a more conventional programming sequence has the advantage of giving students an immediate appreciation for the breadth of computer science, allowing them to more easily decide whether this is a field they might wish to study in depth. The primary disadvantage of this approach, however, is that it adds one course to the size of the major and delays by a term the completion of the introductory sequence.

In our discussions, the CC2001 Task Force saw no reason why it would not be possible to create a successful breadth-first sequence, particularly if one abandons the view that the introductory sequence must be two semesters long. The basic idea is to take the material in the first-year courses—the introductory programming sequence and the discrete mathematics courses—and reassemble them in a way that provides early exposure to the breadth of the field. Unfortunately, we have not been able to identify models that meet our acceptance criterion of successful implementation by faculty other than the originator. We therefore have presented two separate implementations of a breadth-first approach:

- A one-semester course (CS100B) that serves as a prerequisite to a more traditional programming sequence
- A preliminary implementation of a breadth-first introductory sequence (CS101B/102B/103B) that seeks to accomplish in three semesters what has proven to be difficult in two

Another approach to providing breadth in the curriculum is to offer a survey of the field *after* the completion of the introductory programming sequence. This "breadth-second" approach means that students begin with a programming-based introduction to ensure they have the necessary implementation skills and an early chance to appreciate the range of topics that are all part of computer science. While we feel that such an experiment is worth pursuing, we have not yet found models that meet our acceptance criteria.

7.6.5 Algorithms-first

In this approach, the basic concepts of computer science are introduced using pseudocode instead of an executable language. Introducing students to basic algorithmic concepts and constructs apart from any particular executable language minimizes the preoccupation with syntactic detail that successful program execution typically demands. Instead, this approach requires that students reason about and explain the algorithms they construct, tracing them by hand and mind. Students work with a range of data and control structures without having to contend with the various peculiarities that popular programming languages inevitably introduce. Moreover, because students are freed from the need to execute their programs, this approach permits students to experience the range of such constructs more rapidly. Once students grasp the algorithmic foundations and the range of data and control structures used in the pseudocode, they can then move on to a more conventional language, either partway through the first course or, at the latest, the beginning of the second course. Because students have experienced a wider range of both data and control structures early, they progress through conventional programming work more rapidly, allowing class time to focus more explicitly on issues of effective programming practices and systematic debugging skills.

By eliminating some of the time spent on syntax and the details of a particular programming environment, an introductory course that follows the algorithms-first approach can include additional theoretical topics, such as estimations of efficiency and the rudiments of computability. This approach is useful in two respects:

1. For nonmajors, it permits some access to the "science" of computer science.
2. For computer science majors, it permits them to encounter appropriate aspects of theory from the very beginning of their course of study, minimizing the risk that they will later experience coursework in theory as an irrelevant curricular appendage.

At the same time, the algorithms-first approach has several critical weaknesses. Students at the introductory level want to experience the power and satisfaction that come from making computers actually *do* something. Courses focused only on constructing algorithms in pseudocode frustrate this motivation and desire. It is therefore useful to combine the algorithms-first approach with laboratory-based exposure to modern application software that provides students with applied computing experience. This strategy helps students develop a practical skill set that may be of greater relevance to nonmajors than conventional programming. By synchronizing the laboratory-and-project agenda in software applications with the lecture-and-homework coverage of algorithms, students experience the relevance of, for example, data structures in the context of database work, control structures in the context of spreadsheet development, and high-level design in the context of Web page creation.

Relying on pseudocode, however, also has the effect of freeing students from the need to demonstrate that their algorithms work in the context of a functioning implementation. While the process of getting a program to compile and execute correctly is sometimes frustrating, it is also a critical skill that students must master early in their education. The process of debugging in the pseudocode environment differs from the process of debugging an executable program. The former is characterized by desk-checking and reasoning about the algorithm; the latter usually involves interpreting symptoms and learning to do the detective work associated with finding programming errors. Both skills are important, and it is difficult to assess how the algorithms-first approach affects the students' facility with the debugging process.

The final concern about the algorithms-first approach is that it requires substantial grading effort. While it is certainly inappropriate to assess introductory programming assignments solely on successful execution in a set of test cases, being able to make such tests helps graders identify algorithmic errors more easily. Evaluating pseudocode for correctness is a harder challenge that typically requires extensive use of course assistants.

In this report, the algorithms-first approach is illustrated by the following courses:

> CS111A. Introduction to Algorithms and Applications
> CS112A. Programming Methodology

The first course focuses on algorithms and applications early, and then offers an introduction to object-oriented programming toward the end. The second course provides intensive coverage of object-oriented programming to ensure that students are up to speed on these techniques.

7.6.6 Hardware-first

The hardware-first approach teaches the basics of computer science beginning at the machine level and building up toward more abstract concepts. The basic philosophy of this approach is that students should learn about computing in a step-by-step fashion with as little mystification as possible. The syllabus begins with switching circuits, uses those to make simple registers and arithmetic units, and then embeds those in a simple von Neumann machine. Only after establishing the hardware foundation does the course go on to consider programming in a higher-level language.

The courses that comprise this model are

> CS111H. Introduction to the Computer
> CS112H. Object-Oriented Programming Techniques

The first course in the sequence covers the computer from the bottom up; the second uses that foundation to build up the students' programming skills and provide a solid introduction to object-oriented techniques.

Such an approach works well for students who prefer to understand the process of computation in reductionist detail. It is less effective at encouraging students to see the holistic concepts beyond the mechanics of implementation. The hardware-first approach is also at odds with the growing centrality of software and the tendency of increasingly sophisticated virtual machines to separate the programming process from the underlying hardware. At the same time, we believe that such a course might be particularly viable in a computing engineering program, where early exposure to hardware issues is essential.

Chapter 8
Intermediate Courses

The intermediate courses in the curriculum are designed to provide a solid foundation that serves as a base for more advanced study of particular topics. At the same time, it is important to keep in mind that the introductory courses described in Chapter 7 and the intermediate courses described here together do *not* constitute a complete curriculum. All undergraduate programs will include a significant amount of additional elective material of the type described in Chapter 9. In this chapter, we propose four implementations for the intermediate level curriculum:

- A traditional approach in which each course addresses a single topic
- A compressed approach that organizes courses around broader themes
- An intensive systems-based approach
- A Web-based approach that uses networking as its organizing principle

These implementations are representative models rather than prescriptive standards. In each case, there are other workable options that apply similar philosophies to develop a different set of courses. Moreover, it is possible to create hybrid approaches by combining elements from different models, as discussed in section 8.3. The most important consideration is whether a particular implementation ensures that all students encounter the units in the required core at some point in the curriculum.

8.1 Issues in the design of the intermediate courses

As with the introductory courses, individual faculty and institutions have crafted different approaches to the intermediate-level courses. This level of variety and the pedagogical experimentation that makes it possible are healthy signs attesting to the vitality of education in our discipline. The members of the CC2001 Task Force, however, are concerned that most of the existing models focus on relatively compartmentalized topics; only a few models seek to build a curriculum around more abstract themes that cut across the discipline. In a 1992 article entitled "We can teach software better" [Shaw92], Mary Shaw expressed this point as follows:

> Let's organize our courses around ideas rather than around artifacts. This helps make the objectives of the course clear to both students and faculty. Engineering schools don't teach boiler design—they teach thermodynamics. Yet two of the mainstay software courses—"compiler construction" and "operating systems"—are system-artifact dinosaurs.

We believe that this advice remains both applicable and insightful. In existing computer science curricula, many courses continue to be focused around artifacts. We believe it is important for both curriculum designers and individual instructors to break away from this legacy and experiment with alternative models.

Previous reports have focused on broad themes that unify the practice of computer science. Computing Curricula 1991, for example, identified three broad processes and twelve recurring concepts that permeate the study of computer science, as shown in Figure 8-1. Similarly, the ACM model curriculum for a liberal arts degree in computer science [Gibbs86, Walker96] organized its intermediate-level courses on four central themes of computer science—hardware, software, algorithms, and theory—leading to a course in each area.

Figure 8-1. Processes and themes from Computing Curricula 1991

The Three Processes	*The Twelve Recurring Themes*
Theory: • Definitions and axioms • Theorems • Proofs • Definitions and axioms	Binding
	Complexity of large problems
	Conceptual and formal models
	Consistency and completeness
Abstraction: • Data collection and hypothesis formation • Modeling and prediction • Design of an experiment • Analysis of results	Efficiency
	Evolution
	Levels of abstraction
	Ordering in space
Design: • Requirements • Specifications • Design and implementation • Testing and analysis	Ordering in time
	Reuse
	Security
	Tradeoffs and consequences

At the very least, we believe it is important to recognize that even the artifact-based approaches must remain sensitive to current technology. As Mary Shaw observed, the traditional curriculum includes courses about operating systems and compilers, which are no longer as central to the discipline as they once were. In today's world, networks and component-based systems are more important to the practice of the field. In a rapidly changing field like computer science, focusing too narrowly on specific applications, vendors, or implementations leaves students vulnerable to the problem of obsolescence.

8.2 Sample approaches for the intermediate level

The subsections that follow describe the four intermediate tracks—topic-based, compressed, systems-based, and Web-based—that are proposed in this report, along with an additional section describing hybrid approaches. To emphasize which 200-level courses go together, the descriptions in these sections use the subscripts T, C, S, and W to identify a course with its model. For example, the discussion of the topic-based approach uses the designation CS220T to refer to the intermediate course in architecture. The description of the compressed approach refers to CS220C. In fact, these two courses are the same. At the 200-level, the course number uniquely identifies the material, and the subscripts identify which track or tracks include that course. In the actual course description in Appendix B, the header line identifies all the tracks that use the approach. In this case, the header line is

CS220{C,S,T}. Computer Architecture

which shows that the compressed, systems-based, and topic-based approaches all include this course.

8.2.1 A traditional topic-based approach

The most common approach to the intermediate courses is to apportion the material into units based on the traditional divisions of the field. Students take separate courses in each core area: a course in architecture, a course in operating systems, a course in algorithms, and so on. It is not necessary, however, to require separate courses in every area covered by the body of knowlege. Some areas with few core units, such as graphics, can be integrated into the introductory curriculum; others, such as human-computer interaction, can be incorporated into advanced courses that explore the nature of professional practice in the discipline.

As a sample implementation of this model, we propose the following set of courses:

CS210T. Algorithm Design and Analysis
CS220T. Computer Architecture
CS225T. Operating Systems
CS230T. Net-centric Computing
CS260T. Artificial Intelligence
CS270T. Databases
CS280T. Social and Professional Issues
CS290T. Software Development
CS490. Capstone Project

This model is close to what many departments and programs currently do, so it has the advantage of being well tested. The classes will generally be familiar to most faculty, and instructional resources—such as syllabi, texts, and problem sets—are readily available.

At the same time, this model is highly susceptible to the problem of "artifact-based courses" described in section 8.1. In addition, some institutions may have problems with the size of this model. Students must complete nine intermediate courses, along with one introductory sequence described in Chapter 7. For large schools, offering nine intermediate courses may not be a problem. However, for schools with limited space in their major, nine intermediate courses may be beyond what their program can support. The compressed approach described in the following section offers one approach to reducing the size of the curriculum, as do the hybrid approaches in section 8.3.

8.2.2 A compressed approach

For the most part, the topic-based approach devotes a full course to each of the major areas in the body of knowledge. Most of these areas, however, do not include 40 hours of core material, which means that the intermediate courses in the topic-based approach cover additional topics beyond what is required for the core. For institutions that must reduce the number of intermediate courses, the most straightforward approach is to combine individual topics into *thematic courses* that integrate material from related areas of computer science. In addition to making the core smaller, this strategy also begins to address the problem of classes that focus too narrowly on "software artifacts."

As an example, it is certainly possible to combine the material on artificial intelligence from CS260T with the material on databases from CS270T to create an integrated course that looks at these ideas together. Similarly, it is possible to merge the core topics in software engineering with those in the social and professional areas. Our compressed model represents a particularly aggressive approach to combining topics that reduces the nine courses proposed in the traditional model to the following set of five courses:

CS210C. Algorithm Design and Analysis
CS220C. Computer Architecture
CS226C. Operating Systems and Networking
CS262C. Information and Knowledge Management
CS292C. Software Development and Professional Practice

This implementation covers the required core units but saves four courses over the topic-based approach. As a result, this approach may prove useful in environments where it is important to keep the number of intermediate courses to a minimum. Such pressures may exist in small colleges with few faculty members or in any institution that has been unable to recruit sufficient faculty to teach a larger curriculum.

It is not necessary, of course, to go quite so far in terms of reducing the number of intermediate courses as the compressed model does. Section 8.3 outlines several hybrid approaches that adopt some of the strategies from the compressed model to create intermediate course sequences that are intermediate in size between the five-course compressed model and the nine-course traditional model. At the same time, it is important to avoid being too aggressive in seeking to reduce the number of courses. We strongly recommend against trying to pack the required units into the theoretical minimum of seven courses implied by the fact that the core contains 280 hours of material. Overpacking the curriculum creates courses that lack coherent themes and leaves too little time for individual instructors to adapt and enhance the material.

8.2.3 A systems-based approach

Ultimately, the theories and practices of computer science find expression in the development of high-quality computer systems. This section defines a computer science curriculum that uses systems development as a unifying theme. It includes more technical and professional material than the other models, while retaining a reasonable level of coverage of the theoretical topics. Computer science theory remains essential, both as a foundation for understanding practice and providing students with a lasting knowledge base that remains valid despite changes in technology.

A minimal implementation of the systems-based approach consists of the following courses beyond the introductory sequence:

CS120. Introduction to Computer Organization
CS210s. Algorithm Design and Analysis
CS220s. Computer Architecture
CS226s. Operating Systems and Networking
CS240s. Programming Language Translation
CS255s. Computer Graphics
CS260s. Artificial Intelligence
CS271s. Information Management
CS291s. Software Development and Systems Programming
CS490. Capstone Project

Although their titles suggest that these courses focus on single areas, it is important to use the encompassing notion of a system as a unifying theme. This system perspective must permeate all aspects of the curriculum and include a combination of theory, practice, application, and attitudes.

8.2.4 A Web-based approach

This model has grown out of a grass-roots demand for curricular structures that focus more attention on the Internet and the World Wide Web, using these domains to serve as a common foundation for the curriculum as a whole. The following courses represent one attempt to develop such a model:

CS130. Introduction to the World Wide Web
CS210w. Algorithm Design and Analysis
CS221w. Architecture and Operating Systems
CS222w. Architectures for Networking and Communication
CS230w. Net-centric Computing
CS250w. Human-Computer Interaction

CS255w. Computer Graphics
CS261w. AI and Information
CS292w. Software Development and Professional Practice

8.3 Hybrid approaches

As noted in the introduction to this chapter, the four intermediate approaches outlined in this report—the traditional approach, the compressed approach, the systems-based approach, and the Web-based approach—should be viewed as representative models that represent only a few of the possibilities available. In many cases, it is possible to combine elements of two or more approaches to create a new hybrid curriculum that may meet more effectively the needs of a particular institution. In creating such a hybrid, however, it is important to ensure that the resulting curriculum in fact covers the required core topics.

Figure 8-2 outlines three hybrid approaches that meet the condition of covering the full set of core topics when used in conjunction with any of the introductory sequences described in Chapter 7. Other combinations are possible as well.

All of the approaches described in this chapter—the four specific models and the various hybrids—all have a common goal: to present the fundamental ideas and enduring concepts of computer science that every student must learn to work successfully in the field. In doing so, these intermediate courses lay the foundation for more advanced work in computer science.

Figure 8-2. Hybrid approaches

An eight-course hybrid that adds one cross-cutting course to a traditional model:
  CS210t. Algorithm Design and Analysis
  CS220t. Computer Architecture
  CS226c. Operating Systems and Networking
  CS260t. Artificial Intelligence
  CS270t. Databases
  CS280t. Social and Professional Issues
  CS290c. Software Development
  CS490. Capstone Project

A seven-course hybrid that mixes the Web-based and the compressed approach:
  CS130. Introduction to the World Wide Web
  CS210w. Algorithm Design and Analysis
  CS221w. Architecture and Operating Systems
  CS222w. Operating Systems
  CS230w. Net-centric Computing
  CS262c. Information and Knowledge Management
  CS292c. Software Development and Professional Practice

A six-course hybrid that mixes the traditional and the compressed approach:
  CS210t. Algorithm Design and Analysis
  CS220t. Computer Architecture
  CS225t. Operating Systems
  CS230t. Net-centric Computing
  CS262c. Information and Knowledge Management
  CS292c. Software Development and Professional Practice

Chapter 9
Completing the Curriculum

The primary purpose of Chapters 7 and 8 is to outline a variety of approaches for covering the core units in the body of knowledge. As we have emphasized on several occasions in this report, the computer science core does not in itself constitute a complete curriculum. To complete the curriculum, computer science programs must also ensure that students have the background knowledge and skills they need to succeed as well as the chance to do advanced work that goes beyond the boundaries of the core. This chapter offers strategies and guidelines in each of these areas. Section 9.1 describes a set of general requirements that support the broad education of computer science students. Section 9.2 outlines a set of advanced courses to provide depth in the curriculum, which is followed by a discussion of project courses in section 9.3. Finally, section 9.4 provides an overview of a few curricular models that address these goals for a variety of institutions.

9.1 General requirements

A successful computer science graduate needs many skills beyond the technical ones found in the CS body of knowledge. For example, computer science students must have a certain level of mathematical sophistication, familiarity with the methods of science, a sense of how computing is applied in practice, effective communication skills, and the ability to work productively in teams. This chapter outlines several general recommendations for computer science programs seeking to meet these goals.

9.1.1 Mathematical rigor

Mathematics techniques and formal mathematical reasoning are integral to most areas of computer science. The Computing Curricula 1991 report identified theory as one of the three primary foundations of computer science, and we believe strongly that the same principle holds true today. Computer science depends on mathematics for many of its fundamental definitions, axioms, theorems, and proof techniques. In addition, mathematics provides a language for working with ideas relevant to computer science, specific tools for analysis and verification, and a theoretical framework for understanding important computing ideas. For example, functional programming and problem solving draw directly on the mathematical concepts and notations for functions; algorithmic analysis depends heavily on the mathematical topics of counting, permutations and combinations, and probability; discussions of concurrency and deadlock draw heavily from graph theory; and both program verification and computability build on formal logic and deduction. Thus, it is critical for computer science programs to include enough mathematics so that students understand the theoretical underpinnings of the discipline.

Given the pervasive role of mathematics within computer science, the CS curriculum must include mathematical concepts early and often. Basic mathematical concepts should be introduced early within a student's course work, and later courses should use these concepts regularly. While different colleges and universities will need to adjust their prerequisite structure to reflect local needs and opportunities, it is important for upper-level computer science courses to make use of the mathematical content developed in earlier courses. This dependency, moreover, should be reflected in the formal prerequisite structure.

In developing these recommendations, the CC2001 Task Force has concluded that computer science programs must take responsibility for ensuring that students get the mathematics they need, especially in terms of discrete mathematics. To this end, the CC2001 report defines a new knowledge area consisting of the discrete mathematics required for an undergraduate program. That area—Discrete Structures (DS)—specifies the units and topics that we believe are essential to every undergraduate program. The material on discrete structures can be presented in separate courses or integrated more directly into the curriculum by presenting the mathematical material together with the computer science topics that depend on it. In either case, it is essential to make sure that the curriculum emphasizes the use of discrete mathematical techniques throughout the undergraduate program.

The CC2001 Task Force makes the following recommendations with respect to the mathematical content of the computer science curriculum:

- *Discrete mathematics.* All students need exposure to the tools of discrete mathematics. When possible, it is best for students to take more than one course in this area, but all programs should include enough exposure to this area to cover the core topics in the DS area. Strategies for integrating discrete mathematics into the introductory curriculum are discussed in section 7.4.
- *Additional mathematics.* Students should take additional mathematics to develop their sophistication in this area. That mathematics might consist of courses in any number of areas including statistics, calculus, linear algebra, numerical methods, number theory, geometry, or symbolic logic. The choice should depend on program objectives, institutional requirements, and the needs of the individual student.

9.1.2 The scientific method

As noted in Computing Curricula 1991, the process of abstraction (data collection, hypothesis formation and testing, experimentation, analysis) represents a vital component of logical thought within the field of computer science. The scientific method represents a basis methodology for much of the discipline of computer science, and students should have a solid exposure to this methodology.

To develop a firm understanding of the scientific method, students must have direct hands-on experience with hypothesis formulation, experimental design, hypothesis testing, and data analysis. While a curriculum may provide this experience in various ways, it is vital that students must "do science"—not just "read about science."

The CC2001 Task Force therefore makes the following recommendations about science:

- Students must develop an understanding of the scientific method and experience this mode of inquiry in courses that provide some exposure to laboratory work.
- Students may acquire their scientific perspective in a variety of domains, depending on program objectives and their area of interest.

9.1.3 Familiarity with applications

With the broad range of applications of computing in today's society, computer scientists must be able to work effectively with people from other disciplines. To this end, the CC2001 Task Force recommends that all computer science students should:

- Engage in an in-depth study of some subject that uses computing in a substantive way.

Computing students have a wide range of interests and professional goals. For many students, study of computing together with an application area will be extremely useful. Such work might be accomplished in several ways. One approach is to integrate case studies into computer science courses in a way that emphasizes the importance of understanding the application domain. Other approaches might include an extended internship experience or the equivalent of a full semester's work that would count toward a major in that discipline. Such opportunities certainly exist in such fields as psychology, sociology, economics, biology, business, or any of the science or engineering disciplines. With some creativity, it is also possible to find applications to areas that might be considered farther afield, often through innovative approaches beyond the scope of a standard computer science curriculum.

9.1.4 Communications skills

A widely heard theme among employers is that computer scientists must be able to communicate effectively with colleagues and clients. Because of the importance of good communication skills in nearly all computing careers, computer science students must sharpen their oral and writing skills in a variety of contexts—both inside and outside of computer science courses. In particular, students in computer science programs should be able to

- Communicate ideas effectively in written form
- Make effective oral presentations, both formally and informally
- Understand and offer constructive critiques of the presentations of others

While institutions may adopt different strategies to accomplish these goals, the program of each computer science student must include numerous occasions for improving writing and practicing oral communication in a way that emphasizes both speaking and active listening skills.

At a minimum, a computer science curriculum should require

- Course work that emphasizes the mechanics and process of writing
- At least one formal oral presentation to a group
- The opportunity to critique at least one oral presentation

Furthermore, the computer science curriculum should integrate writing and verbal discussion consistently in substantive ways ways. Communication skills should not be seen as separate but should instead be fully incorporated into the computer science curriculum and its requirements.

9.1.5 Working in teams

Few computer professionals can expect to work in isolation for very much of the time. Software projects are usually implemented by groups of people working together as a team. Computer science students therefore need to learn about the mechanics and dynamics of effective team participation as part of their undergraduate education. Moreover, because the value of working in teams (as well as the difficulties that arise) does not become evident in small-scale projects, students need to engage in team-oriented projects that extend over a reasonably long period of time, possibly a full semester or a significant fraction thereof.

To ensure that students have the opportunity to acquire these skills as undergraduates, the CC2001 Task Force recommends that all computer science programs include the following:

- Opportunities to work in teams beginning relatively early in the curriculum.
- A significant project that involves a complex implementation task in which both the design and implementation are undertaken by a small student team. This project is

often scheduled for the last year of undergraduate study, where it can serve as a capstone for the undergraduate experience. Strategies for structuring this project experience are discussed in section 9.3 later in this chapter.

The experience that students derive from a significant team project can be enhanced by using teams that cross disciplinary boundaries. As an example, computer science students can be paired with students in biology to conduct a project in the emerging area of biocomputation. Such a project will require expertise from both disciplines, along with strategies to support effective communication across the disciplinary boundary. The ABET 2000 report [ABET2000] specifically endorses the concept of interdisciplinary team projects, and the CC2001 Task Force agrees that such projects can provide a rich experience for students, both inside and outside of computer science.

9.1.6 The complementary curriculum

Particularly in times of intense demand for computer science graduates, institutions feel pressured to ensure that graduates have specific skills to meet the needs of employers. On the one hand, the goal of producing graduates with the skills necessary for employment is certainly a positive one. On the other hand, it is important to keep in mind that students are best served not by mastering specific skills that may soon be obsolete, but instead by gaining an enduring understanding of theory and practice that will allow them to maintain their currency over the long term. The best way to think about this aspect of student preparation is that both employers and the students themselves should see computer science graduates as agents of change capable of moving into employment with skills and expectations that prove of enduring value to those organizations.

To empower students in this way, the curriculum must encourage them to develop a set of transferable skills that enhance their overall efficacy. To some extent, these skills include those listed in the preceding sections. But they also include skills that are not typically developed through coursework, such as the ability to write an effective résumé, manage time effectively, conduct library research, maintain professional responsibility, remain up to date, engage in life-long learning, and so on. This constellation of skills has been identified as the *complementary curriculum*.

One way to ensure that students develop these skills is to weave them into the fabric of the traditional curriculum. There is, however, always a danger that elements of the complementary curriculum absorb so much time that they overwhelm the technical material. There are delicate issues of balance here, and curriculum and course designers must find the proper mix.

9.2 Advanced courses

We use the term *advanced course* to mean courses whose content is substantially beyond the material of the core. The units in the body of knowledge give testimony to the rich set of possibilities that exist for such courses, but few if any institutions will be able to offer courses covering every unit in detail. Institutions will wish to orient such courses to their own areas of expertise, guided by the needs of students, the expertise of faculty members, and the needs of the wider community.

The CC2001 Task Force has benefited from the work of one of its pedagogy focus groups, which produced a set of advanced courses using the framework provided by the body of knowledge. A set of potential course titles for each knowledge area appears in Figure 9-1. We have, however, decided not to include in the printed report full descriptions of the advanced courses unless those courses are part of one of the curricular

Figure 9-1. Advanced courses by area

Discrete Structures (DS)
CS301. Combinatorics
CS302. Probability and Statistics
CS303. Coding and Information Theory

Computational Science (CN)
CS304. Computational Science
CS305. Numerical Analysis
CS306. Operations Research
CS307. Simulation and Modeling
CS308. Scientific Computing
CS309. Computational Biology

Algorithms and Complexity (AL)
CS310. Advanced Algorithmic Analysis
CS311. Automata and Language Theory
CS312. Cryptography
CS313. Geometric Algorithms
CS314. Parallel Algorithms

Architecture and Organization (AR)
CS320. Advanced Computer Architecture
CS321. Parallel Architectures
CS322. System on a Chip
CS323. VLSI Development
CS324. Device Development

Operating Systems (OS)
CS325. Advanced Operating Systems
CS326. Concurrent and Distributed Systems
CS327. Dependable Computing
CS328. Fault Tolerance
CS329. Real-Time Systems

Net-Centric Computing (NC)
CS330. Advanced Computer Networks
CS331. Distributed Systems
CS332. Wireless and Mobile Computing
CS333. Cluster Computing
CS334. Data Compression
CS335. Network Management
CS336. Network Security
CS337. Enterprise Networking
CS338. Programming for the World Wide Web

Programming Languages (PL)
CS340. Compiler Construction
CS341. Programming Language Design
CS342. Programming Language Semantics
CS343. Programming Paradigms
CS344. Functional Programming
CS345. Logic Programming
CS346. Scripting Languages

Human-Computer Interaction (HC)
CS350. Human-Centered Design and Evaluation
CS351. Graphical User Interfaces
CS352. Multimedia Systems Development
CS353. Interactive Systems Development
CS354. Computer-Supported Cooperative Work

Graphics and Visual Computing (GV)
CS355. Advanced Computer Graphics
CS356. Computer Animation
CS357. Visualization
CS358. Virtual Reality
CS359. Genetic Algorithms

Intelligent Systems (IS)
CS360. Intelligent Systems
CS361. Automated Reasoning
CS362. Knowledge-Based Systems
CS363. Machine Learning
CS364. Planning Systems
CS365. Natural Language Processing
CS366. Agents
CS367. Robotics
CS368. Symbolic Computation
CS369. Genetic Algorithms

Information Management (IM)
CS370. Advanced Database Systems
CS371. Database Design
CS372. Transaction Processing
CS373. Distributed and Object Databases
CS374. Data Mining
CS375. Data Warehousing
CS376. Multimedia Information Systems
CS377. Digital Libraries

Social and Professional Issues (SP)
CS380. Professional Practice
CS381. Social Context of Computing
CS382. Computers and Ethics
CS383. Computing Economics
CS384. Computer Law
CS385. Intellectual Property
CS386. Privacy and Civil Liberties

Software Engineering (SE)
CS390. Advanced Software Development
CS391. Software Engineering
CS392. Software Design
CS393. Software Engineering and Formal Specification
CS394. Empirical Software Engineering
CS395. Software Process Improvement
CS396. Component-Based Computing
CS397. Programming Environments
CS398. Safety-Critical Systems

tracks described in Chapter 8. Instead, we plan to create Web pages for these courses, which will be accessible from the CC2001 Web page. By doing so, we will reduce the size of the printed document and, at the same time, allow the documentation associated with each advanced course to remain more up to date.

9.3 Project courses

As discussed in section 9.1.5, the CC2001 Task Force believes it is essential for all undergraduates to complete a significant team project that encompasses both design and implementation. Depending on the structure of the institution, there are several workable strategies for providing this type of practical experience. In some cases, it may be possible to work with local companies to create internships in which students have the opportunity to engage in projects in an industry setting. More often, however, computer science departments will need to offer this type of project experience through the curricular structure.

The course descriptions in Appendix B offer several models for including project work in the curriculum. The first strategy is simply to include a project component as part of the required intermediate or advanced course that covers the core material on software engineering. This strategy is illustrated by the course

CS292{C,W}. Software Development and Professional Practice

which includes a team project along with a significant amount of additional material. As long as students have sufficient time to undertake the design and implementation of a significant project, this approach is workable. The projects in such courses, however, tend to be relatively small in scale, simply because the time taken up by the software engineering material cuts into the time available for the project.

As an alternative, the CC2001 Task Force recommends that curricula include a capstone project that allows students to bring together all the skills and concepts that they have previously learned during their undergraduate courses. Such a course might include a small amount of additional material, but the major focus must be on the project. Appendix B includes both

CS490. Capstone Project

which provides a one-semester capstone and the two-semester sequence

CS491. Capstone Project I
CS492. Capstone Project II

The two-semester version offers students much more time to complete a large project, but may not be feasible given the time constraints of the undergraduate program in the United States.

9.4 Sample curricula

One of the great difficulties in designing curriculum guidelines is the enormous variation that exists between programs at different types of universities and colleges. Given the range of expectations for degree programs—particularly internationally but also within the United States—it is impossible to come up with a single model that fits all institutions. Chapters 7 and 8 offer several different approaches for the introductory and intermediate levels of the curriculum that can presumably be adapted to many different institutions. The purpose of this section is to illustrate how the complete curriculum could be embedded into degree programs at a range of institutional types.

Perhaps the most significant variable among academic programs is the number of computer science courses required for an undergraduate degree. In institutions outside the United States, university students typically focus on a single subject, with perhaps a few additional courses in closely related fields. Under this type of educational system, a student might take 3 to 4 computer science courses in the first year, 4 to 5 in the second, and 5 to 6 in each of the third and fourth years. An undergraduate at such an institution would therefore complete 17 to 21 computer science courses in a four-year degree program. In the United States, this level of concentration is extremely rare. At universities, for example, students typically take 12 to 15 computer science courses as undergraduates, filling out their programs with general education requirements and electives. Students at liberal-arts colleges take 9 to 12 computer science courses, rounding out their education with a strong liberal-arts experience and often a second major or minor in another field of study. Thus, the number of computer science courses that constitute an undergraduate degree can vary by as much as a factor of two.

It is important to realize that a smaller curriculum does *not* mean a weaker curriculum. Any curriculum that follows the guidelines proposed in this report must provide a rigorous grounding in the fundamentals of computer science. Regardless of the characteristics and expectations of the educational institution, every curriculum must

- Cover all 280 hours of core material in the CS body of knowledge
- Require sufficient advanced coursework to provide depth in at least one area of computer science
- Include an appropriate level of supporting mathematics
- Offer students exposure to "real world" professional skills such as research experience, teamwork, technical writing, and project development

The next three sections describe curricular models designed to fit the needs of the following broad classes of institution:

1. A research-oriented university in the United States
2. A university in which undergraduate education is focused on a single discipline, as is typically the case in countries outside North America
3. An institution, such as a liberal-arts college in the United States, with a small computer science department

9.4.1 Curriculum model for a research university in the United States

The purpose of this model is to show the correspondence between CC2001 and what is typically done in undergraduate programs in U.S. research universities. These programs typically have a fairly large faculty capable of providing considerable depth and breadth in computer science. It is often an implicit goal that all students will have sufficient depth for both graduate study and work in industry. For many of these schools, another goal is for their students to have a smooth path between taking the first two years of the degree at a two-year institution, such as a community college in the United States, and the rest of the degree at the university.

In designing a university curriculum, any combination of an introductory track described in Chapter 7 with either the traditional, systems, or Web-based intermediate curriculum from Chapter 8 can be made to work. The most common choices of introductory sequences in such settings are the two- and three-course versions of the imperative and objects-first introductions, described in sections 7.6.1 and 7.6.2, respectively. It is important to note, however, that these implementations are not simply an instantiation of current practice. Each of these sequences puts a significant amount of modern material in such areas as networking and databases into the required introductory and intermediate courses. In many research universities today, that material is found only in advanced elective courses, which may therefore be missing from some student programs.

Figure 9-2. University model (US)

	semester 1	semester 2
year 1	CS101I. Programming Fundamentals Calculus I	CS102I. The Object-Oriented Paradigm CS115. Discrete Structures for Computer Science Calculus II
year 2	CS103I. Data Structures and Algorithms Science course I	CS120. Introduction to Computer Organization Science course II Probability and Statistics
year 3	CS210T. Algorithm Design and Analysis CS220T. Computer Architecture Advanced mathematics elective	CS225T. Operating Systems CS280T. Social and Professional Issues CS elective Undergraduate research project
year 4	CS230T. Net-centric Computing CS262T. Information and Knowledge Management CS290T. Software Development Undergraduate research project	CS490. Capstone Project CS elective CS elective

Figure 9-2 outlines the structure of a curriculum designed for a U.S. research university. The sections that follow offer additional notes on the design decisions that affect the overall structure of the model.

Introductory and intermediate courses

Any of the introductory sequences followed by anything other than the highly compressed model is appropriate for the research university setting. The curriculum outlined in Figure 9-2, for example, uses a three-course imperative introductory sequence and the traditional approach to the intermediate level, with the following modifications:

1. We have added the optional course CS120 (Introduction to Computer Organization), as outlined in the discussion of the systems-based approach.

2. We have replaced the pair of "traditional" courses in artificial intelligence and databases, CS260 and CS270, with the combined course CS262 (Information and Knowledge Management), as outlined in the discussion of the compressed approach.

CS120 is optional in that all of its core units are covered in other courses. If CS120 is included, the later courses will be able to go into greater depth. If it is not, it might be replaced by another CS elective or simply deleted from the curriculum. CS120 is included in this example because such programs often desire earlier and deeper coverage of systems material than the pure traditional approach offers, and also because CS120 is a course that can be easily offered at two-year colleges.

One of the great strengths of the CC2001 core is the requirement of material in information management and intelligent systems. Many schools have put almost all such material into elective courses. For this curriculum, we suggest one required course combining the two, with the expectation that many schools would additionally continue to run advanced electives in both.

Science and mathematics

A deep grounding in science and mathematics is one of the usual goals of research university computer science programs. We therefore require two semesters of science. In keeping with the desire for mathematical depth and maturity, we require the following courses in mathematics:

• One semester of discrete structures, represented by Discrete Structures for Computer Science. Institutions that wish to offer a more thorough grounding in this material could easily expand this coverage by implementing the two-semester sequence Discrete Structures I-Discrete Structures II.

52

- An introduction to calculus at the level necessary to take advanced math electives such as logic, linear algebra, and abstract algebra. Depending on the institution, the calculus requirement might range from a one-semester course to a sequence with three or more courses. On the whole, we believe that it is often more appropriate for computer science students to take less calculus and more courses in discrete mathematics or other material more directly relevant to the practice of computer science. In many institutions, however, the structure of the mathematics curriculum may be outside the control of the computer science program, leaving relatively little flexibility for the department.

- One semester of probability and statistics.

- At least one additional semester of advanced mathematics taken as an elective.

Completing the curriculum

To complete their degree programs, students must be exposed to additional material beyond what exists in the required core. In many institutions, it makes sense to allow students to determine what areas they would like to pursue. Thus, one approach to the problem of completing the curriculum is simply to require students to include some number of elective courses in their program. Departments, however, have the option to achieve more specific educational objectives by adjusting the degree requirements. For example, a program may ensure breadth by requiring the electives to be in different areas. Conversely, a program may seem to ensure depth in a subfield by requiring students to take a sequence of advanced courses in the same area. Depending on local strengths and interests, some schools may choose to require one or more advanced courses explicitly. As an example, schools that are particularly concerned with mathematical foundations may require CS310 (Advanced Algorithmic Analysis).

In addition to the advanced material, an undergraduate program must also expose students to the issues involved in programming large-scale systems. Implementing such a requirement allows for wide variations in strategy. Students might gain their experience with programming in the large through either a one-semester capstone project (CS490), a two-semester capstone project (CS491-CS492), or an advanced software development course (CS390).

For undergraduates, one of the great strengths of a research university is that the faculty are actively engaged in the process of extending the frontiers of the discipline. For many students, however, that aspect of the academic mission is largely invisible, because relatively few have the opportunity to participate in research projects during their undergraduate years. Students who have the chance to participate gain significantly from that experience in the following ways:

- They get to experience firsthand the excitement associated with creative research.

- They develop a strong connection to a faculty member who can serve as a mentor.

- They establish a track record of project experience that will prove useful to them, both in industry and in securing admission to graduate programs.

9.4.2 A discipline-based model

In the United States and Canada, students at a university generally take a large fraction of their course work *outside* their area of specialization. In other countries, this generalist approach to university education is rare. Instead, students are expected to concentrate on a single field of study, possibly augmented by a few courses in closely related disciplines. We refer to such curricula as *discipline based*. The discipline-based approach is typical of computer science curricula in England, for example, where such programs have a

Figure 9-3. Discipline-based model

	semester 1	semester 2
year 1	CS101O. Introduction to Object-Oriented Programming CS105. Discrete Structures I CS120. Introduction to Computer Organization	CS102O. Objects and Data Abstraction CS106. Discrete Structures II Probability and statistics
year 2	CS103O. Algorithms and Data Structures CS210S. Algorithm Design and Analysis CS220S. Computer Architecture CS271S. Information Management	CS226S. Operating Systems and Networking CS240S. Programming Language Translation CS255S. Computer Graphics CS291S. Software Development and Systems Programming
year 3	CS260S. Artificial Intelligence CS380. Professional Practice CS elective CS491. Capstone Project I	CS326. Concurrent and Distributed Systems CS393. Software Engineering and Formal Specification CS elective CS492. Capstone Project II

three-year duration. Other countries often use a four-year model, but it is relatively easy to tailor the basic discipline-based model to fit local conditions.

Discipline-based curricula typically offer some level of flexibility at all levels of the program. In the first year, for example, the flexibility comes from the opportunity students have to widen their perspective through the choice of electives. Those electives may address some interesting application area, for example, and so enhance or broaden the student's overall education. Those electives may also be used to provide opportunities for exploration if the student is unsure of the intended nature of the final degree. The precise details here will vary from institution to institution and depend on matters such as the entry qualifications for the specific program of study. For instance, some institutions may require that applicants already hold a relatively advanced qualification in mathematics, or even in computer science itself. Then the details of the program need to be adjusted to reflect such considerations.

Another opportunity for flexibility occurs in the final year where optional advanced classes allow a student to specialize, often with a view to exploring or enhancing career prospects in a particular direction. By this stage it is expected that courses are leading students to the frontiers of their subject, at least when viewed from the perspective on an undergraduate education.

A three-year implementation of a discipline-based curriculum appears in Figure 9-3. This curriculum reflects the following design decisions beyond the general guidelines proposed in this report:

- *Programming is difficult to teach and requires considerable time and attention in the curriculum.* The courses that provide students with a foundation in programming are critical to the curriculum. Students must have frequent and repeated opportunities to practice their programming skills throughout their degree program in a way that allows later courses to build on the work of earlier ones.

- *The overall program must include extensive opportunities for students to develop practical skills.* Most courses in a computer science program must include a laboratory component that requires students to develop their technical skills and acquire an understanding of effective professional practice. Students must not be allowed to pass a course without demonstrating an appropriate level of mastery of the associated practice.

- *The sample curriculum does not include a specific course in science but instead assumes that this material can be integrated into the elective structure.* The experimental method can be addressed in the context of a course on Human Computer Interaction, for example; teaching such material in the setting of computer science is far preferable to teaching it in isolation.

Figure 9-4. Small department model

	semester 1	*semester 2*
year 1	CS111O. Object-Oriented Programming CS105. Discrete Structures I	CS112O. Object-Oriented Design and Methodology CS106. Discrete Structures II
year 2	CS210C. Algorithm Design and Analysis CS220C. Computer Architecture	CS226C. Operating Systems and Networking Mathematics elective
year 3	CS262C. Information and Knowledge Management CS elective	CS292C. Software Development and Professional Practice CS elective
year 4	CS elective	CS490. Capstone Project

- *Insofar as possible, it is important to teach supporting material in the context of its application to computer science.* The comment in the previous point about teaching material in context applies broadly in the curriculum. Much of the supporting material—including mathematics, certain transferable skills, professional practice, and so on—can be taught more effectively in context.

9.4.3 A small department model

This curricular model is designed for computer science programs in small departments. We use the term "small department" in an informal way, since what is considered "small" at one school may be thought of as "rather large" at another. In general, the following model would be appropriate for departments with fewer than five or six faculty, but may nonetheless be attractive to larger departments as well.

The primary effect of a small faculty on the design of the curriculum is that the number of computer science courses in the program will be less than that typically found at larger schools. For example, the university model for U.S. universities described in section 9.4.1 contains 15 computer science courses; the discipline-based model from section 9.4.2 contains 21. Offering this many courses would not be possible in a department with five or six faculty members. A major in a small department might typically include 9 to 11 computer science courses, along with supporting mathematics classes and a project.

The small-department model is illustrated in Figure 9-4, which specifies a total of 14 courses, organized into the following groups:

1.	Supporting mathematics courses	3
2.	Introductory computer science courses	2
3.	Intermediate computer science courses	5
4.	Advanced computer science electives	3
5.	Capstone project	1
	Total courses	14

The courses in each of these groupings are described in more detail in the sections that follow.

Supporting mathematics courses

The number of supporting mathematics courses often depends on how much space is available in the curriculum. While four or five supporting courses is certainly desirable, it may not be possible to require that level of mathematics and satisfy all the other requirements of an undergraduate degree. We therefore recommend the following *minimum* mathematics requirement, with the caveat that, if room is available, additional mathematics courses would be a desirable addition:

CS105. Discrete Structures I

CS106. Discrete Structures II

A minimum of one additional mathematics elective, chosen to support the interests of the student and the advanced electives that are used to complete the program

We have specified the two-semester approach to discrete mathematics because the topics covered in these courses are the most important area of mathematics for computer science majors. Currently, most schools offer a one-semester course. However, there is now so much material to be covered that a two-semester sequence can be far more effective than a single course.

The third required mathematics course is not specified. Instead, it should be selected in conjunction with the student's advisor based on the interests of the student and the advanced courses they plan on taking. It might include more advanced calculus, linear algebra, mathematical logic, mathematical modeling, or numerical analysis.

Introductory computer science courses

For the introductory computer science courses, we recommend either of the following two-course sequences described in Chapter 7:

CS111o. Object-Oriented Programming

CS112o. Object-Oriented Design and Methodology

or

CS111ғ. Introduction to Functional Programming

CS112ғ. Objects and Algorithms

Both of these introductory sequences focus on important conceptual issues, such as problem solving, design specifications, and language paradigms, rather than the syntactic details of a specific programming language. Either sequence would be a good fit with a small department curriculum because they both introduce students to many fundamental ideas and enduring concepts in a small number of classes.

Intermediate computer science courses

For the intermediate course sequence, we selected the compressed approach presented in Section 8.2.2. This model contains five required courses that cover all 280 hours of required core material. These five courses are:

CS210c. Algorithm Design and Analysis

CS220c. Computer Architecture

CS226c. Operating Systems and Networking

CS262c. Information and Knowledge Management

CS292c. Software Development and Professional Practice

There are several reasons why this intermediate course sequence is appropriate for a small program. First, the core has been compressed into five courses. This compression allows the full 280 hours to be covered by a program with limited room in its major. Even small programs should be able to offer a five-course core. Second, and perhaps even more important, this sequence of courses is quite different from a typical "artifacts based" core that offers a separate class for various software artifacts, such as compilers, operating systems, data bases, networks, graphics, and the World Wide Web. Instead, this model includes a number of "crosscutting" courses that integrate related material from different areas of computer science. For example, CS262c (Information and Knowledge Management) incorporates material from both artificial intelligence and databases, along with such algorithm-oriented topics as data compression and encryption. Finally, the issues of ethics and professionalism have not been relegated to a single course independent of and unrelated to the rest of the curriculum. This important material has instead been incorporated into many intermediate courses. For example, CS262c treats the ownership of intellectual property, while CS292c (Software Development and Professional Practice) includes modules on the social context of computing, ethical and professional responsibilities, and risks and liabilities in software development.

Advanced computer science electives

Advanced courses serves three purposes, as follows:

1. Exposing the student to advanced material beyond the core
2. Demonstrating applications of fundamental concepts presented in the core courses
3. Providing students with a depth of knowledge in at least one subarea of computer science

As with the number of required mathematics courses, the exact number of electives in a given program will typically be a function of how much room is available in the curriculum, as well as college distribution requirements. However, the number of electives should be large enough to provide depth in at least one subarea of computer science. We propose a minimum of three advanced electives, while realizing that some schools may enlarge or decrease this number based on local conditions. We feel that three elective courses can provide sufficient opportunity for depth of study while keeping the overall program to a manageable size.

To ensure that students develop a reasonable level of depth in at least one subarea, it makes sense to require that a minimum of two out of three electives be chosen from a single area within the body of knowledge. The advanced courses are listed by area in Figure 9-1.

Capstone project

The final component of this curricular model is CS490, Capstone Project. This course provides students with opportunities to enhance skills that may not be easy to accomplish in the traditional classroom setting, such as working in teams, interacting with users, developing formal problem specifications, reviewing the research journals, building prototypes, scientific writing, and making oral presentations.

The most popular model for a capstone is a team-oriented, software engineering effort in which students design a solution to an information-based problem and work in teams to implement that solution. However, there is another model that might be more attractive to outstanding students who are thinking about graduate study and research, as opposed to private-sector employment. For these students, an alternative capstone format is a research experience that includes some original work, a review of the scientific literature, and an investigation of a proposed solution, followed by a scientific paper and/or an oral presentation of the results. It is important to remember that these are undergraduates and be realistic about the amount and quality of research expected. Even so, it may be more worthwhile to expose outstanding students to the challenges of research than to have them design and build yet another program.

Finally, each school must determine how long the capstone project will last. To get the most out of it (especially a research-based capstone), a year-long project is ideal. However, the resources available to a small department may constrain the project experience to a single semester.

9.4.4 Programs for two-year colleges

In the United States, a large fraction of computer science students begin their studies in two-year colleges rather than at four-year institutions. As a result, computer science programs in these institutions are a critical target audience for the Computing Curricula 2001 project. Because two-year colleges have specific characteristics and concerns that are in some respects different from those of four-year programs, the CC2001 Task Force—in conjunction with the Two-Year College Committee of the ACM and its newly formed counterpart in IEEE-CS—has decided to publish a separate report that offers more specific recommendations for the two-year college community.

Even though the recommendations for two-year colleges are included in a separate report, there are several aspects of the two-year college model that are important for U.S. four-year institutions as well. The central concern that links the programs in two- and four-year institutions is that of *articulation,* which refers to the process of determining how two-year college students can make an effective transition to a four-year model to complete their undergraduate study. The issue of articulation is extremely important for four-year institutions that accept students from the two-year schools and is therefore worth some discussion in this report.

Programs at two-year colleges generally fall into one of two categories—career or transfer—depending on the nature of the institution and the needs of local industry. A career program typically provides a broad educational foundation as well as the specific knowledge, skills, and abilities needed to proceed directly into the work environment. Students graduating from a two-year career program typically enter the work force immediately. Once they have gained work experience, some graduates of career-oriented programs may return to a four-year institution to complete their undergraduate degree, and some may move immediately in that direction. In a transfer-oriented program, most students are expected to transfer to a four-year program. Unless the two-year curriculum was specifically designed to enable such transfers, however, students will often need to take additional courses at the introductory or early intermediate levels.

Careful articulation of courses and programs between two- and four-year institutions facilitates the transfer of students from one institution to the other. The overall goal of articulation is to make that transfer process as seamless as possible. Efficient and effective articulation requires accurate assessment of courses and programs as well as meaningful communication and cooperation. That articulation process, however, is complex for the following reasons:

1. Students at two-year colleges are likely to come from outside the traditional student population and therefore have a greater variety of experiences than their four-year counterparts.

2. Because many two-year college curricula offer internship or coop programs, the background of students from two-year colleges often contains a blend of theory and practical skills that may be difficult to map into a traditional four-year program.

3. Courses do not always correspond on a one-to-one basis in the two-year and four-year programs. Even so, it is often possible to identify a sequence of courses in one institution that matches a sequence in the other, even though the number of courses in the two sequences may differ.

In light of this complexity, it is important for institutions to view the articulation process as a negotiated exercise that must be carried out in an ongoing fashion.

Faculty of both institutions must ensure that programs are clearly defined, that program objectives are followed responsibly, and that students are evaluated effectively against these defined standards. When program exit points are specified in an articulation agreement, faculty at the two-year institution must cover sufficient material to prepare students to pursue further academic work at least as well as students at the four-year institution.

A fully articulated transfer program typically provides a path into a four-year program and sufficient coursework to prepare the students to take advanced courses in the four-year program. As a result, transfer students are able to enter the four-year program as juniors, right along with their counterparts who started at the four-year school. We believe that institutions that base their early curricula on the models presented in Chapters 7 and 8 will be well positioned to design effective articulation programs that enable such smooth transitions.

Chapter 10
Professional Practice

As we enter the 21st century, an unprecedented opportunity exists to make professional practice a seamless part of the curriculum in computer science and other computing disciplines. Understanding professional practice is critical for most computer science students since the vast majority will enter the workforce upon graduation. In this chapter, we explore various strategies for incorporating professional practice into the computer science curriculum. The individual sections review the underlying rationale, current practice in education, support for professional practice from both the private and public sector, techniques for incorporating professional practice into a curriculum, and strategies for assessing the effectiveness of those techniques.

10.1 Rationale

The need to incorporate professional practice into the curriculum is based on real-world issues, such as the needs of the public and private sector, the public's demand for higher quality products, the increasing number of software liability cases, and the need to promote life-long learning after graduation. In most cases, students enter school without a complete knowledge of or appreciation for these issues, which is a source of frustration both for those who teach these students and for those who hire them. Indeed, as students learn more about professional practice and the underlying issues, they become more interested in their studies and how they can work well with others. Incorporating professional practice into the curriculum can therefore serve as a catalyst to awaken and broaden a student's interest in computing.

Both the private and public sectors have a vested interest in students learning professional practice. They find that students who have experience with the realities of professional work understand the value of interpersonal skills in collaborating with team members and clients, maintain their focus on producing high-quality work, contribute their time and talents to worthy outside causes, engage in life-long learning, and participate in improvements in their firm. Each year, for example, the National Association of Colleges and Employers conducts a survey to determine what qualities employers consider most important in applicants seeking employment [NACE2001]. In 2001, the top ten factors were

1. Communication skills (verbal and written)
2. Honesty/integrity
3. Teamwork skills
4. Interpersonal skills
5. Motivation/initiative
6. Strong work ethic
7. Analytical skills
8. Flexibility/adaptability
9. Computer skills
10. Self-confidence

That employers are candidates with these general qualities underscores the importance of making professional practice a central component of the curriculum.

The growing demand for better, less defect-ridden products has also increased the pressure to incorporate professional practice into the curriculum. Haphazard software engineering techniques are widely recognized as a significant factor in producing software with a high number of defects. As a result, clients are demanding proof of sound software processes before they will sign a contract with a software provider. In particular, after losing millions of dollars on unworkable or undelivered software, U.S. Government bodies, such as the Department of Defense, require all government contractors to operate at Level 3 of the Software Engineering Institute's Capability Maturity Model [Paulk95]. To meet these guidelines, contractors must have a solid, sound, organization-wide, and reliable process in place to develop software. Unsatisfied clients, particularly those who do not know their software providers well, are taking their software providers into court to recover their costs, force completion of software, or seek compensation for damages. Students therefore need to understand the value of establishing face-to-face relationships with clients, agreeing to requirements that can be implemented, and producing the highest quality software possible.

Both the IEEE and the ACM promote the development of professional responsibility in several ways.

- They develop and promote codes of ethics [ACM2001, IEEE2001, SEEPP98] to which members are expected to adhere. These codes, in general, promote honesty, integrity, maintenance of high standards of quality, leadership, support of the public interest, and life-long learning.
- They sponsor established subgroups—the Society on Social Implications of Technology (SSIT) and the Special Interest Group on Computers and Society (SIGCAS)—that focus directly on ethical and professional issues.
- They develop and refine curricular guidelines, such as the ones in this report and its predecessors.
- They participate in the development of accreditation guidelines that ensure the inclusion of professional practice in the curriculum [ABET2000, CSAB2000].
- They support the formation of student chapters which encouraged students to develop a mature attitude toward professional practice.
- They provide opportunities for lifelong professional development through technical publications, conferences, and tutorials.

Both students and society must be educated as to what they can and should expect from people professionally trained in the computing discipline. Students, for example, need to understand the importance of professional conduct on the job and the ramifications of negligence. They also need to recognize that the professional societies, through their codes of ethics and established subgroups emphasizing professional practice, can provide a support network that enables them to stand up for what is ethically right. By laying the groundwork for this support network as part of an undergraduate program, students can avoid the sense of isolation that young professionals often feel and be well equipped to practice their profession in a mature and ethical way.

10.2 Current practice in education

Many strategies currently exist for incorporating professional practice into the curriculum. One of the most common characteristics of these strategies are courses that help students strengthen their communication, problem-solving, and technical skills. These skills may be fostered in computing courses or, alternatively, in courses outside the computer science department, such as a speech class in a communication department or a technical writing class in an English department. Accreditation bodies, however, usually require not only that students *acquire* these skills—either through general education requirements or through courses required specifically for computer science—but also that students *apply* these skills in their later courses.

The level of coverage assigned to professional practice varies depending on institutional commitment, departmental resources, and faculty interest. For example, in 1999, Laurie King (Department of Mathematics and Computer Science at Holy Cross College) conducted an informal survey concerning the inclusion of ethics in curricula through the ACM SIGCSE list. Of the 74 schools that responded, 40 schools had enough coverage of ethics that would meet CSAB Criteria 2000 [CSAB2000]. Although many schools clearly did not consider this material to be essential, it is encouraging that more than half of the schools did. With the growing emphasis on professionalism in accreditation criteria, it is likely that other schools will strengthen their commitment to teaching professional practice.

The following list outlines several potential mechanisms for incorporating additional material on professional practice:

- *Senior capstone courses.* These courses typically form a one- to a two-semester sequence during the student's last year. Usually, students must work in teams to design and implement projects, where those projects must involve consideration of real-world issues including cost, safety, efficiency, and suitability for the intended user. The projects may be developed solely for the class, but may also involve other on- or off-campus clients. Although the emphasis of the course is on project work and student presentations, some material on intellectual property rights, copyrights, patents, law, and ethics may be included.

- *Professionalism, ethics, and law courses.* These courses are one semester long and expose students to issues of professional practice, ethical behavior, and computer law. Topics included may be history of computing, impact of computers on society, computing careers, legal and ethical responsibilities, and the computing profession.

- *Practicum/internship/co-op programs.* These programs are sponsored by the institution (preferably) or department to allow students to have the opportunity to work in industry full- or part-time before graduation. At least one to two coordinators should be hired to oversee the program and it is helpful to have one coordinator at the college level as well as to have a part-time coordinator within a department. Students typically work during the summers and/or from one to three nonconsecutive semesters while they are engaged in their undergraduate degree. The students who do a co-op or internship generally do so off-campus and so may interrupt their education for a summer or a semester. Students are usually paid for their work, but in some cases may also be allowed course credit.

- *Team-based implementation courses.* These courses emphasize the process of software development and typically include a team project. Course topics include software processes, software management, economics, risk management, requirements engineering, design, implementation, maintenance, software retirement, software quality assurance, ethics, and teamwork. Topic coverage is usually broad rather than in-depth.

Many courses outside the computer science department can also help students to develop stronger professional practice. Such courses include, but are not limited to, philosophical ethics, psychology, business management, economics, technical communications, and engineering design.

10.3 Supporting professional practice

Support for including more professional practice in the curriculum can come from many sources. The sections that follow look at the responsibilities of the public and private sectors; the relationship between academic preparation and the work environment; and the roles of university administrations, faculty, and students in making professional practice an educational priority.

10.3.1 The private and public sectors

Most students graduating from universities go on to employment in the private or public sector. In their role as the primary consumer of graduating students, industry and government play an important role in helping educational institutions promote professional practice. As an example, students who take advantage of industrial co-ops or government internships may mature faster in their problem-solving skills and become more serious about their education. Such internships may also help the institutions that offer them, in that a student who has an internship with a company may choose to work there again after graduation. With private/public sector support, professional practice coverage is given a necessary augmentation both inside and outside the classroom.

One of the most important ways that the private and public sectors can support the education process is to encourage their employees to play a greater role in helping to train students. These employees can offer support in a number of ways:

• They can function in the role of mentors to students working on projects.

• They can give special presentations to classes for telling students and faculty about their firm, their work, and their development processes.

• They can take part-time positions as adjunct instructors to strengthen a university's course offerings.

• They can provide in-house training materials and/or classes to faculty and students in specialized research, process, or software tool areas.

• They can serve on industrial advisory boards, which allows them to provide valuable feedback to the department and institution about the strengths and weaknesses of the students.

In each of these ways, institutions in the private and public sectors can establish important lines of communication with the educational institutions that provide them with their future employees.

In addition to the various opportunities that take place on campus, industry and government also contribute to the development of strong professional practice by bringing students and faculty into environments outside of academia. Students and faculty may take field trips to local firms and begin to establish better relationships. Over a longer term, co-op, practicum, and internship opportunities give students a better understanding of what life on the job will be like. In addition, students may become more interested in their studies and use that renewed interest to increase their marketable potential. Students may also form a bond with particular employers and be more likely to return to that firm after graduation. For faculty, consulting opportunities establish a higher level of trust between the faculty member and the company. As a result of these initiatives, employers, students, and faculty know more about each other and are more willing to promote each other's welfare.

In what remains one of the most important forms of support, private and public sectors may also make donations or grants to educational institutions and professional societies in the form of hardware, software, product discounts, money, time, and the like. Often, these donations and grants are critical in providing updated resources, such as lab hardware and software, and in funding student scholarships/awards as well as faculty teaching/research awards. They serve to sponsor student programming, design, and educational contests. Grants can enable more research and projects to be accomplished. At this level, private/public sectors help to ensure the viability/progress of future education and advances in the computing field.

Through patience, long-term commitment, understanding of each other's constraints, and learning each other's value systems, private/public sectors and education can work together to produce students skilled in professional practice and behaviors. Their cooperative agreement is essential for producing students who value a high ethical standard and the safety of the people who use the products the students will develop as professionals.

10.3.2 Modeling local and international work environments

Just as industry representatives increasingly seek graduates who are "job ready," most students expect to practice computing in the workplace upon graduation without significant additional training. Although the educational experience differs from that of the workplace, educators need to ease the transition from academia to the business world by:

- Mimicking the computing resources of the work environment
- Teaching students how to work in teams
- Providing significant project experiences

Introducing these points into the curriculum makes it possible to model significant issues in the local and international work environment. Faculty can discuss and have students apply international, intercultural, and workplace issues within the context of computing resources, teamwork, and projects.

Because computing environments change rapidly and several different ones exist, it is not possible to predict the exact environment that students will use upon graduation. As a result, it is not advisable to focus attention in the curriculum on a particular set of tools. Exposure to a wide variety of computing platforms and software tools provides good preparation for professional work, resulting in flexible learners rather than students who immaturely cling to their one familiar environment.

Learning how to work in teams is not a natural process for many students, but it is nonetheless extremely important. Students should learn to work in both small and large teams so that they acquire planning, budgeting, organizational, and interpersonal skills. Ample course material should support the students in their teamwork. The lecture material may include project scheduling, communication skills, the characteristics of well-functioning and malfunctioning teams, and sources of stress for team environments. Assessment can be based on the result of the team's work, the individual work of the members, or some combination thereof. Team member behavior may also play a factor in the assessment.

Significant project experiences can enhance the problem-solving skills of students by exposing them to problems that are not well defined or that do not have straightforward solutions. Such projects may be a controlled, in-class experience or have a certain amount of unpredictability that occurs with an outside client. The project should serve to stretch the student beyond the typical one-person assignments that exercise basic skills in a knowledge area. Beyond that, projects can also cut across several knowledge areas, thereby helping students to bring all their basic skills together.

10.3.3 Administration, faculty, and student roles

At the highest institutional level, the administration must support faculty professional and departmental development activities. Such activities may include consulting work, professional society and community service, summer fellowships, obtaining certifications and professional licensure, achieving accreditation, forming industrial advisory boards with appropriate charters, establishing co-op/internship/practicum programs for course credit, and creating more liaisons with the private and public sectors. Such activities can be extremely time-consuming. They are, however, enormously valuable to both the individual and the institution, which must take these activities into account in decisions of promotion and tenure.

Faculty and students can work together by jointly adopting, promoting, and enforcing professional society ethical and professional behavior guidelines. Faculty should join professional societies and help to establish student chapters of those societies at their institutions. Through the student chapters, awards may be given for significant achievement in course work, service to the community, or related professional activities. In addition, student chapters may provide a forum for working with potential employers and be instrumental in obtaining donations, speakers, and mentors from outside the institution.

10.4 Incorporating professional practice into the curriculum

The incorporation of professional practice must be a conscious and proactive effort because much of the material must be interwoven into the fabric of existing curricula. For example, the introductory courses in the major can include discussion and assignments on the impact of computing on society and the importance of professional practice. As students progress into their sophomore-level courses, they can start to keep records of their work as a professional might do in the form of requirements, design, and test documents.

Additional material, such as computer history, techniques for tackling ill-defined problems, teamwork with individual accountability, real-life ethics issues, standards and guidelines, and the philosophical basis for ethical arguments, may also be covered either in a dedicated course or distributed throughout the curriculum. The distributed approach has the advantage of presenting this material in the context of a real application area. On the other hand, the distributed approach can be problematical in that professional practice is often minimized in the scramble to find adequate time for the technical material. Projects, however, may provide a natural outlet for much of this material particularly if faculty can recruit external clients needing non-critical systems. When they engage in service-learning projects in the community or work with external clients, students begin to see the necessity for ethical behavior in very different terms. As a result, those students learn much more effectively how to meet the needs of the client's ill-defined problem. No matter how professional practice is integrated into the curriculum, however, it is critical that this material be reinforced with exercises, projects, and exams.

For departments with adequate faculty and resources, courses dedicated to teaching professional practice may be appropriate. These courses include those in professional practice, ethics, and computer law, as well as senior capstone and other appropriate courses. More advanced courses on software economics, quality, safety, and security may be included as well. As noted at the end of section 10.2, these courses may be from disciplines outside of computer science and still have a profound effect on the professional development of students.

10.5 Assessing professional practice work

Faculty can promote the positive assessment of professional practice work by establishing an infrastructure where student work is evaluated under common standards and where professional completion of assigned work is actively encouraged. The infrastructure may be built upon the following:

- Using outcomes-based assessment strategies
- Reviewing assignments, projects, and exams for appropriate inclusion of professional practice material
- Establishing sound measurements on student work to show student progress and improvement
- Getting students involved in the review and assessment process so that they understand the assessment process
- Employing professionals in the private and public sectors to help assess student project work
- Using standardized tests to measure overall student progress
- Taking postgraduation surveys of alumni to see how well alumni thought their education prepared them for their careers
- Obtaining accreditation to demonstrate that certain education standards for professional practice have been met

The assessment process should encourage students to employ good technical practice and high standards of integrity. It should discourage students from attempting to complete work without giving themselves enough time or in a haphazard manner, such as starting and barely completing work the night before an assignment is due. The assessment process should hold students accountable on an individual basis even if they work collectively in a team. It should have a consistent set of measurements so that students become accustomed to using them and learn how to associate them with progress or lack thereof.

Chapter 11
Characteristics of CS Graduates

While consideration of the body of knowledge is one major issue in determining whether a specific program meets the necessary requirements to be called a computer science degree, other issues must also be addressed. Typically, these issues are concerned with the overall nature of the discipline, the breadth and depth of a program, plus other factors relating to practical, personal, and transferable skills.

In general terms, institutions are expected to define outcomes and objectives that characterize their particular programs and indicate that their curricula are at the level of a undergraduate degree in computer science. Degree programs in computer science can take various forms, each of which could prepare students for different but valid careers. At one extreme, a degree program might provide opportunities for students to take courses on a wide range of topics spanning the entire area of computer science. Graduates from such programs would have great flexibility and might be of particular value either in emerging areas where specialist courses may not be established or in contexts where their ability to span the field would be useful. At another extreme, a program might take one very specific aspect of computer science and cover it in depth. The graduates from such programs would typically tend to seek opportunities in the area of specialization they have studied, whether it be the development of multimedia systems, network design, formal verification for safety-critical systems, electronic commerce, or other specialties that emerge and become important. Despite such differences in emphasis and content, however, there are certain minimal characteristics that are expected of any graduate in computer science. The purpose of this chapter is to explore what those characteristics should be.

The material in this chapter draws heavily on a report designed to identify the desired characteristics of computer science graduates in the United Kingdom [QAA2000]. Its purpose is to define standard thresholds that all graduates of computer science programs are expected to achieve. To a large extent, the characteristics for graduates outlined in the chapter cover the same ground as the curricular objectives outlined in the earlier chapters. The difference is primarily one of perspective. Looking at the objectives of an academic program in terms of the characteristics of its graduates makes it easier to design assessment measures that ensure that those objectives are being met.

11.1 General characteristics of computer science graduates

While the characteristics that one expects of graduates are related to the learning objectives associated with the core units, the expectations one assigns to those who complete an undergraduate degree in computer science reflect a more global level of student achievement. The learning objectives detailed in Appendix A specify what a student must know at the conclusion of any particular unit. In this section, the goal is to identify the characteristics that a successful graduate should possess. At a broad level, these characteristics can be expressed as follows:

- *System-level perspective.* The objectives associated with individual units in the body of knowledge tend to emphasize isolated concepts and skills that can lead to a fragmented view of the discipline. Graduates of a computer science program must develop a high-level understanding of systems as a whole. This understanding must transcend the implementation details of the various components to encompass an appreciation for the structure of computer systems and the processes involved in their construction and analysis.

- *Appreciation of the interplay between theory and practice.* A fundamental aspect of computer science is the balance between theory and practice and the essential link between them. Graduates of a computer science program must understand not only the theoretical underpinnings of the discipline but also how that theory influences practice.

- *Familiarity with common themes.* In the course of an undergraduate program in computer science, students will encounter many recurring themes such as abstraction, complexity, and evolutionary change. Graduates should recognize that these themes have broad application to the field of computer science and must not compartmentalize them as relevant only to the domains in which they were introduced.

- *Significant project experience.* To ensure that graduates can successfully apply the knowledge they have gained, all students in computer science programs must be involved in at least one substantial software project. Such a project demonstrates the practical application of principles learned in different courses and forces students to integrate material learned at different stages of the curriculum.

- *Adaptability.* One of the essential characteristics of computer science over its relatively brief history has been an enormous pace of change. Graduates of a computer science program must possess a solid foundation that allows them to maintain their skills as the field evolves. Strategies for achieving this adaptability are described in section 11.3.

11.2 Capabilities and skills

Students of computer science must develop a wide range of capabilities and skills. Some of those skills are specific to degrees in computer science; others are more generic and would be expected of any graduate of a technical discipline. These capabilities and skills may be divided into three general categories:

- Cognitive capabilities relating to intellectual tasks specific to computer science
- Practical skills relating to computer science
- Additional transferable skills that may be developed in the context of computer science but which are of a general nature and applicable in many other contexts as well

The required capabilities and skills are outlined in Figure 11-1. In each case, the institution must ensure that the skills in each of these categories—cognitive, practical, and general—receive sufficient coverage in the curriculum that all students will have had the necessary background before graduation.

11.3 Coping with change

An essential requirement of any computer science degree is that it should enable graduates to cope with—and even benefit from—the rapid change that is a continuing feature of the computing field. But how does one achieve this goal in practice? At one level, the pace of change represents a challenge to academic staff who must continually update courses and equipment. At another level, however, it suggests a shift in pedagogy away from the transmission of specific material, which will quickly become dated, toward modes of instruction that encourage students to acquire knowledge and skills on their own.

Fundamentally, teaching students to cope with change requires instilling in those students an attitude that promotes continued study throughout a career. To this end, a computer science curriculum must strive to meet the following challenges:

- Adopt a teaching methodology that emphasizes learning as opposed to teaching, with students continually being challenged to think independently.

Figure 11-1. Capabilities and skills for computer science graduates

Cognitive capabilities and skills relating to computer science

- *Knowledge and understanding.* Demonstrate knowledge and understanding of essential facts, concepts, principles, and theories relating to computer science and software applications.

- *Modeling.* Use such knowledge and understanding in the modeling and design of computer-based systems in a way that demonstrates comprehension of the tradeoff involved in design choices.

- *Requirements.* Identify and analyze criteria and specifications appropriate to specific problems, and plan strategies for their solution.

- *Critical evaluation and testing.* Analyze the extent to which a computer-based system meets the criteria defined for its current use and future development.

- *Methods and tools.* Deploy appropriate theory, practices, and tools for the specification, design, implementation, and evaluation of computer-based systems.

- *Professional responsibility.* Recognize and be guided by the social, professional, and ethical issues involved in the use of computer technology.

Practical capabilities and skills relating to computer science

- *Design and implementation.* Specify, design, and implement computer-based systems.

- *Evaluation.* Evaluate systems in terms of general quality attributes and possible tradeoffs presented within the given problem.

- *Information management.* Apply the principles of effective information management, information organization, and information-retrieval skills to information of various kinds, including text, images, sound, and video.

- *Human-computer interaction.* Apply the principles of human-computer interaction to the evaluation and construction of a wide range of materials including user interfaces, Web pages, and multimedia systems.

- *Risk assessment.* Identify any risks or safety aspects that may be involved in the operation of computing equipment within a given context.

- *Tools.* Deploy effectively the tools used for the construction and documentation of software, with particular emphasis on understanding the whole process involved in using computers to solve practical problems.

- *Operation.* Operate computing equipment and software systems effectively.

Additional transferable skills

- *Communication.* Make succinct presentations to a range of audiences about technical problems and their solutions.

- *Teamwork.* Be able to work effectively as a member of a development team.

- *Numeracy.* Understand and explain the quantitative dimensions of a problem.

- *Self management.* Manage one's own learning and development, including time management and organizational skills

- *Professional development.* Keep abreast of current developments in the discipline to continue one's own professional development.

- Assign challenging and imaginative exercises that encourage student initiative.
- Present a sound framework with appropriate theory that ensures that the education is sustainable.
- Ensure that equipment and teaching materials remain up to date.
- Make students aware of information resources and appropriate strategies for staying current in the field.
- Encourage cooperative learning and the use of communication technologies to promote group interaction.
- Convince students of the need for continuing professional development to promote life-long learning.

11.4 Benchmarking standards

In seeking to define an appropriate set of objectives for computer science graduates, the authors of the UK benchmarking report [QAA2000] recognized that establishing a minimum standard may discourage both faculty and students from pushing for excellence beyond that minimum. To avoid this danger, the UK report provides benchmarking standards to assess various levels of achievement. At the lowest level, the report identifies a *threshold standard* consisting of a set of objectives that any graduate must be able to meet. The report goes on to identify a somewhat *modal standard* corresponding to the expected level of the average student.

Defining objectives for the threshold and modal standards represents a valuable opportunity for a department engaged in undergraduate computer science education. Setting such objectives makes it easier to understand the overall impact of the curriculum and makes it possible to assess the effectiveness of the educational process. While these objectives will certainly vary by the type of program and the characteristics of individual institutions, the objectives shown in Figure 11-2, which are adapted from the UK benchmarking report, may provide a useful model for local implementations.

Even though these benchmarking standards are defined only for the minimum and the average, it is nevertheless important for programs in computer science to provide opportunities for students of the highest caliber to achieve their full potential. Such students will be creative and innovative in their application of the principles covered in the curriculum; they will be able to contribute significantly to the analysis, design, and development of systems which are complex, and fit for purpose; and they will be able to exercise critical evaluation and review of both their own work and the work of others. Inasmuch as human ingenuity and creativity have fostered the rapid development of the discipline of computer science in the past, programs in computer science should not limit those who will lead the development of the discipline in the future.

Figure 11-2. Standards for achievement

Threshold standard representing the minimum level

- Demonstrate a requisite understanding of the main body of knowledge and theories of computer science.

- Understand and apply essential concepts, principles, and practices in the context of well-defined scenarios, showing judgment in the selection and application of tools and techniques.

- Produce work involving problem identification, analysis, design, and development of a software system, along with appropriate documentation. The work must show some problem-solving and evaluation skills, drawing on some supporting evidence, and demonstrate a requisite understanding of and appreciation for quality.

- Demonstrate the ability to work as an individual under guidance and as a team member.

- Identify appropriate practices within a professional, legal, and ethical framework.

- Appreciate the need for continuing professional development.

- Discuss applications based on the body of knowledge.

Modal standard representing the average level

- Demonstrate a sound understanding of the main areas of the body of knowledge and the theories of computer science, with an ability to exercise critical judgment across a range of issues.

- Analyze and apply a range of concepts, principles, and practices of the subject in the context of loosely specified problems, showing effective judgment in the selection and use of tools and techniques.

- Produce work involving problem identification, analysis, design, and development of a software system, along with appropriate documentation. The work must show a range of problem-solving and evaluation skills, draw on supporting evidence, and demonstrate a good understanding of the need for quality.

- Demonstrate the ability to work as an individual with minimum guidance and as either a leader or member of a team.

- Follow appropriate practices within a professional, legal, and ethical framework.

- Identify mechanisms for continuing professional development and life-long learning.

- Explain a wide range of applications based on the body of knowledge.

Chapter 12
Computing across the Curriculum

As we describe in Chapter 1, the CC2001 Task Force appointed a set of pedagogy focus groups to look at the curriculum from a broad perspective that would supplement the perspective provided by the body of knowledge. By adopting a more holistic approach, the pedagogy focus groups sought to identify unifying themes among the different areas that might well be missed in a strictly bottom-up, area-based assessment of the discipline.

Most of the pedagogy focus groups were charged with making recommendations regarding specific aspects of the undergraduate computer science curriculum. The focus group on "Computing across the curriculum" had a more inclusive charge, which consisted in part of articulating those aspects of computer science relevant to all citizens and academic disciplines and proposing guidelines for the role computer science can play in helping students achieve that knowledge.

This chapter consists of the report of that group, which addresses the responsibilities of computer science departments to the college and university community as a whole. In its report, the pedagogy focus groups interpreted the phrase "computing across the curriculum" to describe curricula (i.e., courses and/or course modules) targeted at students other than computer science majors. While computer science students might enroll in such courses, they are designed primarily to meet the needs of students outside computing. These courses represent one of the ways that computer science is attempting to address the issues of the expanding nature of the discipline.

This chapter is organized into three parts. In section 12.1, we discuss the important role that general-education courses play within the academic community and argue that developing and teaching these courses must be viewed as part of the mission of a computer science department. In section 12.2, we outline the process of course specification, design, implementation, and assessment. This section also includes questions to facilitate the design process; the set of questions is not complete but can act as a starting point for identifying essential educational goals. In section 12.3, we identify and describe three distinct courses formats that computer science departments might choose to offer.

12.1 Goals and rationale

Computer science departments exist within the broader context of a college or university setting, which typically includes such divisions as social sciences, humanities, and fine arts. Earlier chapters in this report have documented the dramatic growth of computing and the enormous impact that computing is making on virtually every field of study. Today, computer science is not only an area of study in its own right but an important supporting area for many other disciplines. The urban planner constructing a demographic database, the graphics designer utilizing CAD/CAM software, and the economist creating computer models are all examples of people exploiting important developments in computing to assist them with their professional work. The pervasiveness of computing and information technology creates both an opportunity and a responsibility to provide high-quality classroom instruction for an audience that reaches well beyond our own students. While we must, of course, make sure that we provide a solid educational program for our majors, we must not lose sight of the important academic services we also provide to students in other fields.

When financial resources are tight or when there may not be enough personnel to meet the needs within computer science itself, departments will feel pressure to focus their limited resources on their own students by reducing the offerings to students outside the department. We believe that such a policy—while understandable from the departmental perspective—is inappropriate for the university as a whole. Given the impact of computing on all aspects of society, every university has a responsibility to offer courses in computer science for all students. Because such courses are most effectively taught by computer science departments, universities must make sure that those departments have the resources to (1) educate students in the discipline of computer science, and (2) help students from other disciplines understand and use computing and information technology. Both missions are vitally important.

12.2 Process questions

A useful model for the course development process is, appropriately enough, the software development process. As with software, the course development process can be divided into four phases: specification, design, implementation, and assessment.

12.2.1 Course specification

The design of a general-education course entails asking and answering a number of important questions. But to whom should these questions be addressed? Who should have the primary responsibility for specifying the goals and content of a general-education course in computer science? While computing faculty must, of course, be fully involved in helping to formulate specifications, we must be careful not to dictate them. It is important that an in-depth discussion of course goals occur both *inside* and *outside* computer science to ensure that course design is driven by curricular needs and not simply by a desire to teach a certain type of class. In the past, mathematics departments have been criticized for creating introductory courses that focus almost exclusively on pure mathematics, even though many students are interested in and need more applied topics. Computer science should not repeat this mistake. While we should offer assistance during course design, we must also listen and respond to the needs of students and faculty from other departments.

There are four possible goals of a general-education course in computing:

1. To satisfy general student interest in learning more about computing
2. To meet institutional distribution requirements in the physical and/or mathematical sciences
3. To give students knowledge of and experience with the effective use of computing technology in their own discipline
4. To provide a broader understanding of information technology required for effective participation in society

Such courses may be taught to a wide audience of students from throughout the college or to a narrow group of students for a more specific purpose. For example, many institutions have a general education requirement relating to computer literacy. On the other hand, a computer science department might teach a computer graphics course only for art students. It is relatively easy to agree that when a course is designed for a specific subset of students, the faculty in the targeted discipline must provide significant input about the concepts and skills to be covered. We believe that the same is true even when a course is designed for a much broader range of students.

The first step in developing new general-education courses is identifying a curricular need that is not currently being met. This may be done either reactively or proactively. Computing departments should certainly respond to requests from faculty or industry representatives for a new course that could be quite useful to their students or employees. Alternately, computer science can approach other departments with a proposal for a new course that covers material not included in the existing curriculum. Regardless of how a need is identified, if there is interest expressed by all parties, the next step is to identify the target audience and seek input from everyone with a stake in the course's content and structure. A number of questions are appropriate to pose at this time:

- What need will this course meet that is not currently being met by existing courses in the curriculum?

- Who is the target audience for this course? Which departments and programs within the university are likely stakeholders in the course? What type of student will enroll? Do we have some way to measure the interest and demand for such a course? Will the students we are trying to reach have room for this new course within their existing program?

- How will teaching the course affect our own department? Will it have an adverse impact on our ability to teach computer science majors?

- How will credit be awarded? Will the course count for general education or distribution credit, major or minor credit in some program(s), or university elective? Will the course, instead, be offered only as training or continuing education credit?

- Who will teach the course? Will it be team-taught? Who receives credit for developing and teaching it? Do we have sufficient faculty to teach this course even when people are on leave? If not, how can we retrain existing faculty or hire additional faculty with the necessary skills?

In addition to reviewing the responses to these, and similar, questions, departments should carefully read and examine the National Research Council report *Being Fluent with Information Technology* [CSTB99]. This report addresses the fundamental goals and purposes of general-education courses in computing, and it lays an excellent foundation for understanding the issue of computing across the curriculum. This report, along with the responses of client departments to the above questions, will provide the input needed for a detailed course design.

12.2.2 Course design

Once a curricular need has been clearly identified and all departments support the development of a course to meet this need, the next step is course design. Course design involves identifying explicit educational goals and objectives by specifying the technical skills and concepts to be included in the course syllabus and the educational outcomes that we want our students to have. To do so, it is important to pose these basic questions:

- What specific computing skills should be included in the course, and are these skills important and current to the field of study? What level of expertise in these skills do we want our students to achieve?

- What fundamental and enduring computing concepts should be included in the course, and how do these concepts relate to and support the computing skills being taught?

- What, if any, social and ethical issues should be included in the course to complement the technical material being presented?

As in the discussion of course specification in the preceding section, we recommend that departments use the National Research Council's (NRC) Fluency Report [CSTB99] as a guide. This report identifies three distinct types of knowledge that are appropriate to consider for inclusion in a general-education course:

- *Computer-specific skills.* This class of knowledge refers to the ability to use contemporary computing applications and includes such skills as word processing, browsing the World Wide Web, and MatLab programming. These skills need to be clearly identified and included during course design. However, as they may be short-lived, the specific set of skills needs to be periodically reexamined and updated if necessary.

- *Fundamental and enduring computing concepts.* As mentioned in the NRC Fluency Report, "Concepts explain the how and why of information technology, and they give insight into its opportunities and limitations. Concepts are the raw material for understanding new information technology as it evolves." Enduring computing concepts includes ideas that transcend any specific vendor, package, or skill set. Examples might include algorithms, complexity, machine organization, information representations, modeling, and abstraction. Understanding these fundamental concepts is essential to the effective use of computer-specific skills. While skills are fleeting, fundamental concepts are enduring and provide long-lasting benefits to students, critically important in a rapidly changing discipline.

- *General intellectual capabilities.* This class of knowledge consists of broad intellectual skills important in virtually every area of study, not simply computer science. These skills allow students to apply information technology to complex tasks in effective and useful ways. Examples include problem solving, debugging, logical reasoning, and effective oral and written communication skills. These capabilities are beneficial to all students and help to develop and improve a student's overall intellectual ability.

The NRC report gives specific examples of all three types of knowledge, and it stresses that a well designed class must include ideas from all three. A course that focuses only on skills acquisition may be useful in the short-run but will quickly become dated and of little benefit to those who take it. Similarly, a class that addresses only abstract ideas and general concepts may not provide the skills that students needs to make effective use of computing technology. The NRC report emphasizes that effective course design involves the appropriate balance of material among these three types of knowledge.

12.2.3 Course implementation

Once the general course content and goals have been established, developers can turn their attention to implementation-specific details about how the proposed course will be structured by asking themselves the following questions:

- Should the class be taught using a large lecture format or small discussion sections? Should it include a formal laboratory? Informal laboratory? No laboratory?

- What learning activities are most useful for developing specific technical skills? Should there be few large projects? More smaller projects? Team assignments? What about written papers and/or oral presentations to improve communication skills?

- How can we best evaluate students' learning? What types of projects and/or examinations will be most effective at measuring student success in meeting course goals?

- What instructor expertise is necessary for teaching the course? Do we have such expertise in one individual or would it be better to use a team-teaching approach?

- Do we have adequate educational resources (e.g., computers, laboratories) to offer this course?

- Will there be sufficient student interest to generate adequate enrollment? How often should the course be offered? How many credits should the course be and how many times a week will it meet?

The answers to these and other implementation questions will often be determined not by lofty academic goals but by local concerns and resource constraints that are beyond the scope of this report. These factors could include such issues as enrollment pressures, financial considerations, student populations, college distribution requirements, faculty interests, space limitations, and the working relationship between computer science and other departments. But, regardless of how they may be answered, a department should be able, based on responses to these questions, to implement a general-education course that goes a long way toward meeting the desired goals.

12.2.4 Course assessment

Following implementation, a department is ready to offer the new general-education course to the college community. This leaves only the final step in the course development process—assessment. After the course has been offered once or twice, its design and implementation should be carefully reviewed and evaluated. The data needed for assessment can be collected in a number of ways: written student evaluations, in-class observations, and personal interviews with students and faculty from the client departments. Once the course has been taught for a few years, it is also a good idea to interview graduates regarding the value of this course to their professional work environment.

Some of the questions that should be asked during course assessment include the following:

- Does this course meet its stated goals? If not, should we redesign it or simply eliminate it from the program and consider an alternative approach?

- Has any important topic been omitted? Is anything unnecessarily included?

- Based on examination results and course evaluations, do students completing the course possess the desired skills, knowledge, and capabilities?

- Is the client department satisfied with our course offering? If not, what can we do to improve their satisfaction?

The design and implementation of a general-education course is not a one-time process but rather a "work in progress" that must be updated and modified as we gain additional experience. Course design must include regular reviews and redesign, just as in the software development process. Such reviews are especially important in light of the rapidly changing nature of our field.

12.3 Course models

We have identified three types of courses that can be offered by a computer science department: general fluency, area-wide, and single discipline. These three approaches are described in the following sections.

12.3.1 General fluency

These courses address skills and concepts that are appropriate for all students at an institution, regardless of their specific field of study. General fluency courses are not concerned with providing specific computer-related skills to a particular discipline. Instead, they are meant to satisfy general student interests in computing, to meet college distribution requirements, and to help produce more informed citizens with respect to information technology.

One popular general fluency course involves a broad overview of the discipline of computer science, much like the breadth-first course CS100B described in Appendix B. Another possibility is a broad-based introduction to networking and communications—including both conceptual and technical issues as well as discussions of the applications and uses of networks, and the positive and negative impacts of communications technology on society. Another example might be a course entitled "Computing and Ethics" that examines the social, legal, moral, and ethical issues of computing—certainly something of importance to virtually all students.

12.3.2 Area-wide or multidisciplinary courses

Area-wide courses serve several departments that share a common need for particular computing skills and concepts. They share the characteristic that most, if not all, prerequisite material comes from outside computing. The following examples illustrate this category:

- A computational science course offered for science majors
- A computational modeling course for economics, finance, management, and business majors
- An artificial intelligence course for cognitive psychology, linguistics, and philosophy majors
- A computer graphics course for art and graphic design students and other fine arts majors

The NRC Fluency Report also includes a number of examples of this type of area-wide course. For example, the report describes a class on the applications of information technology to social research, including computerized databases, Web searching, sampling, data analysis, and statistical software. Such a course has obvious appeal to many of the social sciences including sociology, anthropology, and political science.

Computer science may work with other departments to identify this type of specialized need, or the impetus may come from one or more of the affected departments. Computer science may be asked to teach such a course because only its faculty have the necessary technical expertise. Alternately, it may be team taught using one faculty member from computer science and another from a client department.

At schools with limited enrollments, such as private liberal arts colleges and smaller state colleges, there is a better chance of success with a general-education course that is attractive to many departments rather than just one. For example, a course in Computational Physics might be difficult to justify at a small institution with few physics majors. However, an area-wide course entitled something like Computational Science would not only appeal to physicists but biologists, chemists, geologists, and economists as well, significantly increasing the likelihood of its success.

12.3.3 Single-discipline courses

These courses are narrower in focus than those discussed in the two preceding sections, and they are generally offered to a homogeneous group of students majoring in a single department. For example, many of us are familiar with a course in discrete mathematics offered by mathematics essentially for computer science. This type of course would fit into the single-discipline category.

Examples of such courses are the Computational Physics course described in the preceding section or a course in Computational Biology. The NRC Fluency Report describes a course offered to economics students that uses spreadsheets and simulation packages to create models of economic problems or historical events to demonstrate the factors contributing to the outcome. In each case, such a course could be offered jointly by computer science and the relevant department to ensure that both the computer science aspects and the domain-specific aspects received the appropriate level of coverage. While much of the technical material in such a class comes from the department supplying the domain expertise, it is important to remember that the course remains a general-education class, and therefore should include fundamental and enduring computer concepts, in addition to specific computational skills.

12.4 Summary

In this chapter, we have argued the fundamental importance of well-crafted general-education courses; provided guidelines for the design, implementation, and assessment of these service courses; and, finally, presented examples of three distinct types of courses that departments may want to consider. When designing and developing these courses, computer science faculty must always be mindful of the needs of the intended audience and carefully design a course to meet those needs. We must not do this in a vacuum but, instead, seek the advice of colleagues outside our department when developing the goals, content, learning activities, and outcomes of these courses.

Most nonmajors will take only a single course in computer science. Thus, it is important that we carefully design these courses to make them as useful as possible. We must present both computer-specific skills as well as broad fundamental concepts that together allows students to develop a rich, full, and long-lasting understanding of the material.

Chapter 13
Institutional Challenges

This report is designed primarily as a resource for colleges and universities seeking to develop or improve undergraduate programs in computer science. To this end, the appendices to this report offer an extensive analysis of the structure and scope of computer science knowledge along with a detailed set of course descriptions that represent viable approaches to the undergraduate curriculum. Implementing a curriculum successfully, however, requires each institution to consider broad strategic and tactical issues that transcend such details. The purpose of this chapter is to enumerate some of these issues and illustrate how addressing those concerns affects curriculum design.

13.1 The need for local adaptation

The task of designing a computer science curriculum is a difficult one in part because so much depends on the characteristics of the individual institution. Even if every institution could agree on a common set of knowledge and skills for undergraduate education, there would nonetheless be many additional factors that would influence curriculum design. These factors include the following:

- *The type of institution and the expectations for its degree programs.* As we discuss in section 9.3, institutions vary enormously in the structure and scope of undergraduate degree requirements. The number of courses that institutions require of computer science majors can vary by almost a factor of two depending on the institution type. A curriculum that works well at a liberal-arts college in the United States may be completely inappropriate for a research university elsewhere in the world.

- *The range of postgraduate options that students pursue.* Institutions whose primary purpose is to prepare a skilled workforce for the information technology profession presumably have different curricular goals than those seeking to prepare research students for graduate study. Individual schools must ensure that the curriculum they offer gives students the necessary preparation for their eventual academic and career paths.

- *The preparation and background of entering students.* Students at different institutions—and often within a single institution—vary substantially in their level of preparation. As a result, computer science departments often need to tailor their introductory offerings so that they meet the needs of their students.

- *The faculty resources available to an institution.* The number of faculty in a computer science department may vary from as little as three or four at a small college or a private liberal-arts college to 40 or 50 at a large research university. The flexibility and options available in these smaller programs are obviously a great deal less. Therefore, faculty in smaller departments need to set priorities for how they will use their limited resources.

- *The interests and expertise of the faculty.* Individual curricula often vary according to the specific interests and knowledge base of the department, particularly at smaller institutions where expertise is concentrated in particular areas.

Creating a workable curriculum requires finding an appropriate balance among these factors, which will require different choices at every institution. There can be no single curriculum that works for everyone. Every college and university will need to consider the various models proposed in this document and design an implementation that meets the need of that environment.

13.2 Principles for curriculum design

Despite the fact that curriculum design requires significant local adaptation, curriculum designers can draw on several key principles to help in the decision-making process. These principles include the following:

- *The curriculum must reflect the integrity and character of computer science as an independent discipline.* Computer science is a discipline in it own right. That discipline, moreover, is characterized by a combination of theory, practice, knowledge, and skills. Any computer science curriculum should therefore ensure that practice is guided both by theory and a spirit of professionalism.

- *The curriculum must respond to rapid technical change and encourage students to do the same.* Computer science is a vibrant and fast-changing discipline. As we discuss in Chapter 3, the enormous pace of change means that computer science programs must update their curricula on a regular basis. Equally importantly, the curriculum must teach students to respond to change as well. Computer science graduates must keep up to date with modern developments and should indeed be excited by the prospect of doing so. One of the most important goals of a computer science program should be to produce students who are life-long learners.

- *Curriculum design must be guided by the outcomes you hope to achieve.* Throughout the process of defining a computer science curriculum, it is essential to consider the goals of the program and the specific capabilities students must have at its conclusion. These goals—and the associated techniques for determining whether the goals are met—provide the foundation for the entire curriculum. In the United States and elsewhere, accreditation bodies have focused increasing attention on the definition of goals and assessment strategies. Programs that seek to defend their effectiveness must be able to demonstrate that their curricula in fact accomplish what they intend.

- *The curriculum as a whole should maintain a consistent ethos that promotes innovation, creativity, and professionalism.* Students respond best when they understand what it is expected of them. It is unfair to students to encourage particular modes of behavior in early courses, only to discourage that same behavior in later courses. Throughout the entire curriculum, students should be encouraged to use their initiative and imagination to go beyond the minimal requirements. At the same time, students must be encouraged from the very beginning to maintain a professional and responsible attitude toward their work.

- *Ensure that the curriculum is accessible to a wide range of students.* All too often, computer science programs attract a homogeneous population that includes relatively few women or students whose ethic, social, or economic background are not those of the dominant culture. Although many of the factors that lead to this imbalance lie outside the university, every institution should seek to ensure greater diversity, both by eliminating bias in the curriculum and by actively encouraging a broader group of students to take part.

- *The curriculum must provide students with a capstone experience that gives them a chance to apply their skills and knowledge to solve a challenging problem.* The culmination of an undergraduate computer science degree should include a final-year project that requires students to use a range of practices and techniques in solving a substantial problem. There are aspects of the computer science discipline that cannot be presented adequately in the formal classroom setting. These skills can be learned only in the framework of an independent capstone experience.

13.3 The need for adequate computing resources

Higher education is, of course, always subject to resource limitations of various kinds. At some level, all educational programs must take costs into account and cannot do everything that they might wish to do if they were somehow freed from economic constraints. In many respects, those limitations are no more intense in computer science than they are in other academic fields. It is, for example, no longer the case that adequate computing hardware lies outside the reach of academic institutions, as it did in the early days of the discipline. Over the last 20 years, computers have become commodity items, which makes the hardware far more affordable.

At the same time, it is essential for institutions to recognize that computing costs are real. These costs, moreover, are by no means limited to the hardware. Software also represents a substantial fraction of the overall cost of computing, particularly if one includes the development costs of courseware. Providing adequate support staff to maintain the computing facilities represents another large expense. To be successful, computer science programs must receive adequate funding to support the computing needs of both faculty and students.

Over the last few years, computer science has become—like biology, chemistry, and physics—a laboratory science with formal, scheduled laboratories included in many of its courses. The laboratory component leads to an increased need for staff to assist in both the development of materials and the teaching of laboratory sections. This development will add to the academic support costs of a high-quality computer science program.

To a certain extent, the costs of courseware and other academic resources can be reduced by taking advantage of the tremendous range of resources available from the World Wide Web. A list of the major existing courseware repositories is maintained on the ACM Special Interest Group in Computer Science Education (SIGCSE) home page at `http://www.acm.org/sigcse/`.

13.4 Attracting and retaining faculty

One of the most daunting problems that computer science departments face is the problem of attracting faculty. In most academic fields, the number of faculty applicants is much larger than the number of available positions. In computer science, there are often more advertised positions than candidates [Myers98, Roberts99], although there are some signs that the crisis is easing with decreasing student enrollments in the wake of the economic downturn. The shortage of faculty applicants, coupled with the fact that computer scientists command high salaries outside academia, makes it difficult to attract and retain faculty.

To mitigate the effects of the faculty shortage, we recommend that institutions adopt the following strategies:

- *Adopt an aggressive plan for faculty recruitment.* Scarcity is in itself no reason to abandon the search; the shortage of candidates simply means that computer science departments need to look harder. Being successful is usually a matter of initiative and persistence. Departments must start the recruiting process very early and should consider reaching out to a wide range of potential applicants, including overseas students and people currently working in industry.

- *Create academic positions that focus on teaching.* As in most disciplines, faculty positions in computer science typically require a doctorate and involve both research and teaching. If there were a sufficient pool of candidates with the right credentials and skills, insisting on these qualification would cause no problem. Given the shortage of faculty candidates, it is not clear whether computer science departments can afford such selectivity. It is not necessary for every institution to maintain a research program in computer science. At the same time, it is hard to imagine that any university today could get away without offering courses in this area. Opening faculty positions to those who enjoy teaching but are not drawn to academic research increases the size of the available pool.

- *Make sure that faculty receive the support they need to stay in academia.* Studies undertaken by the National Science Foundation in the 1980s found that faculty members who left academia for industry typically did not cite economics as their primary motivation [Curtis83]. Instead, they identified a range of concerns about the academic work environment—huge class sizes, heavy teaching loads, inadequate research support, the uncertainty of tenure, and bureaucratic hassles—that the NSF study refers to collectively as "institutional disincentives." As enrollments in computer science courses increase, it is critical for institutions to ensure that faculty workloads remain manageable.

- *Get undergraduates involved as course assistants.* The crisis in computer science education arises from the fact that there are too few teachers to serve the needs of too many undergraduates. One of the best ways to meet the increasing student demand is to get those undergraduates involved in the teaching process. Using undergraduates as course assistants not only helps alleviate the teaching shortfall but also provides a valuable educational experience to the student assistants [Roberts95].

13.5 Conclusion

There is no single formula for success in designing a computer science curriculum. Although we believe that the recommendations of this report and the specific strategic suggestions in this chapter will prove useful to a wide variety of institutions, every computer science program must adapt those recommendations and strategies to match the characteristics of the particular institution. It is, moreover, important to evaluate and modify curricular programs on a regular basis to keep up with the rapid changes in the field. The computer science curricula in place today are the product of many years of experimentation and refinement by computer science educators in their own institutions. The curricula of the future will depend just as much on the creativity that follows in the wake of this report to build even better computer science programs for undergraduates throughout the world.

Acknowledgments

Many people have contributed to the CC2001 project since its inception at the end of 1998. The following individuals have served on at least one of the focus groups: Ishfaq Ahmad, Robert Aiken, Anne Applin, Richard H. Austing, Scott Badman, Donald J. Bagert, Bruce Barnes, Mordechai (Moti) Ben-Ari, Julia Benson, Russell C. Bjork, Kevin W. Bowyer, Kim Bruce, Amy S. Bruckman, Bob Campbell, James Caristi, Doris Carver, Carl K. Chang, Morris Chang, Yiming Chen, Ashraful Chowdhury, Alan Clements, C. Fay Cover, Thad Crews, George T. Crocker, James H. Cross II, Steve Cunningham, Nell Dale, Andrea Danyluk, Gordon Davies, Susan Dean, Thomas G. Dietterich, John P. Dougherty, Sarah Douglas, J. Philip East, Dick Eckhouse, Gerald Engel, Edward Feigenbaum, Sue Fitzgerald, Ken Ford, Edward A. Fox, Josephine Freedman, Jose Galaviz, Dick Gayler, Benjamin Goldberg, Dina Golden, Don Gotterbarn, Saul Greenberg, Mark Guzdial, Cindy Hanchey, Elizabeth Hawthorne, Pat Hayes, Chris Haynes, Xudong He, Jim Hendler, Tom Hilburn, Wayne Horn, Cay Horstmann, Chuck Huff, Joseph Hummel, Phillip Hutto, John Impagliazzo, Michel Israel, Robert Jacob, Anil Jain, Carol Janik, Barbara Jennings, Ricardo Jiménez-Peris, Keith Jolly, Rhys Price Jones, Ioannis Kakadiaris, Willis King, Karl Klee, Timothy Klingler, Peter Knoke, Richard E. Korf, Norbert Kubilus, Amruth Kumar, Francis Lau, Gary Leavens, J. A. N. Lee, Ernst Leiss, James Lin, Cheng-Wen Liu, Ming T. (Mike) Liu, Tim Long, Philip Machanick, Raghu Machiraj, Raghu Machiraju, John Mallozzi, Bill Marion, C. Dianne Martin, Marta Patiño Martínez, Bruce R. Maxim, W. Michael McCracken, Chris McDonald, Andrew McGettrick, Susan Mengel, Dan Myers, John Mitchell, Michael Murphy, Walid Najjar, Thomas L. Naps, Patricia Nettnin, Gary Nutt, Yale Patt, Holly Patterson-McNeill, Richard E. Pattis, T. S. Pennington, Judy Porter, Jenny Preece, Anne-Louise Radimsky, Brad Richards, Eric Roberts, Ingrid Russell, Sartaj Sahni, Ahmed Sameh, Carolyn Schauble, G. Michael Schneider, Henning Schulzrinne, Russ Shackelford, Alfred Shin, Charles Shipley, Ben Shneiderman, Shai Simonson, Robert Sloan, Carl Smith, Milan Sonka, Sylvia Sorkin, Pradip Srimani, Lynn Andrea Stein, George Stockman, Devika Subramanian, Bobby Thrash, D. Singh Tomer, Frank Tong, Marilyn Mantei Tremaine, Alan Underwood, Ron Vetter, Henry Walker, David Waltz, Wenping Wang, Yun Wang, Tony Wasserman, Laurie Honour Werth, Curt M. White, Ed Wilkens, Barry Wilkinson, Terry Winograd, Ursula Wolz, and Anita Wright.

We also want to thank the many people who attended the various CC2001 workshops over the last two years for all the feedback that they provided to the steering committee. The input we received during those meetings has had a profound effect on the structure and scope of this report.

Finally, we are grateful to the Association for Computing Machinery, the Computer Society of the Institute for Electrical and Electronic Engineers, and the National Science Foundation for supporting this effort.

Bibliography

[Abelson85] Harold Abelson and Gerald Jay Sussman with Julie Sussman. Structure and Interpretation of Computer Programs. Cambridge, MA: MIT Press, 1985.

[ABET2000] Accreditation Board for Engineering and Technology. Accreditation Policy and Procedure Manual. Baltimore, MD: ABET, Inc., November 2000. `http://www.abet.org/images/policies.pdf`.

[ACM65] ACM Curriculum Committee on Computer Science. An undergraduate program in computer science—preliminary recommendations. Communications of the ACM, 8(9):543-552, September 1965.

[ACM68] ACM Curriculum Committee on Computer Science. Curriculum '68: Recommendations for the undergraduate program in computer science. Communications of the ACM, 11(3):151-197, March 1968.

[ACM78] ACM Curriculum Committee on Computer Science. Curriculum '78: Recommendations for the undergraduate program in computer science. Communications of the ACM, 22(3):147-166, March 1979.

[ACM99] ACM Two-Year College Education Committee. Guidelines for Associate-Aegree and Certificate Programs to Support Computing in a Networked Environment. New York: The Association for Computing Machinery, September 1999.

[ACM2001] Association for Computing Machinery. ACM Code of Ethics and Professional Conduct. New York: The Association for Computing Machinery, May 2001. `http://www.acm.org/constitution/code.html`.

[AP2000] Advanced Placement Program. Introduction of Java in 2003-2004. The College Board, December 20, 2000. `http://www.collegeboard.org/ap/computer-science`.

[BCS89a] British Computer Society and The Institution of Electrical Engineers. Undergraduate curricula for software engineers. London: British Computer Society, June 1989.

[BCS89b] British Computer Society and The Institution of Electrical Engineers. Software in safety-related systems. London: British Computer Society, October 1989.

[Beidler85] John Beidler, Richard Austing, and Lillian Cassel. Computing programs in small colleges. Communications of the ACM, 28(6):605-611, June 1985.

[Bennett86] W. Bennett. A position paper on guidelines for electrical and computer engineering education. IEEE Transactions in Education, E-29(3):175-177, August 1986.

[Bott91] Frank Bott, Allison Coleman, Jack Eaton, and Diane Rowland. Professional Issues in Software Engineering. London: Pitman, 1991.

[Carnegie92] Carnegie Commission on Science, Technology, and Government. Enabling the Future: Linking Science and Technology to Societal Goals. New York: Carnegie Commission, September 1992.

[COSINE67] COSINE Committee. Computer Science in Electrical Engineering. Washington, DC: Commission on Engineering Education, September 1967.

[CSAB86] Computing Sciences Accreditation Board. Defining the computing sciences professions. October 1986. `http://www.csab.org/comp_sci_profession.html`.

[CSAB2000]   Computing Sciences Accreditation Board. Criteria for accrediting programs in computer science in the United States. Version 1.0, January 2000. `http://www.csab.org/criteria2k_v10.html`.

[CSTB94]   Computing Science and Telecommunications Board. Realizing the Information Future. Washington DC: National Academy Press, 1994.

[CSTB99]   Computing Science and Telecommunications Board. Being Fluent with Information Technology. Washington DC: National Academy Press, 1999.

[Curtis83]   Kent K. Curtis. Computer Manpower: Is There a Crisis? Washington DC: National Science Foundation, 1983. `http://www.acm.org/sigcse/papers/curtis83/`.

[Davis97]   Gordon B. Davis, John T. Gorgone, J. Daniel Couger, David L. Feinstein, and Herbert E. Longnecker, Jr. IS'97 model curriculum and guidelines for undergraduate degree programs in information systems. Association of Information Technology Professionals, 1997. `http://webfoot.csom.umn.edu/faculty/gdavis/curcomre.pdf`.

[Denning89]   Peter J. Denning, Douglas E. Comer, David Gries, Michael C. Mulder, Allen B. Tucker, A. Joe Turner, and Paul R. Young. Computing as a discipline. Communications of the ACM, 32(1):9-23, January 1989.

[Denning98]   Peter J. Denning. Computing the profession. Educom Review, November 1998.

[Denning99]   Peter J. Denning. Our seed corn is growing in the commons. Information Impacts Magazine, March 1999. `http://www.cisp.org/imp/march_99/denning/03_99denning.htm`.

[EAB83]   Educational Activities Board. The 1983 model program in computer science and engineering. Technical Report 932, Computer Society of the IEEE, December 1983.

[EAB86]   Educational Activities Board. Design education in computer science and engineering. Technical Report 971, Computer Society of the IEEE, October 1986.

[EC77]   Education Committee of the IEEE Computer Society. A curriculum in computer science and engineering. Publication EHO119-8, Computer Society of the IEEE, January 1977.

[Gibbs86]   Norman E. Gibbs and Allen B. Tucker. Model curriculum for a liberal arts degree in computer science. Communications of the ACM, 29(3):202-210, March 1986.

[Gorgone2000]   John T. Gorgone, Paul Gray, David L. Feinstein, George M. Kasper, Jerry N. Luftman, Edward A. Stohr, Joseph S. Valacich, and Rolf T. Wigand. MSIS 2000: Model curriculum and guidelines for graduate degree programs in information systems. Association for Computing Machinery and Association for Information Systems, January 2000. `http://cis.bentley.edu/ISA/pages/documents/msis2000jan00.pdf`.

[IEEE2001]   Institute for Electrical and Electronic Engineers. IEEE Code of Ethics. Piscataway, NJ: IEEE, May 2001. `http://www.ieee.org/about/whatis/code.html`.

[Kelemen99]   Charles F. Kelemen (editor), Owen Astrachan, Doug Baldwin, Kim Bruce, Peter Henderson, Dale Skrien, Allen Tucker, and Charles Ban Loan. Computer Science Report to the CUPM Curriculum Foundations Workshop in Physics and Computer Science. Report from a workshop at Bowdoin College, October 28-31, 1999.

[Koffman84]   Elliot P. Koffman, Philip L. Miller, and Caroline E. Wardle. Recommended curriculum for CS1: 1984 a report of the ACM curriculum task force for CS1. Communications of the ACM, 27(10):998-1001, October 1984.

[Koffman85] Elliot P. Koffman, David Stemple, and Caroline E. Wardle. Recommended curriculum for CS2, 1984: A report of the ACM curriculum task force for CS2. Communications of the ACM, 28(8):815-818, August 1985.

[Lee98] Edward A. Lee and David G. Messerschmitt. Engineering and education for the future. IEEE Computer, 77-85, January 1998.

[Lidtke99] Doris K. Lidtke, Gordon E. Stokes, Jimmie Haines, and Michael C. Mulder. ISCC '99: An information systems-centric curriculum '99, July 1999. http://www.iscc.unomaha.edu.

[Martin96]   C. Dianne Martin, Chuck Huff, Donald Gotterbarn, Keith Miller. Implementing a tenth strand in the CS curriculum. Communications of the ACM, 39(12):75-84, December 1996.

[Mulder75] Michael C. Mulder. Model curricula for four-year computer science and engineering programs: Bridging the tar pit. Computer, 8(12):28-33, December 1975.

[Mulder84]   Michael C. Mulder and John Dalphin. Computer science program requirements and accreditation—an interim report of the ACM/IEEE Computer Society joint task force. Communications of the ACM, 27(4):330-335, April 1984.

[Mulder98] Fred Mulder and Tom van Weert. Informatics in higher education: Views on informatics and noninformatics curricula. Proceedings of the IFIP/WG3.2 Working Conference on Informatics (computer science) as a Discipline and in Other Disciplines: What Is in Common? London: Chapman and Hall, 1998.

[Myers98] J. Paul Myers, Jr. and Henry M. Walker. The state of academic hiring in computer science: An interim review. SIGCSE Bulletin, 30(4):32a-35a, December 1998.

[NACE2001] National Association of Colleges and Employers. Job outlook '01 (online version). http://www.jobweb.com

[Neumann95] Peter G. Neumann. Computer Related Risks. New York: ACM Press, 1995.

[NSF96] National Science Foundation Advisory Committee. Shaping the Future: New Expectations for Undergraduate Education in Science, Mathematics, Engineering, and Technology. Washington DC: National Science Foundation, 1996.

[NTIA99]   National Telecommunications and Information Administration. Falling through the Net: Defining the Digital Divide. Washington, DC: Department of Commerce, November 1999.

[Nunamaker82] Jay F. Nunamaker, Jr., J. Daniel Couger, Gordon B. Davis. Information systems curriculum recommendations for the 80s: Undergraduate and graduate programs. Communications of the ACM, 25(11):781-805, November 1982.

[OTA88] Office of Technology Assessment. Educating Scientists and Engineers: Grade School to Grad School. OTA-SET-377. Washington, DC: U.S. Government Printing Office, June 1988.

[Paulk95]   Mark Paulk, Bill Curtis, Mary Beth Chrissis, and Charles Weber. The Capability Maturity Model: Guidelines for Improving the Software Process. Reading, MA: Addison-Wesley, 1995.

[QAA2000] Quality Assurance Agency for Higher Education. A Report on Benchmark Levels for Computing. Gloucester, England: Southgate House, 2000.

[Ralston80] Anthony Ralston and Mary Shaw. Curriculum '78—Is computer science really that unmathematical. Communications of the ACM, (23)2:67-70, February 1980.

[Roberts95] Eric Roberts, John Lilly, and Bryan Rollins. Using undergraduates as teaching assistants in introductory programming courses: An update on the Stanford experience. SIGCSE Bulletin, (27)1:48-52, March 1995.

[Roberts99] Eric Roberts. Conserving the seed corn: Reflections on the academic hiring crisis. SIGCSE Bulletin (31)4:4-9, December 1999.

[SAC67] President's Science Advisory Commission. Computers in Higher Education. Washington, DC: The White House, February 1967.

[SEEPP98] IEEE-CS/ACM Joint Task Force on Software Engineering Ethics and Professional Practices (SEEPP). Software engineering code of ethics and professional practice (Version 5.2). `http://www.acm.org/serving/se/code.htm`.

[Shaw85] Mary Shaw. The Carnegie-Mellon Curriculum for Undergraduate Computer Science. New York: Springer-Verlag, 1985.

[Shaw91] Mary Shaw and James E Tomayko. Models for Undergraduate Courses in Software Engineering. Pittsburgh: Software Engineering Institute, Carnegie Mellon University, January 1991.

[Shaw92] Mary Shaw. We can teach software better. Computing Research News, 4(4):2-12, September 1992.

[SIGCHI92] Special Interest Group on Computer-Human Interaction. ACM SIGCHI Curricula for Human-Computer Interaction. New York: Association for Computing Machinery, 1992.

[SWEBOK2001] Software Engineering Coordinating Committee. Guide to the Software Engineering Body of Knowledge (SWEBOK). Stone Man Version 0.95. A Project of the IEEE Computer Society, May 2001. `http://www.swebok.org/stoneman/version095.html/`.

[Tucker91] Allen B. Tucker, Bruce H. Barnes, Robert M. Aiken, Keith Barker, Kim B. Bruce, J. Thomas Cain, Susan E. Conry, Gerald L. Engel, Richard G. Epstein, Doris K. Lidtke, Michael C. Mulder, Jean B. Rogers, Eugene H. Spafford, and A. Joe Turner. Computing Curricula '91. Association for Computing Machinery and the Computer Society of the Institute of Electrical and Electronics Engineers, 1991.

[Walker96] Henry M. Walker and G. Michael Schneider. A revised model curriculum for a liberal arts degree in computer science. Communications of the ACM, 39(12):85-95, December 1996.

[Zadeh68] Lofti A. Zadeh. Computer science as a discipline. Journal of Engineering Education, 58(8):913-916, April 1968.

Appendix A
The CS Body of Knowledge

This appendix to the Computing Curricula 2001 report defines the knowledge domain that is likely to be taught in an undergraduate curriculum in computer science. The underlying rationale for this categorization scheme and additional details about its history, structure, and application are included in the full task force report. Because we expect the appendices to have wider circulation than the full report, the task force feels it is important to include in each appendix a summary of the fundamental concepts that are necessary to understand the recommendations. The most important concepts are outlined in the sections that follow.

Structure of the body of knowledge

The CS body of knowledge is organized hierarchically into three levels. The **area**—the highest level of the hierarchy—represents a particular disciplinary subfield. Each area is identified by a two-letter abbreviation, such as OS (operating systems) or PL (programming languages). The areas are broken down into smaller divisions called **units,** which represent individual thematic modules within an area. Each unit is identified by adding a numeric suffix to the area name; as an example, OS3 is a unit on *concurrency.* Each unit is further subdivided into a set of **topics**—the hierarchy's lowest level.

Core and elective units

In updating the body of knowledge from the framework established in Computing Curricula 1991, the CC2001 Task Force has to take account of the fact that the computing discipline has expanded to such an extent that it is impossible for undergraduates to learn every topic that has at one time been considered fundamental to the discipline. The task force has therefore sought to define a minimal **core** consisting of that material that essentially everyone teaching computer science agrees is essential to anyone obtaining an undergraduate degree in this field. Material offered as part of an undergraduate program that falls outside the core is considered to be **elective.** By insisting on a broad consensus in the definition of the core, the task force hopes to keep the core as small as possible, giving institutions the freedom to tailor the elective components of the curriculum in ways that meet their individual needs.

In discussing the CC2001 recommendations during their development, we have found that it helps to emphasize the following points:

- *The core is not a complete curriculum.* Because the core is defined as minimal, it does not, by itself, constitute a complete undergraduate curriculum. Every undergraduate program must include additional elective units from the body of knowledge, although the CC2001 report does not define what those units will be.

- *Core units are not necessarily limited to a set of introductory courses taken early in the undergraduate curriculum.* Although many of the units defined as core are indeed introductory, there are also some core units that clearly must be covered only after students have developed significant background in the field. For example, the task force believes that all students must develop a significant application as some point during their undergraduate program. The material that is essential to successful management of projects at this scale is therefore part of the core, since it is required of all students. At the same time, the project course experience is very likely to come toward the end of a student's undergraduate program. Similarly, introductory courses may include elective units alongside the coverage of core material. The designation *core* simply means *required* and says nothing about the level of the course in which it appears.

Assessing the time required to cover a unit

To give readers a sense of the time required to cover a particular unit, the CC2001 report must define a metric that establishes a standard of measurement. Choosing such a metric has proven difficult, because no standard measure is recognized throughout the world. For consistency with the earlier curriculum reports, the task force has chosen to express time in **hours,** corresponding to the in-class time required to present the material in a traditional lecture-oriented format. To dispel potential confusion, however, it is important to underscore the following observations about the use of lecture hours as a measure:

- *The task force does not seek to endorse the lecture format.* Even though we have used a metric with its roots in a classical, lecture-oriented form, the task force believes that there are other styles—particular given recent improvements in educational technology—that can be at least as effective. For some of these styles, the notion of *hours* may be difficult to apply. Even so, the time specifications should at least serve as a comparative measure, in the sense that a 5-hour unit will presumably take roughly five times as much time to cover as a 1-hour unit, independent of the teaching style.

- *The hours specified do not include time spent outside of class.* The time assigned to a unit does not include the instructor's preparation time or the time students spend outside of class. As a general guideline, the amount of out-of-class work is approximately three times the in-class time. Thus, a unit that is listed as requiring 3 hours will typically entail a total of 12 hours (3 in class and 9 outside).

- *The hours listed for a unit represent a minumum level of coverage.* The time measurements we have assigned for each unit should be interpreted as the *minimum* amount of time necessary to enable a student to perform the learning objectives for that unit. It is always appropriate to spend more time on a unit than the mandated minimum.

Details of the CS body of knowledge

A summary of the body of knowledge—showing the areas, units, which units are core, and the minimum time required for each—appears as Figure A-1. The details of each area follow as separate sections.

Figure A-1. Computer science body of knowledge with core topics underlined

DS. Discrete Structures (43 core hours)
DS1. Functions, relations, and sets (6)
DS2. Basic logic (10)
DS3. Proof techniques (12)
DS4. Basics of counting (5)
DS5. Graphs and trees (4)
DS6. Discrete probability (6)

PF. Programming Fundamentals (38 core hours)
PF1. Fundamental programming constructs (9)
PF2. Algorithms and problem solving (6)
PF3. Fundamental data structures (14)
PF4. Recursion (5)
PF5. Event-driven programming (4)

AL. Algorithms and Complexity (31 core hours)
AL1. Basic algorithmic analysis (4)
AL2. Algorithmic strategies (6)
AL3. Fundamental computing algorithms (12)
AL4. Distributed algorithms (3)
AL5. Basic computability (6)
AL6. The complexity classes P and NP
AL7. Automata theory
AL8. Advanced algorithmic analysis
AL9. Cryptographic algorithms
AL10. Geometric algorithms
AL11. Parallel algorithms

AR. Architecture and Organization (36 core hours)
AR1. Digital logic and digital systems (6)
AR2. Machine level representation of data (3)
AR3. Assembly level machine organization (9)
AR4. Memory system organization and architecture (5)
AR5. Interfacing and communication (3)
AR6. Functional organization (7)
AR7. Multiprocessing and alternative architectures (3)
AR8. Performance enhancements
AR9. Architecture for networks and distributed systems

OS. Operating Systems (18 core hours)
OS1. Overview of operating systems (2)
OS2. Operating system principles (2)
OS3. Concurrency (6)
OS4. Scheduling and dispatch (3)
OS5. Memory management (5)
OS6. Device management
OS7. Security and protection
OS8. File systems
OS9. Real-time and embedded systems
OS10. Fault tolerance
OS11. System performance evaluation
OS12. Scripting

NC. Net-Centric Computing (15 core hours)
NC1. Introduction to net-centric computing (2)
NC2. Communication and networking (7)
NC3. Network security (3)
NC4. The Web as an example of client-server computing (3)
NC5. Building Web applications
NC6. Network management
NC7. Compression and decompression
NC8. Multimedia data technologies
NC9. Wireless and mobile computing

PL. Programming Languages (21 core hours)
PL1. Overview of programming languages (2)
PL2. Virtual machines (1)
PL3. Introduction to language translation (2)
PL4. Declarations and types (3)
PL5. Abstraction mechanisms (3)
PL6. Object-oriented programming (10)
PL7. Functional programming
PL8. Language translation systems
PL9. Type systems
PL10. Programming language semantics
PL11. Programming language design

Note: The numbers in parentheses represent the minimum number of hours required to cover this material in a lecture format. It is always appropriate to include mor

HC. Human-Computer Interaction (8 core hours)
HC1. Foundations of human-computer interaction (6)
HC2. Building a simple graphical user interface (2)
HC3. Human-centered software evaluation
HC4. Human-centered software development
HC5. Graphical user-interface design
HC6. Graphical user-interface programming
HC7. HCI aspects of multimedia systems
HC8. HCI aspects of collaboration and communication

GV. Graphics and Visual Computing (3 core hours)
GV1. Fundamental techniques in graphics (2)
GV2. Graphic systems (1)
GV3. Graphic communication
GV4. Geometric modeling
GV5. Basic rendering
GV6. Advanced rendering
GV7. Advanced techniques
GV8. Computer animation
GV9. Visualization
GV10. Virtual reality
GV11. Computer vision

IS. Intelligent Systems (10 core hours)
IS1. Fundamental issues in intelligent systems (1)
IS2. Search and constraint satisfaction (5)
IS3. Knowledge representation and reasoning (4)
IS4. Advanced search
IS5. Advanced knowledge representation and reasoning
IS6. Agents
IS7. Natural language processing
IS8. Machine learning and neural networks
IS9. AI planning systems
IS10. Robotics

IM. Information Management (10 core hours)
IM1. Information models and systems (3)
IM2. Database systems (3)
IM3. Data modeling (4)
IM4. Relational databases
IM5. Database query languages
IM6. Relational database design
IM7. Transaction processing
IM8. Distributed databases
IM9. Physical database design
IM10. Data mining
IM11. Information storage and retrieval
IM12. Hypertext and hypermedia
IM13. Multimedia information and systems
IM14. Digital libraries

SP. Social and Professional Issues (16 core hours)
SP1. History of computing (1)
SP2. Social context of computing (3)
SP3. Methods and tools of analysis (2)
SP4. Professional and ethical responsibilities (3)
SP5. Risks and liabilities of computer-based systems (2)
SP6. Intellectual property (3)
SP7. Privacy and civil liberties (2)
SP8. Computer crime
SP9. Economic issues in computing
SP10. Philosophical frameworks

SE. Software Engineering (31 core hours)
SE1. Software design (8)
SE2. Using APIs (5)
SE3. Software tools and environments (3)
SE4. Software processes (2)
SE5. Software requirements and specifications (4)
SE6. Software validation (3)
SE7. Software evolution (3)
SE8. Software project management (3)
SE9. Component-based computing
SE10. Formal methods
SE11. Software reliability
SE12. Specialized systems development

CN. Computational Science (no core hours)
CN1. Numerical analysis
CN2. Operations research
CN3. Modeling and simulation
CN4. High-performance computing

Discrete Structures (DS)

DS1. Functions, relations, and sets [core]
DS2. Basic logic [core]
DS3. Proof techniques [core]
DS4. Basics of counting [core]
DS5. Graphs and trees [core]
DS6. Discrete probability [core]

Discrete structures is foundational material for computer science. By *foundational* we mean that relatively few computer scientists will be working primarily on discrete structures, but that many other areas of computer science require the ability to work with concepts from discrete structures. Discrete structures includes important material from such areas as set theory, logic, graph theory, and combinatorics.

The material in discrete structures is pervasive in the areas of data structures and algorithms but appears elsewhere in computer science as well. For example, an ability to create and understand a formal proof is essential in formal specification, in verification, and in cryptography. Graph theory concepts are used in networks, operating systems, and compilers. Set theory concepts are used in software engineering and in databases.

As the field of computer science matures, more and more sophisticated analysis techniques are being brought to bear on practical problems. To understand the computational techniques of the future, today's students will need a strong background in discrete structures.

Finally, we note that while areas often have somewhat fuzzy boundaries, this is especially true for discrete structures. We have gathered together here a body of material of a mathematical nature that computer science education must include, and that computer science educators know well enough to specify in great detail. However, the decision about where to draw the line between this area and the Algorithms and Complexity area (AL) on the one hand, and topics left only as supporting mathematics on the other hand, was inevitably somewhat arbitrary. We remind readers that there are vital topics from those two areas that some schools will include in courses with titles like discrete structures.

DS1. Functions, relations, and sets [core]

Minimum core coverage time: 6 hours

Topics:

> Functions (surjections, injections, inverses, composition)
> Relations (reflexivity, symmetry, transitivity, equivalence relations)
> Sets (Venn diagrams, complements, Cartesian products, power sets)
> Pigeonhole principle
> Cardinality and countability

Learning objectives:

1. Explain with examples the basic terminology of functions, relations, and sets.

2. Perform the operations associated with sets, functions, and relations.

3. Relate practical examples to the appropriate set, function, or relation model, and interpret the associated operations and terminology in context.

4. Demonstrate basic counting principles, including uses of diagonalization and the pigeonhole principle.

DS2. Basic logic [core]

Minimum core coverage time: 10 hours

Topics:

> Propositional logic
> Logical connectives
> Truth tables
> Normal forms (conjunctive and disjunctive)
> Validity
> Predicate logic
> Universal and existential quantification
> Modus ponens and modus tollens
> Limitations of predicate logic

Learning objectives:

1. Apply formal methods of symbolic propositional and predicate logic.

2. Describe how formal tools of symbolic logic are used to model algorithms and real-life situations.

3. Use formal logic proofs and logical reasoning to solve problems such as puzzles.

4. Describe the importance and limitations of predicate logic.

DS3. Proof techniques [core]

Minimum core coverage time: 12 hours

Topics:

> Notions of implication, converse, inverse, contrapositive, negation, and contradiction
> The structure of formal proofs
> Direct proofs
> Proof by counterexample
> Proof by contraposition
> Proof by contradiction
> Mathematical induction
> Strong induction
> Recursive mathematical definitions
> Well orderings

Learning objectives:

1. Outline the basic structure of and give examples of each proof technique described in this unit.

2. Discuss which type of proof is best for a given problem.

3. Relate the ideas of mathematical induction to recursion and recursively defined structures.

4. Identify the difference between mathematical and strong induction and give examples of the appropriate use of each.

DS4. Basics of counting [core]

Minimum core coverage time: 5 hours

Topics:

> Counting arguments
> – Sum and product rule
> – Inclusion-exclusion principle
> – Arithmetic and geometric progressions
> – Fibonacci numbers
> The pigeonhole principle
> Permutations and combinations
> – Basic definitions
> – Pascal's identity
> – The binomial theorem
> Solving recurrence relations
> – Common examples
> – The Master theorem

Learning objectives:

1. Compute permutations and combinations of a set, and interpret the meaning in the context of the particular application.

2. State the definition of the Master theorem.

3. Solve a variety of basic recurrence equations.

4. Analyze a problem to create relevant recurrence equations or to identify important counting questions.

DS5. Graphs and trees [core]

Minimum core coverage time: 4 hours

Topics:

> Trees
> Undirected graphs
> Directed graphs
> Spanning trees
> Traversal strategies

Learning objectives:

1. Illustrate by example the basic terminology of graph theory, and some of the properties and special cases of each.

2. Demonstrate different traversal methods for trees and graphs.

3. Model problems in computer science using graphs and trees.

4. Relate graphs and trees to data structures, algorithms, and counting.

DS6. Discrete probability [core]

Minimum core coverage time: 6 hours

Topics:

    Finite probability space, probability measure, events
    Conditional probability, independence, Bayes' theorem
    Integer random variables, expectation

Learning objectives:

1. Calculate probabilities of events and expectations of random variables for elementary problems such as games of chance.

2. Differentiate between dependent and independent events.

3. Apply the binomial theorem to independent events and Bayes' theorem to dependent events.

4. Apply the tools of probability to solve problems such as the Monte Carlo method, the average case analysis of algorithms, and hashing.

Programming Fundamentals (PF)

PF1. Fundamental programming constructs [core]
PF2. Algorithms and problem-solving [core]
PF3. Fundamental data structures [core]
PF4. Recursion [core]
PF5. Event-driven programming [core]

Fluency in a programming language is prerequisite to the study of most of computer science. In the CC1991 report, knowledge of a programming language—while identified as essential—was given little emphasis in the curriculum. The "Introduction to a Programming Language" area in CC1991 represents only 12 hours of class time and is identified as optional, under the optimistic assumption that "increasing numbers of students . . . gain such experience in secondary school." We believe that undergraduate computer science programs must teach students how to use at least one programming language well; furthermore, we recommend that computer science programs should teach students to become competent in languages that make use of at least two programming paradigms. Accomplishing this goal requires considerably more than 12 hours.

This knowledge area consists of those skills and concepts that are essential to programming practice independent of the underlying paradigm. As a result, this area includes units on fundamental programming concepts, basic data structures, and algorithmic processes. These units, however, by no means cover the full range of programming knowledge that a computer science undergraduate must know. Many of the other areas—most notably Programming Languages (PL) and Software Engineering (SE)—also contain programming-related units that are part of the undergraduate core. In most cases, these units could equally well have been assigned to either Programming Fundamentals or the more advanced area.

PF1. Fundamental programming constructs [core]

Minimum core coverage time: 9 hours

Topics:

Basic syntax and semantics of a higher-level language
Variables, types, expressions, and assignment
Simple I/O
Conditional and iterative control structures
Functions and parameter passing
Structured decomposition

Learning objectives:

1. Analyze and explain the behavior of simple programs involving the fundamental programming constructs covered by this unit.

2. Modify and expand short programs that use standard conditional and iterative control structures and functions.

3. Design, implement, test, and debug a program that uses each of the following fundamental programming constructs: basic computation, simple I/O, standard conditional and iterative structures, and the definition of functions.

4. Choose appropriate conditional and iteration constructs for a given programming task.

5. Apply the techniques of structured (functional) decomposition to break a program into smaller pieces.

6. Describe the mechanics of parameter passing.

PF2. Algorithms and problem-solving [core]

Minimum core coverage time: 6 hours

Topics:

Problem-solving strategies
The role of algorithms in the problem-solving process
Implementation strategies for algorithms
Debugging strategies
The concept and properties of algorithms

Learning objectives:

1. Discuss the importance of algorithms in the problem-solving process.

2. Identify the necessary properties of good algorithms.

3. Create algorithms for solving simple problems.

4. Use pseudocode or a programming language to implement, test, and debug algorithms for solving simple problems.

5. Describe strategies that are useful in debugging.

PF3. Fundamental data structures [core]

Minimum core coverage time: 14 hours

Topics:

Primitive types
Arrays
Records
Strings and string processing
Data representation in memory
Static, stack, and heap allocation
Runtime storage management
Pointers and references
Linked structures
Implementation strategies for stacks, queues, and hash tables
Implementation strategies for graphs and trees
Strategies for choosing the right data structure

Learning objectives:

1. Discuss the representation and use of primitive data types and built-in data structures.

2. Describe how the data structures in the topic list are allocated and used in memory.

3. Describe common applications for each data structure in the topic list.

4. Implement the user-defined data structures in a high-level language.

5. Compare alternative implementations of data structures with respect to performance.

6. Write programs that use each of the following data structures: arrays, records, strings, linked lists, stacks, queues, and hash tables.

7. Compare and contrast the costs and benefits of dynamic and static data structure implementations.

8. Choose the appropriate data structure for modeling a given problem.

PF4. Recursion [core]

Minimum core coverage time: 5 hours

Topics:

    The concept of recursion
    Recursive mathematical functions
    Simple recursive procedures
    Divide-and-conquer strategies
    Recursive backtracking
    Implementation of recursion

Learning objectives:

1. Describe the concept of recursion and give examples of its use.
2. Identify the base case and the general case of a recursively defined problem.
3. Compare iterative and recursive solutions for elementary problems such as factorial.
4. Describe the divide-and-conquer approach.
5. Implement, test, and debug simple recursive functions and procedures.
6. Describe how recursion can be implemented using a stack.
7. Discuss problems for which backtracking is an appropriate solution.
8. Determine when a recursive solution is appropriate for a problem.

PF5. Event-driven programming [core]

Minimum core coverage time: 4 hours

Topics:

    Event-handling methods
    Event propagation
    Exception handling

Learning objectives:

1. Explain the difference between event-driven programming and command-line programming.
2. Design, code, test, and debug simple event-driven programs that respond to user events.
3. Develop code that responds to exception conditions raised during execution.

Algorithms and Complexity (AL)

AL1. Basic algorithmic analysis [core]
AL2. Algorithmic strategies [core]
AL3. Fundamental computing algorithms [core]
AL4. Distributed algorithms [core]
AL5. Basic computability [core]
AL6. The complexity classes P and NP [elective]
AL7. Automata theory [elective]
AL8. Advanced algorithmic analysis [elective]
AL9. Cryptographic algorithms [elective]
AL10. Geometric algorithms [elective]
AL11. Parallel algorithms [elective]

Algorithms are fundamental to computer science and software engineering. The real-world performance of any software system depends on only two things: (1) the algorithms chosen and (2) the suitability and efficiency of the various layers of implementation. Good algorithm design is therefore crucial for the performance of all software systems. Moreover, the study of algorithms provides insight into the intrinsic nature of the problem as well as possible solution techniques independent of programming language, programming paradigm, computer hardware, or any other implementation aspect.

An important part of computing is the ability to select algorithms appropriate to particular purposes and to apply them, recognizing the possibility that no suitable algorithm may exist. This facility relies on understanding the range of algorithms that address an important set of well-defined problems, recognizing their strengths and weaknesses, and their suitability in particular contexts. Efficiency is a pervasive theme throughout this area.

AL1. Basic algorithmic analysis [core]

Minimum core coverage time: 4 hours

Topics:

> Asymptotic analysis of upper and average complexity bounds
> Identifying differences among best, average, and worst case behaviors
> Big O, little o, omega, and theta notation
> Standard complexity classes
> Empirical measurements of performance
> Time and space tradeoffs in algorithms
> Using recurrence relations to analyze recursive algorithms

Learning objectives:

1. Explain the use of big O, omega, and theta notation to describe the amount of work done by an algorithm.

2. Use big O, omega, and theta notation to give asymptotic upper, lower, and tight bounds on time and space complexity of algorithms.

3. Determine the time and space complexity of simple algorithms.

4. Deduce recurrence relations that describe the time complexity of recursively defined algorithms.

5. Solve elementary recurrence relations.

AL2. Algorithmic strategies [core]

Minimum core coverage time: 6 hours

Topics:

Brute-force algorithms
Greedy algorithms
Divide-and-conquer
Backtracking
Branch-and-bound
Heuristics
Pattern matching and string/text algorithms
Numerical approximation algorithms

Learning objectives:

1. Describe the shortcoming of brute-force algorithms.

2. For each of several kinds of algorithm (brute force, greedy, divide-and-conquer, backtracking, branch-and-bound, and heuristic), identify an example of everyday human behavior that exemplifies the basic concept.

3. Implement a greedy algorithm to solve an appropriate problem.

4. Implement a divide-and-conquer algorithm to solve an appropriate problem.

5. Use backtracking to solve a problem such as navigating a maze.

6. Describe various heuristic problem-solving methods.

7. Use pattern matching to analyze substrings.

8. Use numerical approximation to solve mathematical problems, such as finding the roots of a polynomial.

AL3. Fundamental computing algorithms [core]

Minimum core coverage time: 12 hours

Topics:

Simple numerical algorithms
Sequential and binary search algorithms
Quadratic sorting algorithms (selection, insertion)
$O(N \log N)$ sorting algorithms (Quicksort, heapsort, mergesort)
Hash tables, including collision-avoidance strategies
Binary search trees
Representations of graphs (adjacency list, adjacency matrix)
Depth- and breadth-first traversals
Shortest-path algorithms (Dijkstra's and Floyd's algorithms)
Transitive closure (Floyd's algorithm)
Minimum spanning tree (Prim's and Kruskal's algorithms)
Topological sort

Learning objectives:

1. Implement the most common quadratic and $O(N \log N)$ sorting algorithms.

2. Design and implement an appropriate hashing function for an application.

3. Design and implement a collision-resolution algorithm for a hash table.

4. Discuss the computational efficiency of the principal algorithms for sorting, searching, and hashing.

5. Discuss factors other than computational efficiency that influence the choice of algorithms, such as programming time, maintainability, and the use of application-specific patterns in the input data.

6. Solve problems using the fundamental graph algorithms, including depth-first and breadth-first search, single-source and all-pairs shortest paths, transitive closure, topological sort, and at least one minimum spanning tree algorithm.

7. Demonstrate the following capabilities: to evaluate algorithms, to select from a range of possible options, to provide justification for that selection, and to implement the algorithm in programming context.

AL4. Distributed algorithms [core]

Minimum core coverage time: 3 hours

Topics:

> Consensus and election
> Termination detection
> Fault tolerance
> Stabilization

Learning objectives:

1. Explain the distributed paradigm.
2. Explain one simple distributed algorithm.
3. Determine when to use consensus or election algorithms.
4. Distinguish between logical and physical clocks.
5. Describe the relative ordering of events in a distributed algorithm.

AL5. Basic computability [core]

Minimum core coverage time: 6 hours

Topics:

> Finite-state machines
> Context-free grammars
> Tractable and intractable problems
> Uncomputable functions
> The halting problem
> Implications of uncomputability

Learning objectives:

1. Discuss the concept of finite state machines.
2. Explain context-free grammars.
3. Design a deterministic finite-state machine to accept a specified language.
4. Explain how some problems have no algorithmic solution.
5. Provide examples that illustrate the concept of uncomputability.

AL6. The complexity classes P and NP [elective]

Topics:

 Definition of the classes P and NP
 NP-completeness (Cook's theorem)
 Standard NP-complete problems
 Reduction techniques

Learning objectives:

1. Define the classes P and NP.

2. Explain the significance of NP-completeness.

3. Prove that a problem is NP-complete by reducing a classic known NP-complete problem to it.

AL7. Automata theory [elective]

Topics:

 Deterministic finite automata (DFAs)
 Nondeterministic finite automata (NFAs)
 Equivalence of DFAs and NFAs
 Regular expressions
 The pumping lemma for regular expressions
 Push-down automata (PDAs)
 Relationship of PDAs and context-free grammars
 Properties of context-free grammars
 Turing machines
 Nondeterministic Turing machines
 Sets and languages
 Chomsky hierarchy
 The Church-Turing thesis

Learning objectives:

1. Determine a language's location in the Chomsky hierarchy (regular sets, context-free, context-sensitive, and recursively enumerable languages).

2. Prove that a language is in a specified class and that it is not in the next lower class.

3. Convert among equivalently powerful notations for a language, including among DFAs, NFAs, and regular expressions, and between PDAs and CFGs.

4. Explain at least one algorithm for both top-down and bottom-up parsing.

5. Explain the Church-Turing thesis and its significance.

AL8. Advanced algorithmic analysis [elective]

Topics:

 Amortized analysis
 Online and offline algorithms
 Randomized algorithms
 Dynamic programming
 Combinatorial optimization

Learning objectives:

1. Use the potential method to provide an amortized analysis of previously unseen data structure, given the potential function.

2. Explain why competitive analysis is an appropriate measure for online algorithms.

3. Explain the use of randomization in the design of an algorithm for a problem where a deterministic algorithm is unknown or much more difficult.

4. Design and implement a dynamic programming solution to a problem.

AL9. Cryptographic algorithms [elective]

Topics:

> Historical overview of cryptography
> Private-key cryptography and the key-exchange problem
> Public-key cryptography
> Digital signatures
> Security protocols
> Applications (zero-knowledge proofs, authentication, and so on)

Learning objectives:

1. Describe efficient basic number-theoretic algorithms, including greatest common divisor, multiplicative inverse mod n, and raising to powers mod n.

2. Describe at least one public-key cryptosystem, including a necessary complexity-theoretic assumption for its security.

3. Create simple extensions of cryptographic protocols, using known protocols and cryptographic primitives.

AL10. Geometric algorithms [elective]

Topics:

> Line segments: properties, intersections
> Convex hull finding algorithms

Learning objectives:

1. Describe and give time analysis of at least two algorithms for finding a convex hull.

2. Justify the Omega(N log N) lower bound on finding the convex hull.

3. Describe at least one additional efficient computational geometry algorithm, such as finding the closest pair of points, convex layers, or maximal layers.

AL11. Parallel algorithms [elective]

Topics:

> PRAM model
> Exclusive versus concurrent reads and writes
> Pointer jumping
> Brent's theorem and work efficiency

Learning objectives:

1. Describe implementation of linked lists on a PRAM.

2. Use parallel-prefix operation to perform simple computations efficiently in parallel.

3. Explain Brent's theorem and its relevance.

Architecture and Organization (AR)

AR1. Digital logic and digital systems [core]
AR2. Machine level representation of data [core]
AR3. Assembly level machine organization [core]
AR4. Memory system organization and architecture [core]
AR5. Interfacing and communication [core]
AR6. Functional organization [core]
AR7. Multiprocessing and alternative architectures [core]
AR8. Performance enhancements [elective]
AR9. Architecture for networks and distributed systems [elective]

The computer lies at the heart of computing. Without it, most of the computing disciplines today would be a branch of theoretical mathematics. To be a professional in any field of computing today, one should not regard the computer as just a black box that executes programs by magic. All students of computing should acquire some understanding and appreciation of a computer system's functional components, their characteristics, their performance, and their interactions. There are practical implications as well. Students need to understand computer architecture in order to structure a program so that it runs more efficiently on a real machine. In selecting a system to use, they should be able to understand the tradeoff among various components, such as CPU clock speed vs. memory size.

The learning outcomes specified for these topics correspond primarily to the core and are intended to support programs that elect to require only the minimum 36 hours of computer architecture of their students. For programs that want to teach more than the minimum, the same topics (AR1-AR7) can be treated at a more advanced level by implementing a two-course sequence. For programs that want to cover the elective topics, those topics can be introduced within a two-course sequence and/or be treated in a more comprehesive way in a third course.

AR1. Digital logic and digital systems [core]

Minimum core coverage time: 6 hours

Topics:

> Overview and history of computer architecture
> Fundamental building blocks (logic gates, flip-flops, counters, registers, PLA)
> Logic expressions, minimization, sum of product forms
> Register transfer notation
> Physical considerations (gate delays, fan-in, fan-out)

Learning objectives:

1. Describe the progression of computer architecture from vacuum tubes to VLSI.

2. Demonstrate an understanding of the basic building blocks and their role in the historical development of computer architecture.

3. Use mathematical expressions to describe the functions of simple combinational and sequential circuits.

4. Design a simple circuit using the fundamental building blocks.

AR2. Machine level representation of data [core]

Minimum core coverage time: 3 hours

Topics:

    Bits, bytes, and words
    Numeric data representation and number bases
    Fixed- and floating-point systems
    Signed and twos-complement representations
    Representation of nonnumeric data (character codes, graphical data)
    Representation of records and arrays

Learning objectives:

1. Explain the reasons for using different formats to represent numerical data.
2. Explain how negative integers are stored in sign-magnitude and twos-complement representation.
3. Convert numerical data from one format to another.
4. Discuss how fixed-length number representations affect accuracy and precision.
5. Describe the internal representation of nonnumeric data.
6. Describe the internal representation of characters, strings, records, and arrays.

AR3. Assembly level machine organization [core]

Minimum core coverage time: 9 hours

Topics:

    Basic organization of the von Neumann machine
    Control unit; instruction fetch, decode, and execution
    Instruction sets and types (data manipulation, control, I/O)
    Assembly/machine language programming
    Instruction formats
    Addressing modes
    Subroutine call and return mechanisms
    I/O and interrupts

Learning objectives:

1. Explain the organization of the classical von Neumann machine and its major functional units.
2. Explain how an instruction is executed in a classical von Neumann machine.
3. Summarize how instructions are represented at both the machine level and in the context of a symbolic assembler.
4. Explain different instruction formats, such as addresses per instruction and variable length vs. fixed length formats.
5. Write simple assembly language program segments.
6. Demonstrate how fundamental high-level programming constructs are implemented at the machine-language level.
7. Explain how subroutine calls are handled at the assembly level.
8. Explain the basic concepts of interrupts and I/O operations.

AR4. Memory system organization and architecture [core]

Minimum core coverage time: 5 hours

Topics:

Storage systems and their technology
Coding, data compression, and data integrity
Memory hierarchy
Main memory organization and operations
Latency, cycle time, bandwidth, and interleaving
Cache memories (address mapping, block size, replacement and store policy)
Virtual memory (page table, TLB)
Fault handling and reliability

Learning objectives:

1. Identify the main types of memory technology.
2. Explain the effect of memory latency on running time.
3. Explain the use of memory hierarchy to reduce the effective memory latency.
4. Describe the principles of memory management.
5. Describe the role of cache and virtual memory.
6. Explain the workings of a system with virtual memory management.

AR5. Interfacing and communication [core]

Minimum core coverage time: 3 hours

Topics:

I/O fundamentals: handshaking, buffering, programmed I/O, interrupt-driven I/O
Interrupt structures: vectored and prioritized, interrupt acknowledgment
External storage, physical organization, and drives
Buses: bus protocols, arbitration, direct-memory access (DMA)
Introduction to networks
Multimedia support
RAID architectures

Learning objectives:

1. Explain how interrupts are used to implement I/O control and data transfers.
2. Identify various types of buses in a computer system.
3. Describe data access from a magnetic disk drive.
4. Compare the common network configurations.
5. Identify interfaces needed for multimedia support.
6. Describe the advantages and limitations of RAID architectures.

AR6. Functional organization [core]

Minimum core coverage time: 7 hours

Topics:

    Implementation of simple datapaths
    Control unit: hardwired realization vs. microprogrammed realization
    Instruction pipelining
    Introduction to instruction-level parallelism (ILP)

Learning objectives:

1. Compare alternative implementation of datapaths.

2. Discuss the concept of control points and the generation of control signals using hardwired or microprogrammed implementations.

3. Explain basic instruction level parallelism using pipelining and the major hazards that may occur.

AR7. Multiprocessing and alternative architectures [core]

Minimum core coverage time: 3 hours

Topics:

    Introduction to SIMD, MIMD, VLIW, EPIC
    Systolic architecture
    Interconnection networks (hypercube, shuffle-exchange, mesh, crossbar)
    Shared memory systems
    Cache coherence
    Memory models and memory consistency

Learning objectives:

1. Discuss the concept of parallel processing beyond the classical von Neumann model.

2. Describe alternative architectures such as SIMD, MIMD, and VLIW.

3. Explain the concept of interconnection networks and characterize different approaches.

4. Discuss the special concerns that multiprocessing systems present with respect to memory management and describe how these are addressed.

AR8. Performance enhancements [elective]

Topics:

    Superscalar architecture
    Branch prediction
    Prefetching
    Speculative execution
    Multithreading
    Scalability

Learning objectives:

1. Describe superscalar architectures and their advantages.

2. Explain the concept of branch prediction and its utility.

3. Characterize the costs and benefits of prefetching.

4. Explain speculative execution and identify the conditions that justify it.

5. Discuss the performance advantages that multithreading can offer in an architecture along with the factors that make it difficult to derive maximum benefits from this approach.

6. Describe the relevance of scalability to performance.

AR9. Architecture for networks and distributed systems [elective]

Topics:

Introduction to LANs and WANs
Layered protocol design, ISO/OSI, IEEE 802
Impact of architectural issues on distributed algorithms
Network computing
Distributed multimedia

Learning objectives:

1. Explain the basic components of network systems and distinguish between LANs and WANs.

2. Discuss the architectural issues involved in the design of a layered network protocol.

3. Explain how architectures differ in network and distributed systems.

4. Discuss architectural issues related to network computing and distributed multimedia.

Operating Systems (OS)

OS1. Overview of operating systems [core]
OS2. Operating system principles [core]
OS3. Concurrency [core]
OS4. Scheduling and dispatch [core]
OS5. Memory management [core]
OS6. Device management [elective]
OS7. Security and protection [elective]
OS8. File systems [elective]
OS9. Real-time and embedded systems [elective]
OS10. Fault tolerance [elective]
OS11. System performance evaluation [elective]
OS12. Scripting [elective]

An operating system defines an abstraction of hardware behavior with which programmers can control the hardware. It also manages resource sharing among the computer's users. The topics in this area explain the issues that influence the design of contemporary operating systems. Courses that cover this area will typically include a laboratory component to enable students to experiment with operating systems.

Over the years, operating systems and their abstractions have become complex relative to typical application software. It is necessary to ensure that the student understands the extent of the use of an operating system prior to a detailed study of internal implementation algorithms and data structures. Therefore, these topics address both the use of operating systems (externals) and their design and implementation (internals). Many of the ideas involved in operating system use have wider applicability across the field of computer science, such as concurrent programming. Studying internal design has relevance in such diverse areas as dependable programming, algorithm design and implementation, modern device development, building virtual environments, caching material across the web, building secure and safe systems, network management, and many others.

OS1. Overview of operating systems [core]

Minimum core coverage time: 2 hours

Topics:

> Role and purpose of the operating system
> History of operating system development
> Functionality of a typical operating system
> Mechanisms to support client-server models, hand-held devices
> Design issues (efficiency, robustness, flexibility, portability, security, compatibility)
> Influences of security, networking, multimedia, windows

Learning objectives:

1. Explain the objectives and functions of modern operating systems.

2. Describe how operating systems have evolved over time from primitive batch systems to sophisticated multiuser systems.

3. Analyze the tradeoffs inherent in operating system design.

4. Describe the functions of a contemporary operating system with respect to convenience, efficiency, and the ability to evolve.

5. Discuss networked, client-server, distributed operating systems and how they differ from single user operating systems.

6. Identify potential threats to operating systems and the security features design to guard against them.

7. Describe how issues such as open source software and the increased use of the Internet are influencing operating system design.

OS2. Operating system principles [core]

Minimum core coverage time: 2 hours

Topics:

Structuring methods (monolithic, layered, modular, micro-kernel models)
Abstractions, processes, and resources
Concepts of application program interfaces (APIs)
Application needs and the evolution of hardware/software techniques
Device organization
Interrupts: methods and implementations
Concept of user/system state and protection, transition to kernel mode

Learning objectives:

1. Explain the concept of a logical layer.

2. Explain the benefits of building abstract layers in hierarchical fashion.

3. Defend the need for APIs and middleware.

4. Describe how computing resources are used by application software and managed by system software.

5. Contrast kernel and user mode in an operating system.

6. Discuss the advantages and disadvantages of using interrupt processing.

7. Compare and contrast the various ways of structuring an operating system such as object-oriented, modular, micro-kernel, and layered.

8. Explain the use of a device list and driver I/O queue.

OS3. Concurrency [core]

Minimum core coverage time: 6 hours

Topics:

States and state diagrams
Structures (ready list, process control blocks, and so forth)
Dispatching and context switching
The role of interrupts
Concurrent execution: advantages and disadvantages
The "mutual exclusion" problem and some solutions
Deadlock: causes, conditions, prevention
Models and mechanisms (semaphores, monitors, condition variables, rendezvous)
Producer-consumer problems and synchronization
Multiprocessor issues (spin-locks, reentrancy)

Learning objectives:

1. Describe the need for concurrency within the framework of an operating system.

2. Demonstrate the potential run-time problems arising from the concurrent operation of many separate tasks.

3. Summarize the range of mechanisms that can be employed at the operating system level to realize concurrent systems and describe the benefits of each.

4. Explain the different states that a task may pass through and the data structures needed to support the management of many tasks.

5. Summarize the various approaches to solving the problem of mutual exclusion in an operating system.

6. Describe reasons for using interrupts, dispatching, and context switching to support concurrency in an operating system.

7. Create state and transition diagrams for simple problem domains.

8. Discuss the utility of data structures, such as stacks and queues, in managing concurrency.

9. Explain conditions that lead to deadlock.

OS4. Scheduling and dispatch [core]

Minimum core coverage time: 3 hours

Topics:

> Preemptive and nonpreemptive scheduling
> Schedulers and policies
> Processes and threads
> Deadlines and real-time issues

Learning objectives:

1. Compare and contrast the common algorithms used for both preemptive and non-preemptive scheduling of tasks in operating systems, such as priority, performance comparison, and fair-share schemes.

2. Describe relationships between scheduling algorithms and application domains.

3. Discuss the types of processor scheduling such as short-term, medium-term, long-term, and I/O.

4. Describe the difference between processes and threads.

5. Compare and contrast static and dynamic approaches to real-time scheduling.

6. Discuss the need for preemption and deadline scheduling.

7. Identify ways that the logic embodied in scheduling algorithms are applicable to other domains, such as disk I/O, network scheduling, project scheduling, and other problems unrelated to computing.

OS5. Memory management [core]

Minimum core coverage time: 5 hours

Topics:

> Review of physical memory and memory management hardware
> Overlays, swapping, and partitions
> Paging and segmentation
> Placement and replacement policies
> Working sets and thrashing
> Caching

Learning objectives:

1. Explain memory hierarchy and cost-performance tradeoffs.

2. Explain the concept of virtual memory and how it is realized in hardware and software.

3. Summarize the principles of virtual memory as applied to caching, paging, and segmentation.

4. Evaluate the tradeoffs in terms of memory size (main memory, cache memory, auxiliary memory) and processor speed.

5. Defend the different ways of allocating memory to tasks, citing the relative merits of each.

6. Describe the reason for and use of cache memory.

7. Compare and contrast paging and segmentation techniques.

8. Discuss the concept of thrashing, both in terms of the reasons it occurs and the techniques used to recognize and manage the problem.

9. Analyze the various memory portioning techniques including overlays, swapping, and placement and replacement policies.

OS6. Device management [elective]

Topics:

> Characteristics of serial and parallel devices
> Abstracting device differences
> Buffering strategies
> Direct memory access
> Recovery from failures

Learning objectives:

1. Explain the key difference between serial and parallel devices and identify the conditions in which each is appropriate.

2. Identify the relationship between the physical hardware and the virtual devices maintained by the operating system.

3. Explain buffering and describe strategies for implementing it.

4. Differentiate the mechanisms used in interfacing a range of devices (including hand-held devices, networks, multimedia) to a computer and explain the implications of these for the design of an operating system.

5. Describe the advantages and disadvantages of direct memory access and discuss the circumstances in which its use is warranted.

6. Identify the requirements for failure recovery.

7. Implement a simple device driver for a range of possible devices.

OS7. Security and protection [elective]

Topics:

>Overview of system security
>Policy/mechanism separation
>Security methods and devices
>Protection, access, and authentication
>Models of protection
>Memory protection
>Encryption
>Recovery management

Learning objectives:

1. Defend the need for protection and security, and the role of ethical considerations in computer use.

2. Summarize the features and limitations of an operating system used to provide protection and security.

3. Compare and contrast current methods for implementing security.

4. Compare and contrast the strengths and weaknesses of two or more currently popular operating systems with respect to security.

5. Compare and contrast the security strengths and weaknesses of two or more currently popular operating systems with respect to recovery management.

OS8. File systems [elective]

Topics:

>Files: data, metadata, operations, organization, buffering, sequential, nonsequential
>Directories: contents and structure
>File systems: partitioning, mount/unmount, virtual file systems
>Standard implementation techniques
>Memory-mapped files
>Special-purpose file systems
>Naming, searching, access, backups

Learning objectives:

1. Summarize the full range of considerations that support file systems.

2. Compare and contrast different approaches to file organization, recognizing the strengths and weaknesses of each.

3. Summarize how hardware developments have lead to changes in our priorities for the design and the management of file systems.

OS9. Real-time and embedded systems [elective]

Topics:

>Process and task scheduling
>Memory/disk management requirements in a real-time environment
>Failures, risks, and recovery
>Special concerns in real-time systems

Learning objectives:

1. Describe what makes a system a real-time system.

2. Explain the presence of and describe the characteristics of latency in real-time systems.

3. Summarize special concerns that real-time systems present and how these concerns are addressed.

OS10. Fault tolerance [elective]

Topics:

> Fundamental concepts: reliable and available systems
> Spatial and temporal redundancy
> Methods used to implement fault tolerance
> Examples of reliable systems

Learning objectives:

1. Explain the relevance of the terms *fault tolerance, reliability,* and *availability.*

2. Outline the range of methods for implementing fault tolerance in an operating system.

3. Explain how an operating system can continue functioning after a fault occurs.

OS11. System performance evaluation [elective]

Topics:

> Why system performance needs to be evaluated
> What is to be evaluated
> Policies for caching, paging, scheduling, memory management, security, and so forth
> Evaluation models: deterministic, analytic, simulation, or implementation-specific
> How to collect evaluation data (profiling and tracing mechanisms)

Learning objectives:

1. Describe the performance metrics used to determine how a system performs.

2. Explain the main evaluation models used to evaluate a system.

OS12. Scripting [elective]

Topics:

> Scripting and the role of scripting languages
> Basic system commands
> Creating scripts, parameter passing
> Executing a script
> Influences of scripting on programming

Learning objectives:

1. Summarize a typical set of system commands provided by an operating system.

2. Demonstrate the typical functionality of a scripting language, and interpret the implications for programming.

3. Demonstrate the mechanisms for implementing scripts and the role of scripts on system implementation and integration.

4. Implement a simple script that exhibits parameter passing.

Net-Centric Computing (NC)

NC1. Introduction to net-centric computing [core]
NC2. Communication and networking [core]
NC3. Network security [core]
NC4. The Web as an example of client-server computing [core]
NC5. Building Web applications [elective]
NC6. Network management [elective]
NC7. Compression and decompression [elective]
NC8. Multimedia data technologies [elective]
NC9. Wireless and mobile computing [elective]

Recent advances in computer and telecommunications networking, particularly those based on TCP/IP, have increased the importance of networking technologies in the computing discipline. Net-centric computing covers a range of subspecialties including computer communication network concepts and protocols, multimedia systems, Web standards and technologies, network security, wireless and mobile computing, and distributed systems.

Mastery of this subject area involves both theory and practice. Learning experiences that involve hands-on experimentation and analysis are strongly recommended as they reinforce student understanding of concepts and their application to real-world problems. Laboratory experiments should involve data collection and synthesis, empirical modeling, protocol analysis at the source code level, network packet monitoring, software construction, and evaluation of alternative design models. All of these are important concepts that can best be understood by laboratory experimentation.

NC1. Introduction to net-centric computing [core]

Minimum core coverage time: 2 hours

Topics:

> Background and history of networking and the Internet
> Network architectures
> The range of specializations within net-centric computing
>> – Networks and protocols
>> – Networked multimedia systems
>> – Distributed computing
>> – Mobile and wireless computing

Learning objectives:

1. Discuss the evolution of early networks and the Internet.

2. Demonstrate the ability to use effectively a range of common networked applications including e-mail, telnet, FTP, newsgroups, and Web browsers, online Web courses, and instant messaging.

3. Explain the hierarchical, layered structure of a typical network architecture.

4. Describe emerging technologies in the net-centric computing area and assess their current capabilities, limitations, and near-term potential.

NC2. Communication and networking [core]

Minimum core coverage time: 7 hours

Topics:

> Network standards and standardization bodies
> The ISO 7-layer reference model in general and its instantiation in TCP/IP
> Circuit switching and packet switching
> Streams and datagrams
> Physical layer networking concepts (theoretical basis, transmission media, standards)
> Data link layer concepts (framing, error control, flow control, protocols)
> Internetworking and routing (routing algorithms, internetworking, congestion control)
> Transport layer services (connection establishment, performance issues)

Learning objectives:

1. Discuss important network standards in their historical context.
2. Describe the responsibilities of the first four layers of the ISO reference model.
3. Discuss the differences between circuit switching and packet switching along with the advantages and disadvantages of each.
4. Explain how a network can detect and correct transmission errors.
5. Illustrate how a packet is routed over the Internet.
6. Install a simple network with two clients and a single server using standard host-configuration software tools such as DHCP.

NC3. Network security [core]

Minimum core coverage time: 3 hours

Topics:

> Fundamentals of cryptography
> Secret-key algorithms
> Public-key algorithms
> Authentication protocols
> Digital signatures
> Examples

Learning objectives:

1. Discuss the fundamental ideas of public-key cryptography.
2. Describe how public-key cryptography works.
3. Distinguish between the use of private- and public-key algorithms.
4. Summarize common authentication protocols.
5. Generate and distribute a PGP key pair and use the PGP package to send an encrypted e-mail message.
6. Summarize the capabilities and limitations of the means of cryptography that are conveniently available to the general public.

NC4. The Web as an example of client-server computing [core]

Minimum core coverage time: 3 hours

Topics:

Web technologies
  – Server-side programs
  – Common gateway interface (CGI) programs
  – Client-side scripts
  – The applet concept
Characteristics of Web servers
  – Handling permissions
  – File management
  – Capabilities of common server architectures
Role of client computers
Nature of the client-server relationship
Web protocols
Support tools for Web site creation and Web management
Developing Internet information servers
Publishing information and applications

Learning objectives:

1. Explain the different roles and responsibilities of clients and servers for a range of possible applications.

2. Select a range of tools that will ensure an efficient approach to implementing various client-server possibilities.

3. Design and build a simple interactive Web-based application (for example, a simple Web form that collects information from the client and stores it in a file on the server).

NC5. Building Web applications [elective]

Topics:

Protocols at the application layer
Principles of Web engineering
Database-driven Web sites
Remote procedure calls (RPC)
Lightweight distributed objects
The role of middleware
Support tools
Security issues in distributed object systems
Enterprise-wide Web-based applications

Learning objectives:

1. Illustrate how interactive client-server Web applications of medium size can be built using different types of Web technologies.

2. Demonstrate how to implement a database-driven Web site, explaining the relevant technologies involved in each tier of the architecture and the accompanying performance tradeoffs.

3. Implement a distributed system using any two distributed object frameworks and compare them with regard to performance and security issues.

4. Discuss security issues and strategies in an enterprise-wide Web-based application.

NC6. Network management [elective]

Topics:

> Overview of the issues of network management
> Use of passwords and access control mechanisms
> Domain names and name services
> Issues for Internet service providers (ISPs)
> Security issues and firewalls
> Quality of service issues: performance, failure recovery

Learning objectives:

1. Explain the issues for network management arising from a range of security threats, including viruses, worms, Trojan horses, and denial-of-service attacks

2. Summarize the strengths and weaknesses associated with different approaches to security.

3. Develop a strategy for ensuring appropriate levels of security in a system designed for a particular purpose.

4. Implement a network firewall.

NC7. Compression and decompression [elective]

Topics:

> Analog and digital representations
> Encoding and decoding algorithms
> Lossless and lossy compression
> Data compression: Huffman coding and the Ziv-Lempel algorithm
> Audio compression and decompression
> Image compression and decompression
> Video compression and decompression
> Performance issues: timing, compression factor, suitability for real-time use

Learning objectives:

1. Summarize the basic characteristics of sampling and quantization for digital representation.

2. Select, giving reasons that are sensitive to the specific application and particular circumstances, the most appropriate compression techniques for text, audio, image, and video information.

3. Explain the asymmetric property of compression and decompression algorithms.

4. Illustrate the concept of run-length encoding.

5. Illustrate how a program like the UNIX `compress` utility, which uses Huffman coding and the Ziv-Lempel algorithm, would compress a typical text file.

NC8. Multimedia data technologies [elective]

Topics:

> Sound and audio, image and graphics, animation and video
> Multimedia standards (audio, music, graphics, image, telephony, video, TV)
> Capacity planning and performance issues
> Input and output devices (scanners, digital camera, touch-screens, voice-activated)
> MIDI keyboards, synthesizers
> Storage standards (Magneto Optical disk, CD-ROM, DVD)
> Multimedia servers and file systems
> Tools to support multimedia development

Learning objectives:

1. For each of several media or multimedia standards, describe in nontechnical language what the standard calls for, and explain how aspects of human perception might be sensitive to the limitations of that standard.

2. Evaluate the potential of a computer system to host one of a range of possible multimedia applications, including an assessment of the requirements of multimedia systems on the underlying networking technology.

3. Describe the characteristics of a computer system (including identification of support tools and appropriate standards) that must host the implementation of one of a range of possible multimedia applications.

4. Implement a multimedia application of modest size.

NC9. Wireless and mobile computing [elective]

Topics:

    Overview of the history, evolution, and compatibility of wireless standards
    The special problems of wireless and mobile computing
    Wireless local area networks and satellite-based networks
    Wireless local loops
    Mobile Internet protocol
    Mobile aware adaption
    Extending the client-server model to accommodate mobility
    Mobile data access: server data dissemination and client cache management
    Software package support for mobile and wireless computing
    The role of middleware and support tools
    Performance issues
    Emerging technologies

Learning objectives:

1. Describe the main characteristics of mobile IP and explain how differs from IP with regard to mobility management and location management as well as performance.

2. Illustrate (with home agents and foreign agents) how e-mail and other traffic is routed using mobile IP.

3. Implement a simple application that relies on mobile and wireless data communications.

4. Describe areas of current and emerging interest in wireless and mobile computing, and assess the current capabilities, limitations, and near-term potential of each.

Programming Languages (PL)

PL1. Overview of programming languages [core]
PL2. Virtual machines [core]
PL3. Introduction to language translation [core]
PL4. Declarations and types [core]
PL5. Abstraction mechanisms [core]
PL6. Object-oriented programming [core]
PL7. Functional programming [elective]
PL8. Language translation systems [elective]
PL9. Type systems [elective]
PL10. Programming language semantics [elective]
PL11. Programming language design [elective]

A programming language is a programmer's principal interface with the computer. More than just knowing how to program in a single language, programmers must understand the different styles of programming promoted by different languages. In their professional life, they will be working with many different languages and styles at once, and will encounter many different languages over the course of their careers. Understanding the variety of programming languages and the design tradeoffs between the different programming paradigms makes it much easier to master new languages quickly. Understanding the pragmatic aspects of programming languages also requires a basic knowledge of programming language translation and runtime features such as storage allocation.

PL1. Overview of programming languages [core]

Minimum core coverage time: 2 hours

Topics:

> History of programming languages
> Brief survey of programming paradigms
>> – Procedural languages
>> – Object-oriented languages
>> – Functional languages
>> – Declarative, nonalgorithmic languages
>> – Scripting languages
> The effects of scale on programming methodology

Learning objectives:

1. Summarize the evolution of programming languages illustrating how this history has led to the paradigms available today.

2. Identify at least one distinguishing characteristic for each of the programming paradigms covered in this unit.

3. Evaluate the tradeoffs between the different paradigms, considering such issues as space efficiency, time efficiency (of both the computer and the programmer), safety, and power of expression.

4. Distinguish between programming-in-the-small and programming-in-the-large.

PL2. Virtual machines [core]

Minimum core coverage time: 1 hour

Topics:

> The concept of a virtual machine
> Hierarchy of virtual machines
> Intermediate languages
> Security issues arising from running code on an alien machine

Learning objectives:

1. Describe the importance and power of abstraction in the context of virtual machines.
2. Explain the benefits of intermediate languages in the compilation process.
3. Evaluate the tradeoffs in performance vs. portability.
4. Explain how executable programs can breach computer system security by accessing disk files and memory.

PL3. Introduction to language translation [core]

Minimum core coverage time: 2 hours

Topics:

> Comparison of interpreters and compilers
> Language translation phases (lexical analysis, parsing, code generation, optimization)
> Machine-dependent and machine-independent aspects of translation

Learning objectives:

1. Compare and contrast compiled and interpreted execution models, outlining the relative merits of each.
2. Describe the phases of program translation from source code to executable code and the files produced by these phases.
3. Explain the differences between machine-dependent and machine-independent translation and where these differences are evident in the translation process.

PL4. Declarations and types [core]

Minimum core coverage time: 3 hours

Topics:

> The conception of types as a set of values with together with a set of operations
> Declaration models (binding, visibility, scope, and lifetime)
> Overview of type-checking
> Garbage collection

Learning objectives:

1. Explain the value of declaration models, especially with respect to programming-in-the-large.
2. Identify and describe the properties of a variable such as its associated address, value, scope, persistence, and size.
3. Discuss type incompatibility.
4. Demonstrate different forms of binding, visibility, scoping, and lifetime management.

5. Defend the importance of types and type-checking in providing abstraction and safety.

6. Evaluate tradeoffs in lifetime management (reference counting vs. garbage collection).

PL5. Abstraction mechanisms [core]

Minimum core coverage time: 3 hours

Topics:

>   Procedures, functions, and iterators as abstraction mechanisms
>   Parameterization mechanisms (reference vs. value)
>   Activation records and storage management
>   Type parameters and parameterized types
>   Modules in programming languages

Learning objectives:

1. Explain how abstraction mechanisms support the creation of reusable software components.

2. Demonstrate the difference between call-by-value and call-by-reference parameter passing.

3. Defend the importance of abstractions, especially with respect to programming-in-the-large.

4. Describe how the computer system uses activation records to manage program modules and their data.

PL6. Object-oriented programming [core]

Minimum core coverage time: 10 hours

Topics:

>   Object-oriented design
>   Encapsulation and information-hiding
>   Separation of behavior and implementation
>   Classes and subclasses
>   Inheritance (overriding, dynamic dispatch)
>   Polymorphism (subtype polymorphism vs. inheritance)
>   Class hierarchies
>   Collection classes and iteration protocols
>   Internal representations of objects and method tables

Learning objectives:

1. Justify the philosophy of object-oriented design and the concepts of encapsulation, abstraction, inheritance, and polymorphism.

2. Design, implement, test, and debug simple programs in an object-oriented programming language.

3. Describe how the class mechanism supports encapsulation and information hiding.

4. Design, implement, and test the implementation of "is-a" relationships among objects using a class hierarchy and inheritance.

5. Compare and contrast the notions of overloading and overriding methods in an object-oriented language.

6. Explain the relationship between the static structure of the class and the dynamic structure of the instances of the class.

7. Describe how iterators access the elements of a container.

PL7. Functional programming [elective]

Topics:

- Overview and motivation of functional languages
- Recursion over lists, natural numbers, trees, and other recursively defined data
- Pragmatics (debugging by divide and conquer; persistency of data structures)
- Amortized efficiency for functional data structures
- Closures and uses of functions as data (infinite sets, streams)

Learning objectives:

1. Outline the strengths and weaknesses of the functional programming paradigm.

2. Design, code, test, and debug programs using the functional paradigm.

3. Explain the use of functions as data, including the concept of closures.

PL8. Language translation systems [elective]

Topics:

Application of regular expressions in lexical scanners
Parsing (concrete and abstract syntax, abstract syntax trees)
Application of context-free grammars in table-driven and recursive-descent parsing
Symbol table management
Code generation by tree walking
Architecture-specific operations: instruction selection and register allocation
Optimization techniques
The use of tools in support of the translation process and the advantages thereof
Program libraries and separate compilation
Building syntax-directed tools

Learning objectives:

1. Describe the steps and algorithms used by language translators.

2. Recognize the underlying formal models such as finite state automata, push-down automata and their connection to language definition through regular expressions and grammars.

3. Discuss the effectiveness of optimization.

4. Explain the impact of a separate compilation facility and the existence of program libraries on the compilation process.

PL9. Type systems [elective]

Topics:

Data type as set of values with set of operations
Data types
   - Elementary types
   - Product and coproduct types
   - Algebraic types
   - Recursive types
   - Arrow (function) types
   - Parameterized types

Type-checking models
Semantic models of user-defined types
  – Type abbreviations
  – Abstract data types
  – Type equality
Parametric polymorphism
Subtype polymorphism
Type-checking algorithms

Learning objectives:

1. Formalize the notion of typing.
2. Describe each of the elementary data types.
3. Explain the concept of an abstract data type.
4. Recognize the importance of typing for abstraction and safety.
5. Differentiate between static and dynamic typing.
6. Differentiate between type declarations and type inference.
7. Evaluate languages with regard to typing.

PL10. Programming language semantics [elective]

Topics:

Informal semantics
Overview of formal semantics
Denotational semantics
Axiomatic semantics
Operational semantics

Learning objectives:

1. Explain the importance of formal semantics.
2. Differentiate between formal and informal semantics.
3. Describe the different approaches to formal semantics.
4. Evaluate the different approaches to formal semantics.

PL11. Programming language design [elective]

Topics:

General principles of language design
Design goals
Typing regimes
Data structure models
Control structure models
Abstraction mechanisms

Learning objectives:

1. Evaluate the impact of different typing regimes on language design, language usage, and the translation process.
2. Explain the role of different abstraction mechanisms in the creation of user-defined facilities.

Human-Computer Interaction (HC)

HC1. Foundations of human-computer interaction [core]
HC2. Building a simple graphical user interface [core]
HC3. Human-centered software evaluation [elective]
HC4. Human-centered software development [elective]
HC5. Graphical user-interface design [elective]
HC6. Graphical user-interface programming [elective]
HC7. HCI aspects of multimedia systems [elective]
HC8. HCI aspects of collaboration and communication [elective]

This list of topics is intended as an introduction to human-computer interaction for computer science majors. Emphasis will be placed on understanding human behavior with interactive objects, knowing how to develop and evaluate interactive software using a human-centered approach, and general knowledge of HCI design issues with multiple types of interactive software. Units HC1 (Foundations of Human-Computer Interaction) and HC2 (Building a simple graphical user interface) will be required for all majors, possibly as modules in the introductory courses. The remaining units will most likely be integrated into one or two elective courses at the junior or senior level.

HC1. Foundations of human-computer interaction [core]

Minimum core coverage time: 6 hours

Topics:

> Motivation: Why care about people?
> Contexts for HCI (tools, Web hypermedia, communication)
> Human-centered development and evaluation
> Human performance models: perception, movement, and cognition
> Human performance models: culture, communication, and organizations
> Accommodating human diversity
> Principles of good design and good designers; engineering tradeoffs
> Introduction to usability testing

Learning objectives:

1. Discuss the reasons for human-centered software development.

2. Summarize the basic science of psychological and social interaction.

3. Differentiate between the role of hypotheses and experimental results vs. correlations.

4. Develop a conceptual vocabulary for analyzing human interaction with software: affordance, conceptual model, feedback, and so forth.

5. Distinguish between the different interpretations that a given icon, symbol, word, or color can have in (a) two different human cultures and (b) in a culture and one of its subcultures.

6. In what ways might the design of a computer system or application succeed or fail in terms of respecting human diversity.

7. Create and conduct a simple usability test for an existing software application.

HC2. Building a simple graphical user interface [core]

Minimum core coverage time: 2 hours

Topics:

> Principles of graphical user interfaces (GUIs)
> GUI toolkits

Learning objectives:

1. Identify several fundamental principles for effective GUI design.
2. Use a GUI toolkit to create a simple application that supports a graphical user interface.
3. Illustrate the effect of fundamental design principles on the structure of a graphical user interface.
4. Conduct a simple usability test for each instance and compare the results.

HC3. Human-centered software evaluation [elective]

Topics:

> Setting goals for evaluation
> Evaluation without users: walkthroughs, KLM, guidelines, and standards
> Evaluation with users: usability testing, interview, survey, experiment

Learning objectives:

1. Discuss evaluation criteria: learning, task time and completion, acceptability.
2. Conduct a walkthrough and a Keystroke Level Model (KLM) analysis.
3. Summarize the major guidelines and standards.
4. Conduct a usability test, an interview, and a survey.
5. Compare a usability test with a controlled experiment.
6. Evaluate an existing interactive system with human-centered criteria and a usability test.

HC4. Human-centered software development [elective]

Topics:

> Approaches, characteristics, and overview of process
> Functionality and usability: task analysis, interviews, surveys
> Specifying interaction and presentation
> Prototyping techniques and tools
>   – Paper storyboards
>   – Inheritance and dynamic dispatch
>   – Prototyping languages and GUI builders

Learning objectives:

1. Explain the basic types and features of human-centered development.
2. Compare human-centered development to traditional software engineering methods.
3. State three functional requirements and three usability requirements.
4. Specify an interactive object with transition networks, OO design, or scenario descriptions.
5. Discuss the pros and cons of development with paper and software prototypes.

HC5. Graphical user-interface design [elective]

Topics:

Choosing interaction styles and interaction techniques
HCI aspects of common widgets
HCI aspects of screen design: layout, color, fonts, labeling
Handling human failure
Beyond simple screen design: visualization, representation, metaphor
Multimodal interaction: graphics, sound, and haptics
3D interaction and virtual reality

Learning objectives:

1. Summarize common interaction styles.
2. Explain good design principles of each of the following: common widgets; sequenced screen presentations; simple error-trap dialog; a user manual.
3. Design, prototype, and evaluate a simple 2D GUI illustrating knowledge of the concepts taught in HC3 and HC4.
4. Discuss the challenges that exist in moving from 2D to 3D interaction.

HC6. Graphical user-interface programming [elective]

Topics:

UIMS, dialogue independence and levels of analysis, Seeheim model
Widget classes
Event management and user interaction
Geometry management
GUI builders and UI programming environments
Cross-platform design

Learning objectives:

1. Differentiate between the responsibilities of the UIMS and the application.
2. Differentiate between kernel-based and client-server models for the UI.
3. Compare the event-driven paradigm with more traditional procedural control for the UI.
4. Describe aggregation of widgets and constraint-based geometry management.
5. Explain callbacks and their role in GUI builders.
6. Identify at least three differences common in cross-platform UI design.
7. Identify as many commonalities as you can that are found in UIs across different platforms.

HC7. HCI aspects of multimedia systems [elective]

Topics:

Categorization and architectures of information: hierarchies, hypermedia
Information retrieval and human performance
 – Web search
 – Usability of database query languages
 – Graphics
 – Sound
HCI design of multimedia information systems
Speech recognition and natural language processing
Information appliances and mobile computing

Learning objectives:

1. Discuss how information retrieval differs from transaction processing.

2. Explain how the organization of information supports retrieval.

3. Describe the major usability problems with database query languages.

4. Explain the current state of speech recognition technology in particular and natural language processing in general.

5. Design, prototype, and evaluate a simple Multimedia Information System illustrating knowledge of the concepts taught in HC4, HC5, and HC7.

HC8. HCI aspects of collaboration and communication [elective]

Topics:

> Groupware to support specialized tasks: document preparation, multiplayer games
> Asynchronous group communication: e-mail, bulletin boards
> Synchronous group communication: chat rooms, conferencing
> Online communities: MUDs/MOOs
> Software characters and intelligent agents

Learning objectives:

1. Compare the HCI issues in individual interaction with group interaction.

2. Discuss several issues of social concern raised by collaborative software.

3. Discuss the HCI issues in software that embodies human intention.

4. Describe the difference between synchronous and asynchronous communication.

5. Design, prototype, and evaluate a simple groupware or group communication application illustrating knowledge of the concepts taught in HC4, HC5, and HC8.

6. Participate in a team project for which some interaction is face-to-face and other interaction occurs via a mediating software environment.

7. Describe the similarities and differences between face-to-face and software-mediated collaboration.

Graphics and Visual Computing (GV)

GV1. Fundamental techniques in graphics [core]
GV2. Graphic systems [core]
GV3. Graphic communication [elective]
GV4. Geometric modeling [elective]
GV5. Basic rendering [elective]
GV6. Advanced rendering [elective]
GV7. Advanced techniques [elective]
GV8. Computer animation [elective]
GV9. Visualization [elective]
GV10. Virtual reality [elective]
GV11. Computer vision [elective]

The area encompassed by Graphics and Visual Computing (GV) is divided into four interrelated fields:

- *Computer graphics.* Computer graphics is the art and science of communicating information using images that are generated and presented through computation. This requires (a) the design and construction of models that represent information in ways that support the creation and viewing of images, (b) the design of devices and techniques through which the person may interact with the model or the view, (c) the creation of techniques for rendering the model, and (d) the design of ways the images may be preserved. The goal of computer graphics is to engage the person's visual centers alongside other cognitive centers in understanding.

- *Visualization.* The field of visualization seeks to determine and present underlying correlated structures and relationships in both scientific (computational and medical sciences) and more abstract datasets. The prime objective of the presentation should be to communicate the information in a dataset so as to enhance understanding. Although current techniques of visualization exploit visual abilities of humans, other sensory modalities, including sound and haptics (touch), are also being considered to aid the discovery process of information.

- *Virtual reality.* Virtual reality (VR) enables users to experience a three-dimensional environment generated using computer graphics, and perhaps other sensory modalities, to provide an environment for enhanced interaction between a human user and a computer-created world.

- *Computer vision.* The goal of computer vision (CV) is to deduce the properties and structure of the three-dimensional world from one or more two-dimensional images. The understanding and practice of computer vision depends on core concepts in computing, but also relates strongly to the disciplines of physics, mathematics, and psychology.

GV1. Fundamental techniques in graphics [core]

Minimum core coverage time: 2 hours

Topics:

> Hierarchy of graphics software
> Using a graphics API
> Simple color models (RGB, HSB, CMYK)
> Homogeneous coordinates
> Affine transformations (scaling, rotation, translation)
> Viewing transformation
> Clipping

Learning objectives:

1. Distinguish the capabilities of different levels of graphics software and describe the appropriateness of each.

2. Create images using a standard graphics API.

3. Use the facilities provided by a standard API to express basic transformations such as scaling, rotation, and translation.

4. Implement simple procedures that perform transformation and clipping operations on a simple two-dimensional image.

5. Discuss the three-dimensional coordinate system and the changes required to extend 2D transformation operations to handle transformations in 3D

GV2. Graphic systems [core]

Minimum core coverage time: 1 hour

Topics:

> Raster and vector graphics systems
> Video display devices
> Physical and logical input devices
> Issues facing the developer of graphical systems

Learning objectives:

1. Describe the appropriateness of graphics architectures for given applications.

2. Explain the function of various input devices.

3. Compare and contrast the techniques of raster graphics and vector graphics.

4. Use current hardware and software for creating and displaying graphics.

5. Discuss the expanded capabilities of emerging hardware and software for creating and displaying graphics.

GV3. Graphic communication [elective]

Topics:

> Psychodynamics of color and interactions among colors
> Modifications of color for vision deficiency
> Cultural meaning of different colors
> Use of effective pseudocolor palettes for images for specific audiences
> Structuring a view for effective understanding
> Image modifications for effective video and hardcopy
> Use of legends to key information to color or other visual data
> Use of text in images to present context and background information
> Visual user feedback on graphical operations

Learning objectives:

1. Explain the value of using colors and pseudocolors.

2. Demonstrate the ability to create effective video and hardcopy images.

3. Identify effective and ineffective examples of communication using graphics.

4. Create effective examples of graphic communication, making appropriate use of color, legends, text, and/or video.

5. Create two effective examples that communicate the same content: one designed for hardcopy presentation and the other designed for online presentation.

6. Discuss the differences in design criteria for hardcopy and online presentations.

GV4. Geometric modeling [elective]

Topics:

Polygonal representation of 3D objects
Parametric polynomial curves and surfaces
Constructive solid geometry (CSG) representation
Implicit representation of curves and surfaces
Spatial subdivision techniques
Procedural models
Deformable models
Subdivision surfaces
Multiresolution modeling
Reconstruction

Learning objectives:

1. Create simple polyhedral models by surface tessellation.

2. Construct CSG models from simple primitives, such as cubes and quadric surfaces.

3. Generate a mesh representation from an implicit surface.

4. Generate a fractal model or terrain using a procedural method.

5. Generate a mesh from data points acquired with a laser scanner.

GV5. Basic rendering [elective]

Topics:

Line generation algorithms (Bresenham)
Font generation: outline vs. bitmap
Light-source and material properties
Ambient, diffuse, and specular reflections
Phong reflection model
Rendering of a polygonal surface; flat, Gouraud, and Phong shading
Texture mapping, bump texture, environment map
Introduction to ray tracing
Image synthesis, sampling techniques, and anti-aliasing

Learning objectives:

1. Explain the operation of the Bresenham algorithm for rendering a line on a pixel-based display.

2. Explain the concept and applications of each of these techniques.

3. Demonstrate each of these techniques by creating an image using a standard API.

4. Describe how a graphic image has been created.

GV6. Advanced rendering [elective]

Topics:

    Transport equations
    Ray tracing algorithms
    Photon tracing
    Radiosity for global illumination computation, form factors
    Efficient approaches to global illumination
    Monte Carlo methods for global illumination
    Image-based rendering, panorama viewing, plenoptic function modeling
    Rendering of complex natural phenomenon
    Nonphotorealistic rendering

Learning objectives:

1. Describe several transport equations in detail, noting all comprehensive effects.

2. Describe efficient algorithms to compute radiosity and explain the tradeoffs of accuracy and algorithmic performance.

3. Describe the impact of meshing schemes.

4. Explain image-based rendering techniques, light fields, and associated topics.

GV7. Advanced techniques [elective]

Topics:

    Color quantization
    Scan conversion of 2D primitive, forward differencing
    Tessellation of curved surfaces
    Hidden surface removal methods
    Z-buffer and frame buffer, color channels (a channel for opacity)
    Advanced geometric modeling techniques

Learning objectives:

1. Describe the techniques identified in this section.

2. Explain how to recognize the graphics techniques used to create a particular image.

3. Implement any of the specified graphics techniques using a primitive graphics system at the individual pixel level.

4. Use common animation software to construct simple organic forms using metaball and skeleton.

GV8. Computer animation [elective]

Topics:

    Key-frame animation
    Camera animation
    Scripting system
    Animation of articulated structures: inverse kinematics
    Motion capture
    Procedural animation
    Deformation

Learning objectives:

1. Explain the spline interpolation method for producing in-between positions and orientations.

2. Compare and contrast several technologies for motion capture.

3. Use the particle function in common animation software to generate a simple animation, such as fireworks.

4. Use free-form deformation techniques to create various deformations.

GV9. Visualization [elective]

Topics:

> Basic viewing and interrogation functions for visualization
> Visualization of vector fields, tensors, and flow data
> Visualization of scalar field or height field: isosurface by the marching cube method
> Direct volume data rendering: ray-casting, transfer functions, segmentation, hardware
> Information visualization: projection and parallel-coordinates methods

Learning objectives:

1. Describe the basic algorithms behind scalar and vector visualization.

2. Describe the tradeoffs of the algorithms in terms of accuracy and performance.

3. Employ suitable theory from signal processing and numerical analysis to explain the effects of visualization operations.

4. Describe the impact of presentation and user interaction on exploration.

GV10. Virtual reality [elective]

Topics:

> Stereoscopic display
> Force feedback simulation, haptic devices
> Viewer tracking
> Collision detection
> Visibility computation
> Time-critical rendering, multiple levels of details (LOD)
> Image-base VR system
> Distributed VR, collaboration over computer network
> Interactive modeling
> User interface issues
> Applications in medicine, simulation, and training

Learning objectives:

1. Describe the optical model realized by a computer graphics system to synthesize stereoscopic view.

2. Describe the principles of different viewer tracking technologies.

3. Explain the principles of efficient collision detection algorithms for convex polyhedra.

4. Describe the differences between geometry- and image-based virtual reality.

5. Describe the issues of user action synchronization and data consistency in a networked environment.

6. Determine the basic requirements on interface, hardware, and software configurations of a VR system for a specified application.

GV11. Computer vision [elective]

Topics:

Image acquisition
The digital image and its properties
Image preprocessing
Segmentation (thresholding, edge- and region-based segmentation)
Shape representation and object recognition
Motion analysis
Case studies (object recognition, object tracking)

Learning objectives:

1. Explain the image formation process.

2. Explain the advantages of two and more cameras, stereo vision.

3. Explain various segmentation approaches, along with their characteristics, differences, strengths, and weaknesses.

4. Describe object recognition based on contour- and region-based shape representations.

5. Explain differential motion analysis methods.

6. Describe the differences in object tracking methods.

Intelligent Systems (IS)

IS1. Fundamental issues in intelligent systems [core]
IS2. Search and constraint satisfaction [core]
IS3. Knowledge representation and reasoning [core]
IS4. Advanced search [elective]
IS5. Advanced knowledge representation and reasoning [elective]
IS6. Agents [elective]
IS7. Natural language processing [elective]
IS8. Machine learning and neural networks [elective]
IS9. AI planning systems [elective]
IS10. Robotics [elective]

The field of artificial intelligence (AI) is concerned with the design and analysis of autonomous agents. These are software systems and/or physical machines, with sensors and actuators, embodied for example within a robot or an autonomous spacecraft. An intelligent system must be able to perceive its environment, to act rationally toward its assigned tasks, and to interact with other agents and with human beings.

These capabilities are covered by topics such as computer vision, planning and acting, robotics, multiagents systems, speech recognition, and natural language understanding. They rely on a broad set of general and specialized knowledge representations and reasoning mechanisms, on problem solving and search algorithms, and on machine learning techniques.

Furthermore, artificial intelligence provides a set of tools for solving problems that are difficult or impractical to solve with other methods. These include heuristic search and planning algorithms, formalisms for knowledge representation and reasoning, machine learning techniques, and methods applicable to sensing and action problems such as speech and language understanding, computer vision, and robotics, among others. The student needs to be able to determine when an AI approach is appropriate for a given problem, and to be able to select and implement a suitable AI method.

IS1. Fundamental issues in intelligent systems [core]

Minimum core coverage time: 1 hour

Topics:

> History of artificial intelligence
> Philosophical questions
> > – The Turing test
> > – Searle's "Chinese Room" thought experiment
> > – Ethical issues in AI
> Fundamental definitions
> > – Optimal vs. human-like reasoning
> > – Optimal vs. human-like behavior
> Philosophical questions
> Modeling the world
> The role of heuristics

Learning objectives:

1. Describe the Turing test and the "Chinese Room" thought experiment.

2. Differentiate the concepts of optimal reasoning and human-like reasoning.

3. Differentiate the concepts of optimal behavior and human-like behavior.

4. List examples of intelligent systems that depend on models of the world.

5. Describe the role of heuristics and the need for tradeoffs between optimality and efficiency.

IS2. Search and constraint satisfaction [core]

Minimum core coverage time: 5 hours

Topics:

> Problem spaces
> Brute-force search (breadth-first, depth-first, depth-first with iterative deepening)
> Best-first search (generic best-first, Dijkstra's algorithm, A*, admissibility of A*)
> Two-player games (minimax search, alpha-beta pruning)
> Constraint satisfaction (backtracking and local search methods)

Learning objectives:

1. Formulate an efficient problem space for a problem expressed in English by expressing that problem space in terms of states, operators, an initial state, and a description of a goal state.

2. Describe the problem of combinatorial explosion and its consequences.

3. Select an appropriate brute-force search algorithm for a problem, implement it, and characterize its time and space complexities.

4. Select an appropriate heuristic search algorithm for a problem and implement it by designing the necessary heuristic evaluation function.

5. Describe under what conditions heuristic algorithms guarantee optimal solution.

6. Implement minimax search with alpha-beta pruning for some two-player game.

7. Formulate a problem specified in English as a constraint-satisfaction problem and implement it using a chronological backtracking algorithm.

IS3. Knowledge representation and reasoning [core]

Minimum core coverage time: 4 hours

Topics:

> Review of propositional and predicate logic
> Resolution and theorem proving
> Nonmonotonic inference
> Probabilistic reasoning
> Bayes' theorem

Learning objectives:

1. Explain the operation of the resolution technique for theorem proving.

2. Explain the distinction between monotonic and nonmonotonic inference.

3. Discuss the advantages and shortcomings of probabilistic reasoning.

4. Apply Bayes' theorem to determine conditional probabilities.

IS4. Advanced search [elective]

Topics:

> Genetic algorithms
> Simulated annealing
> Local search

Learning objectives:

1. Explain what genetic algorithms are and constrast their effectiveness with the classic problem-solving and search techniques.
2. Explain how simulated annealing can be used to reduce search complexity and contrast its operation with classic search techniques.
3. Apply local search techniques to a classic domain.

IS5. Advanced knowledge representation and reasoning [elective]

Topics:

> Structured representation
> – Frames and objects
> – Description logics
> – Inheritance systems
> Nonmonotonic reasoning
> – Nonclassical logics
> – Default reasoning
> – Belief revision
> – Preference logics
> – Integration of knowledge sources
> – Aggregation of conflicting belief
> Reasoning on action and change
> – Situation calculus
> – Event calculus
> – Ramification problems
> Temporal and spatial reasoning
> Uncertainty
> – Probabilistic reasoning
> – Bayesian nets
> – Fuzzy sets and possibility theory
> – Decision theory
> Knowledge representation for diagnosis, qualitative representation

Learning objectives:

1. Compare and contrast the most common models used for structured knowledge representation, highlighting their strengths and weaknesses.
2. Characterize the components of nonmonotonic reasoning and its usefulness as a representational mechanisms for belief systems.
3. Apply situation and event calculus to problems of action and change.
4. Articulate the distinction between temporal and spatial reasoning, explaining how they interrelate.
5. Describe and contrast the basic techniques for representing uncertainty.
6. Describe and contrast the basic techniques for diagnosis and qualitative representation.

IS6. Agents [elective]

Topics:

Definition of agents
Successful applications and state-of-the-art agent-based systems
Agent architectures
– Simple reactive agents
– Reactive planners
– Layered architectures
– Example architectures and applications
Agent theory
– Commitments
– Intentions
– Decision-theoretic agents
– Markov decision processes (MDP)
Software agents, personal assistants, and information access
– Collaborative agents
– Information-gathering agents
Believable agents (synthetic characters, modeling emotions in agents)
Learning agents
Multiagent systems
– Economically inspired multiagent systems
– Collaborating agents
– Agent teams
– Agent modeling
– Multiagent learning
Introduction to robotic agents
Mobile agents

Learning objectives:

1. Explain how an agent differs from other categories of intelligent systems.

2. Characterize and contrast the standard agent architectures.

3. Describe the applications of agent theory, to domains such as software agents, personal assistants, and believable agents.

4. Describe the distinction between agents that learn and those that don't.

5. Demonstrate using appropriate examples how multiagent systems support agent interaction.

6. Describe and contrast robotic and mobile agents.

IS7. Natural language processing [elective]

Topics:

Deterministic and stochastic grammars
Parsing algorithms
Corpus-based methods
Information retrieval
Language translation
Speech recognition

Learning objectives:

1. Define and contrast deterministic and stochastic grammars, providing examples to show the adequacy of each.

2. Identify the classic parsing algorithms for parsing natural language.

3. Defend the need for an established corpus.

4. Give examples of catalog and look up procedures in a corpus-based approach.

5. Articulate the distinction between techniques for information retrieval, language translation, and speech recognition.

IS8. Machine learning and neural networks [elective]

Topics:

> Definition and examples of machine learning
> Supervised learning
> Learning decision trees
> Learning neural networks
> Learning belief networks
> The nearest neighbor algorithm
> Learning theory
> The problem of overfitting
> Unsupervised learning
> Reinforcement learning

Learning objectives:

1. Explain the differences among the three main styles of learning: supervised, reinforcement, and unsupervised.

2. Implement simple algorithms for supervised learning, reinforcement learning, and unsupervised learning.

3. Determine which of the three learning styles is appropriate to a particular problem domain.

4. Compare and contrast each of the following techniques, providing examples of when each strategy is superior: decision trees, neural networks, and belief networks.

5. Implement a simple learning system using decision trees, neural networks, and/or belief networks, as appropriate.

6. Characterize the state of the art in learning theory, including its achievements and its shortcomings.

7. Explain the nearest neighbor algorithm and its place within learning theory.

8. Explain the problem of overfitting, along with techniques for detecting and managing the problem.

IS9. AI planning systems [elective]

Topics:

> Definition and examples of planning systems
> Planning as search
> Operator-based planning
> Propositional planning
> Extending planning systems (case-based, learning, and probabilistic systems)
> Static world planning systems
> Planning and execution
> Planning and robotics

Learning objectives:

1. Define the concept of a planning system.

2. Explain how planning systems differ from classical search techniques.

3. Articulate the differences between planning as search, operator-based planning, and propositional planning, providing examples of domains where each is most applicable.

4. Define and provide examples for each of the following techniques: case-based, learning, and probablistic planning.

5. Compare and contrast static world planning systems with those need dynamic execution.

6. Explain the impact of dynamic planning on robotics.

IS10. Robotics [elective]

Topics:

Overview
  – State-of-the-art robot systems
  – Planning vs. reactive control
  – Uncertainty in control
  – Sensing
  – World models
Configuration space
Planning
Sensing
Robot programming
Navigation and control

Learning objectives:

1. Outline the potential and limitations of today's state-of-the-art robot systems.

2. Implement configuration space algorithms for a 2D robot and complex polygons.

3. Implement simple motion planning algorithms.

4. Explain the uncertainties associated with sensors and how to deal with those uncertainties.

5. Design a simple control architecture.

6. Describe various strategies for navigation in unknown environments, including the strengths and shortcomings of each.

7. Describe various strategies for navigation with the aid of landmarks, including the strengths and shortcomings of each.

Information Management (IM)

IM1. Information models and systems [core]
IM2. Database systems [core]
IM3. Data modeling [core]
IM4. Relational databases [elective]
IM5. Database query languages [elective]
IM6. Relational database design [elective]
IM7. Transaction processing [elective]
IM8. Distributed databases [elective]
IM9. Physical database design [elective]
IM10. Data mining [elective]
IM11. Information storage and retrieval [elective]
IM12. Hypertext and hypermedia [elective]
IM13. Multimedia information and systems [elective]
IM14. Digital libraries [elective]

Information management (IM) plays a critical role in almost all areas where computers are used. This area includes the capture, digitization, representation, organization, transformation, and presentation of information; algorithms for efficient and effective access and updating of stored information, data modeling and abstraction, and physical file storage techniques. It also encompasses information security, privacy, integrity, and protection in a shared environment. The student needs to be able to develop conceptual and physical data models, determine what IM methods and techniques are appropriate for a given problem, and be able to select and implement an appropriate IM solution that reflects all suitable constraints, including scalability and usability.

IM1. Information models and systems [core]

Minimum core coverage time: 3 hours

Topics:

> History and motivation for information systems
> Information storage and retrieval (IS&R)
> Information management applications
> Information capture and representation
> Analysis and indexing
> Search, retrieval, linking, navigation
> Information privacy, integrity, security, and preservation
> Scalability, efficiency, and effectiveness

Learning objectives:

1. Compare and contrast information with data and knowledge.

2. Summarize the evolution of information systems from early visions up through modern offerings, distinguishing their respective capabilities and future potential.

3. Critique/defend a small- to medium-sized information application with regard to its satisfying real user information needs.

4. Describe several technical solutions to the problems related to information privacy, integrity, security, and preservation.

5. Explain measures of efficiency (throughput, response time) and effectiveness (recall, precision).

6. Describe approaches to ensure that information systems can scale from the individual to the global.

IM2. Database systems [core]

Minimum core coverage time: 3 hours

Topics:

> History and motivation for database systems
> Components of database systems
> DBMS functions
> Database architecture and data independence
> Use of a database query language

Learning objectives:

1. Explain the characteristics that distinguish the database approach from the traditional approach of programming with data files.

2. Cite the basic goals, functions, models, components, applications, and social impact of database systems.

3. Describe the components of a database system and give examples of their use.

4. Identify major DBMS functions and describe their role in a database system.

5. Explain the concept of data independence and its importance in a database system.

6. Use a query language to elicit information from a database.

IM3. Data modeling [core]

Minimum core coverage time: 4 hours

Topics:

> Data modeling
> Conceptual models (including entity-relationship and UML)
> Object-oriented model
> Relational data model

Learning objectives:

1. Categorize data models based on the types of concepts that they provide to describe the database structure—that is, conceptual data model, physical data model, and representational data model.

2. Describe the modeling concepts and notation of the entity-relationship model and UML, including their use in data modeling.

3. Describe the main concepts of the OO model such as object identity, type constructors, encapsulation, inheritance, polymorphism, and versioning.

4. Define the fundamental terminology used in the relational data model .

5. Describe the basic principles of the relational data model.

6. Illustrate the modeling concepts and notation of the relational data model.

IM4. Relational databases [elective]

Topics:

> Mapping conceptual schema to a relational schema
> Entity and referential integrity
> Relational algebra and relational calculus

Learning objectives:

1. Prepare a relational schema from a conceptual model developed using the entity-relationship model

2. Explain and demonstrate the concepts of entity integrity constraint and referential integrity constraint (including definition of the concept of a foreign key).

3. Demonstrate use of the relational algebra operations from mathematical set theory (*union, intersection, difference,* and *cartesian product*) and the relational algebra operations developed specifically for relational databases (*select, product, join,* and *division*).

4. Demonstrate queries in the relational algebra.

5. Demonstrate queries in the tuple relational calculus.

IM5. Database query languages [elective]

Topics:

> Overview of database languages
> SQL (data definition, query formulation, update sublanguage, constraints, integrity)
> Query optimization
> QBE and 4th-generation environments
> Embedding nonprocedural queries in a procedural language
> Introduction to Object Query Language

Learning objectives:

1. Create a relational database schema in SQL that incorporates key, entity integrity, and referential integrity constraints.

2. Demonstrate data definition in SQL and retrieving information from a database using the SQL `SELECT` statement.

3. Evaluate a set of query processing strategies and select the optimal strategy.

4. Create a nonprocedural query by filling in templates of relations to construct an example of the desired query result.

5. Embed object-oriented queries into a stand-alone language such as C++ or Java (e.g., `SELECT Col.Method() FROM Object`).

IM6. Relational database design [elective]

Topics:

> Database design
> Functional dependency
> Normal forms (1NF, 2NF, 3NF, BCNF)
> Multivalued dependency (4NF)
> Join dependency (PJNF, 5NF)
> Representation theory

Learning objectives:

1. Determine the functional dependency between two or more attributes that are a subset of a relation.

2. Describe what is meant by 1NF, 2NF, 3NF, and BCNF.

3. Identify whether a relation is in 1NF, 2NF, 3NF, or BCNF.

4. Normalize a 1NF relation into a set of 3NF (or BCNF) relations and denormalize a relational schema.

5. Explain the impact of normalization on the efficiency of database operations, especially query optimization.

6. Describe what is a multivalued dependency and what type of constraints it specifies.

7. Explain why 4NF is useful in schema design.

IM7. Transaction processing [elective]

Topics:

> Transactions
> Failure and recovery
> Concurrency control

Learning objectives:

1. Create a transaction by embedding SQL into an application program.

2. Explain the concept of implicit commits.

3. Describe the issues specific to efficient transaction execution.

4. Explain when and why rollback is needed and how logging assures proper rollback.

5. Explain the effect of different isolation levels on the concurrency control mechanisms.

6. Choose the proper isolation level for implementing a specified transaction protocol.

IM8. Distributed databases [elective]

Topics:

> Distributed data storage
> Distributed query processing
> Distributed transaction model
> Concurrency control
> Homogeneous and heterogeneous solutions
> Client-server

Learning objectives:

1. Explain the techniques used for data fragmentation, replication, and allocation during the distributed database design process.

2. Evaluate simple strategies for executing a distributed query to select the strategy that minimizes the amount of data transfer.

3. Explain how the two-phase commit protocol is used to deal with committing a transaction that accesses databases stored on multiple nodes.

4. Describe distributed concurrency control based on the distinguished copy techniques and the voting method.

5. Describe the three levels of software in the client-server model.

IM9. Physical database design [elective]

Topics:

Storage and file structure
Indexed files
Hashed files
Signature files
B-trees
Files with dense index
Files with variable length records
Database efficiency and tuning

Learning objectives:

1. Explain the concepts of records, record types, and files, as well as the different techniques for placing file records on disk.
2. Give examples of the application of primary, secondary, and clustering indexes.
3. Distinguish between a nondense index and a dense index.
4. Implement dynamic multilevel indexes using B-trees.
5. Explain the theory and application of internal and external hashing techniques.
6. Use hashing to facilitate dynamic file expansion.
7. Describe the relationships among hashing, compression, and efficient database searches.
8. Evaluate costs and benefits of various hashing schemes.
9. Explain how physical database design affects database transaction efficiency.

IM10. Data mining [elective]

Topics:

The usefulness of data mining
Associative and sequential patterns
Data clustering
Market basket analysis
Data cleaning
Data visualization

Learning objectives:

1. Compare and contrast different conceptions of data mining as evidenced in both research and application.
2. Explain the role of finding associations in commercial market basket data.
3. Characterize the kinds of patterns that can be discovered by association rule mining.
4. Describe how to extend a relational system to find patterns using association rules.
5. Evaluate methodological issues underlying the effective application of data mining.
6. Identify and characterize sources of noise, redundancy, and outliers in presented data.
7. Identify mechanisms (online aggregation, anytime behavior, interactive visualization) to close the loop in the data mining process.
8. Describe why the various close-the-loop processes improve the effectiveness of data mining.

IM11. Information storage and retrieval [elective]

Topics:

Characters, strings, coding, text
Documents, electronic publishing, markup, and markup languages
Tries, inverted files, PAT trees, signature files, indexing
Morphological analysis, stemming, phrases, stop lists
Term frequency distributions, uncertainty, fuzziness, weighting
Vector space, probabilistic, logical, and advanced models
Information needs, relevance, evaluation, effectiveness
Thesauri, ontologies, classification and categorization, metadata
Bibliographic information, bibliometrics, citations
Routing and (community) filtering
Search and search strategy, information seeking behavior, user modeling, feedback
Information summarization and visualization
Integration of citation, keyword, classification scheme, and other terms
Protocols and systems (including Z39.50, OPACs, WWW engines, research systems)

Learning objectives:

1. Explain basic information storage and retrieval concepts.

2. Describe what issues are specific to efficient information retrieval.

3. Give applications of alternative search strategies and explain why the particular search strategy is appropriate for the application.

4. Perform Internet-based research.

5. Design and implement a small- to medium-sized information storage and retrieval system.

IM12. Hypertext and hypermedia [elective]

Topics:

Hypertext models (early history, Web, Dexter, Amsterdam, HyTime)
Link services, engines, and (distributed) hypertext architectures
Nodes, composites, and anchors
Dimensions, units, locations, spans
Browsing, navigation, views, zooming
Automatic link generation
Presentation, transformations, synchronization
Authoring, reading, and annotation
Protocols and systems (including Web, HTTP)

Learning objectives:

1. Summarize the evolution of hypertext and hypermedia models from early versions up through current offerings, distinguishing their respective capabilities and limitations.

2. Explain basic hypertext and hypermedia concepts.

3. Demonstrate a fundamental understanding of information presentation, transformation, and synchronization.

4. Compare and contrast hypermedia delivery based on protocols and systems used.

5. Design and implement Web-enabled information retrieval applications using appropriate authoring tools.

IM13. Multimedia information and systems [elective]

Topics:

Devices, device drivers, control signals and protocols, DSPs
Applications, media editors, authoring systems, and authoring
Streams/structures, capture/represent/transform, spaces/domains, compression/coding
Content-based analysis, indexing, and retrieval of audio, images, and video
Presentation, rendering, synchronization, multimodal integration/interfaces
Real-time delivery, quality of service, audio/video conferencing, video-on-demand

Learning objectives:

1. Describe the media and supporting devices commonly associated with multimedia information and systems.

2. Explain basic multimedia presentation concepts.

3. Demonstrate the use of content-based information analysis in a multimedia information system.

4. Critique multimedia presentations in terms of their appropriate use of audio, video, graphics, color, and other information presentation concepts.

5. Implement a multimedia application using a commercial authoring system.

IM14. Digital libraries [elective]

Topics:

Digitization, storage, and interchange
Digital objects, composites, and packages
Metadata, cataloging, author submission
Naming, repositories, archives
Spaces (conceptual, geographical, 2/3D, VR)
Architectures (agents, buses, wrappers/mediators), interoperability
Services (searching, linking, browsing, and so forth)
Intellectual property rights management, privacy, protection (watermarking)
Archiving and preservation, integrity

Learning objectives:

1. Explain the underlying technical concepts in building a digital library.

2. Describe the basic service requirements for searching, linking, and browsing.

3. Critique scenarios involving appropriate and inappropriate use of a digital library, and determine the social, legal, and economic consequences for each scenario.

4. Describe some of the technical solutions to the problems related to archiving and preserving information in a digital library.

5. Design and implement a small digital library.

Social and Professional Issues (SP)

SP1. History of computing [core]
SP2. Social context of computing [core]
SP3. Methods and tools of analysis [core]
SP4. Professional and ethical responsibilities [core]
SP5. Risks and liabilities of computer-based systems [core]
SP6. Intellectual property [core]
SP7. Privacy and civil liberties [core]
SP8. Computer crime [elective]
SP9. Economic issues in computing [elective]
SP10. Philosophical frameworks [elective]

Although technical issues are obviously central to any computing curriculum, they do not by themselves constitute a complete educational program in the field. Students must also develop an understanding of the social and professional context in which computing is done.

This need to incorporate the study of social issues into the curriculum was recognized in the following excerpt from *Computing Curricula 1991* [Tucker91]:

> Undergraduates also need to understand the basic cultural, social, legal, and ethical issues inherent in the discipline of computing. They should understand where the discipline has been, where it is, and where it is heading. They should also understand their individual roles in this process, as well as appreciate the philosophical questions, technical problems, and aesthetic values that play an important part in the development of the discipline.
>
> Students also need to develop the ability to ask serious questions about the social impact of computing and to evaluate proposed answers to those questions. Future practitioners must be able to anticipate the impact of introducing a given product into a given environment. Will that product enhance or degrade the quality of life? What will the impact be upon individuals, groups, and institutions?
>
> Finally, students need to be aware of the basic legal rights of software and hardware vendors and users, and they also need to appreciate the ethical values that are the basis for those rights. Future practitioners must understand the responsibility that they will bear, and the possible consequences of failure. They must understand their own limitations as well as the limitations of their tools. All practitioners must make a long-term commitment to remaining current in their chosen specialties and in the discipline of computing as a whole.

The material in this knowledge area is best covered through a combination of one required course along with short modules in other courses. On the one hand, some units listed as core—in particular, SP2, SP3, SP4, and SP6—do not readily lend themselves to being covered in other traditional courses. Without a standalone course, it is difficult to cover these topics appropriately. On the other hand, if ethical considerations are covered only in the standalone course and not "in context," it will reinforce the false notion that technical processes are void of ethical issues. Thus, it is important that several traditional courses include modules that analyze ethical considerations in the context of the technical subject matter of the course. Courses in areas such as software engineering, databases, computer networks, and introduction to computing provide obvious context for analysis of ethical issues. However, an ethics-related module could be developed for almost any course in the curriculum. It would be explicitly against the spirit of the recommendations to have only a standalone course. Running through all of the issues in this area is the need to speak to the computer practitioner's responsibility to proactively address these issues by both moral and technical actions.

The ethical issues discussed in any class should be directly related to and arise naturally from the subject matter of that class. Examples include a discussion in the database course of data aggregation or data mining, or a discussion in the software engineering course of the potential conflicts between obligations to the customer and obligations to the user and others affected by their work. Programming assignments built around applications such as controlling the movement of a laser during eye surgery can help to address the professional, ethical and social impacts of computing.

There is an unresolved pedagogical conflict between having the core course at the lower (freshman-sophomore) level versus the upper (junior-senior) level. Having the course at the lower level

1. Allows for coverage of methods and tools of analysis (SP3) before analyzing ethical issues in the context of different technical areas

2. Assures that students who drop out early to enter the workforce will still be introduced to some professional and ethical issues.

On the other hand, placing the course too early may lead to the following problems:

1. Lower-level students may not have the technical knowledge and intellectual maturity to support in-depth ethical analysis. Without basic understanding of technical alternatives, it is difficult to consider their ethical implications.

2. Students need a certain level of maturity and sophistication to appreciate the background and issues involved. For that reason, students should have completed at least the discrete mathematics course and the second computer science course. Also, if students take a technical writing course, it should be a prerequisite or corequisite for the required course in the SP area.

3. Some programs may wish to use the course as a "capstone" experience for seniors.

Although items SP2 and SP3 are listed with a number of hours associated, they are fundamental to all the other topics. Thus, when covering the other areas, instructors should continually be aware of the social context issues and the ethical analysis skills. In practice, this means that the topics in SP2 and SP3 will be continually reinforced as the material in the other areas is covered.

SP1. History of computing [core]

Minimum core coverage time: 1 hour

Topics:

> Prehistory—the world before 1946
> History of computer hardware, software, networking
> Pioneers of computing

Learning objectives:

1. List the contributions of several pioneers in the computing field.
2. Compare daily life before and after the advent of personal computers and the Internet.
3. Identify significant continuing trends in the history of the computing field.

SP2. Social context of computing [core]

Minimum core coverage time: 3 hours

Topics:

> Introduction to the social implications of computing
> Social implications of networked communication
> Growth of, control of, and access to the Internet
> Gender-related issues
> International issues

Learning objectives:

1. Interpret the social context of a particular implementation.
2. Identify assumptions and values embedded in a particular design.
3. Evaluate a particular implementation through the use of empirical data.
4. Describe positive and negative ways in which computing alters the modes of interaction between people.
5. Explain why computing/network access is restricted in some countries.

SP3. Methods and tools of analysis [core]

Minimum core coverage time: 2 hours

Topics:

> Making and evaluating ethical arguments
> Identifying and evaluating ethical choices
> Understanding the social context of design
> Identifying assumptions and values

Learning objectives:

1. Analyze an argument to identify premises and conclusion.
2. Illustrate the use of example, analogy, and counter-analogy in ethical argument.
3. Detect use of basic logical fallacies in an argument.
4. Identify stakeholders in an issue and our obligations to them.
5. Articulate the ethical tradeoffs in a technical decision.

SP4. Professional and ethical responsibilities [core]

Minimum core coverage time: 3 hours

Topics:

> Community values and the laws by which we live
> The nature of professionalism
> Various forms of professional credentialing and the advantages and disadvantages
> The role of the professional in public policy
> Maintaining awareness of consequences
> Ethical dissent and whistle-blowing
> Codes of ethics, conduct, and practice (IEEE, ACM, SE, AITP, and so forth)
> Dealing with harassment and discrimination
> "Acceptable use" policies for computing in the workplace

Learning objectives:

1. Identify progressive stages in a whistle-blowing incident.

2. Specify the strengths and weaknesses of relevant professional codes as expressions of professionalism and guides to decision-making.

3. Identify ethical issues that arise in software development and determine how to address them technically and ethically.

4. Develop a computer use policy with enforcement measures.

5. Analyze a global computing issue, observing the role of professionals and government officials in managing the problem.

6. Evaluate the professional codes of ethics from the ACM, the IEEE Computer Society, and other organizations.

SP5. Risks and liabilities of computer-based systems [core]

Minimum core coverage time: 2 hours

Topics:

> Historical examples of software risks (such as the Therac-25 case)
> Implications of software complexity
> Risk assessment and management

Learning objectives:

1. Explain the limitations of testing as a means to ensure correctness.

2. Describe the differences between correctness, reliability, and safety.

3. Discuss the potential for hidden problems in reuse of existing components.

4. Describe current approaches to managing risk, and characterize the strengths and shortcomings of each.

SP6. Intellectual property [core]

Minimum core coverage time: 3 hours

Topics:

> Foundations of intellectual property
> Copyrights, patents, and trade secrets
> Software piracy
> Software patents
> Transnational issues concerning intellectual property

Learning objectives:

1. Distinguish among patent, copyright, and trade secret protection.

2. Discuss the legal background of copyright in national and international law.

3. Explain how patent and copyright laws may vary internationally.

4. Outline the historical development of software patents.

5. Discuss the consequences of software piracy on software developers and the role of relevant enforcement organizations.

SP7. Privacy and civil liberties [core]

Minimum core coverage time: 2 hours

Topics:

> Ethical and legal basis for privacy protection
> Privacy implications of massive database systems
> Technological strategies for privacy protection
> Freedom of expression in cyberspace
> International and intercultural implications

Learning objectives:

1. Summarize the legal bases for the right to privacy and freedom of expression in one's own nation and how those concepts vary from country to country.

2. Describe current computer-based threats to privacy.

3. Explain how the Internet may change the historical balance in protecting freedom of expression.

4. Explain both the disadvantages and advantages of free expression in cyberspace.

5. Describe trends in privacy protection as exemplified in technology.

SP8. Computer crime [elective]

Topics:

> History and examples of computer crime
> "Cracking" ("hacking") and its effects
> Viruses, worms, and Trojan horses
> Crime prevention strategies

Learning objectives:

1. Outline the technical basis of viruses and denial-of-service attacks.

2. Enumerate techniques to combat "cracker" attacks.

3. Discuss several different "cracker" approaches and motivations.

4. Identify the professional's role in security and the tradeoffs involved.

SP9. Economic issues in computing [elective]

Topics:

> Monopolies and their economic implications
> Effect of skilled labor supply and demand on the quality of computing products
> Pricing strategies in the computing domain
> Differences in access to computing resources and the possible effects thereof

Learning objectives:

1. Summarize the rationale for antimonopoly efforts.

2. Describe several ways in which the information technology industry is affected by shortages in the labor supply.

3. Suggest and defend ways to address limitations on access to computing.

4. Outline the evolution of pricing strategies for computing goods and services.

SP10. Philosophical frameworks [elective]

Topics:

Philosophical frameworks, particularly utilitarianism and deontological theories
Problems of ethical relativism
Scientific ethics in historical perspective
Differences in scientific and philosophical approaches

Learning objectives:

1. Summarize the basic concepts of relativism, utilitarianism, and deontological theories.

2. Recognize the distinction between ethical theory and professional ethics.

3. Identify the weaknesses of the "hired agent" approach, strict legalism, naïve egoism, and naïve relativism as ethical frameworks.

Software Engineering (SE)

SE1. Software design [core]
SE2. Using APIs [core]
SE3. Software tools and environments [core]
SE4. Software processes [core]
SE5. Software requirements and specifications [core]
SE6. Software validation [core]
SE7. Software evolution [core]
SE8. Software project management [core]
SE9. Component-based computing [elective]
SE10. Formal methods [elective]
SE11. Software reliability [elective]
SE12. Specialized systems development [elective]

Software engineering is the discipline concerned with the application of theory, knowledge, and practice for effectively and efficiently building software systems that satisfy the requirements of users and customers. Software engineering is applicable to small, medium, and large-scale systems. It encompasses all phases of the life cycle of a software system. The life cycle includes requirement analysis and specification, design, construction, testing, and operation and maintenance.

Software engineering employs engineering methods, processes, techniques, and measurement. It benefits from the use of tools for managing software development; analyzing and modeling software artifacts; assessing and controlling quality; and for ensuring a disciplined, controlled approach to software evolution and reuse. Software development, which can involve an individual developer or a team of developers, requires choosing the tools, methods, and approaches that are most applicable for a given development environment.

The elements of software engineering are applicable to the development of software in any computing application domain where professionalism, quality, schedule, and cost are important in producing a software system.

SE1. Software design [core]

Minimum core coverage time: 8 hours

Topics:

> Fundamental design concepts and principles
> Design patterns
> Software architecture
> Structured design
> Object-oriented analysis and design
> Component-level design
> Design for reuse

Learning objectives:

1. Discuss the properties of good software design.

2. Compare and contrast object-oriented analysis and design with structured analysis and design.

3. Evaluate the quality of multiple software designs based on key design principles and concepts.

4. Select and apply appropriate design patterns in the construction of a software application.

5. Create and specify the software design for a medium-sized software product using a software requirement specification, an accepted program design methodology (for example, structured or object-oriented), and appropriate design notation.

6. Conduct a software design review using appropriate guidelines.

7. Evaluate a software design at the component level.

8. Evaluate a software design from the perspective of reuse.

SE2. Using APIs [core]

Minimum core coverage time: 5 hours

Topics:

> API programming
> Class browsers and related tools
> Programming by example
> Debugging in the API environment
> Introduction to component-based computing

Learning objectives:

1. Explain the value of application programming interfaces (APIs) in software development.

1. Use class browsers and related tools during the development of applications using APIs.

2. Design, implement, test, and debug programs that use large-scale API packages.

SE3. Software tools and environments [core]

Minimum core coverage time: 3 hours

Topics:

> Programming environments
> Requirements analysis and design modeling tools
> Testing tools
> Configuration management tools
> Tool integration mechanisms

Learning objectives:

1. Select, with justification, an appropriate set of tools to support the development of a range of software products.

2. Analyze and evaluate a set of tools in a given area of software development (for example, management, modeling, or testing).

3. Demonstrate the capability to use a range of software tools in support of the development of a software product of medium size.

SE4. Software processes [core]

Minimum core coverage time: 2 hours

Topics:

> Software life-cycle and process models
> Process assessment models
> Software process metrics

Learning objectives:

1. Explain the software life cycle and its phases including the deliverables that are produced.

2. Select, with justification the software development models most appropriate for the development and maintenance of a diverse range of software products.

3. Explain the role of process maturity models.

4. Compare the traditional waterfall model to the incremental model, the object-oriented model, and other apropriate models.

5. For each of various software project scenarios, describe the project's place in the software life cycle, identify the particular tasks that should be performed next, and identify metrics appropriate to those tasks.

SE5. Software requirements and specifications [core]

Minimum core coverage time: 4 hours

Topics:

> Requirements elicitation
> Requirements analysis modeling techniques
> Functional and nonfunctional requirements
> Prototyping
> Basic concepts of formal specification techniques

Learning objectives:

1. Apply key elements and common methods for elicitation and analysis to produce a set of software requirements for a medium-sized software system.

2. Discuss the challenges of maintaining legacy software.

3. Use a common, nonformal method to model and specify (in the form of a requirements specification document) the requirements for a medium-sized software system.

4. Conduct a review of a software requirements document using best practices to determine the quality of the document.

5. Translate into natural language a software requirements specification written in a commonly used formal specification language.

SE6. Software validation [core]

Minimum core coverage time: 3 hours

Topics:

    Validation planning
    Testing fundamentals, including test plan creation and test case generation
    Black-box and white-box testing techniques
    Unit, integration, validation, and system testing
    Object-oriented testing
    Inspections

Learning objectives:

1. Distinguish between program validation and verification.

2. Describe the role that tools can play in the validation of software.

3. Distinguish between the different types and levels of testing (unit, integration, systems, and acceptance) for medium-sized software products.

4. Create, evaluate, and implement a test plan for a medium-sized code segment.

5. Undertake, as part of a team activity, an inspection of a medium-sized code segment.

6. Discuss the issues involving the testing of object-oriented software.

SE7. Software evolution [core]

Minimum core coverage time: 3 hours

Topics:

    Software maintenance
    Characteristics of maintainable software
    Reengineering
    Legacy systems
    Software reuse

Learning objectives:

1. Identify the principal issues associated with software evolution and explain their impact on the software life cycle.

2. Discuss the challenges of maintaining legacy systems and the need for reverse engineering.

3. Outline the process of regression testing and its role in release management.

4. Estimate the impact of a change request to an existing product of medium size.

5. Develop a plan for re-engineering a medium-sized product in response to a change request.

6. Discuss the advantages and disadvantages of software reuse.

7. Exploit opportunities for software reuse in a given context.

SE8. Software project management [core]

Minimum core coverage time: 3 hours

Topics:

Team management
- Team processes
- Team organization and decision-making
- Roles and responsibilities in a software team
- Role identification and assignment
- Project tracking
- Team problem resolution
Project scheduling
Software measurement and estimation techniques
Risk analysis
Software quality assurance
Software configuration management
Project management tools

Learning objectives:

1. Demonstrate through involvement in a team project the central elements of team building and team management.

2. Prepare a project plan for a software project that includes estimates of size and effort, a schedule, resource allocation, configuration control, change management, and project risk identification and management.

3. Compare and contrast the different methods and techniques used to assure the quality of a software product.

SE9. Component-based computing [elective]

Topics:

Fundamentals
- The definition and nature of components
- Components and interfaces
- Interfaces as contracts
- The benefits of components
Basic techniques
- Component design and assembly
- Relationship with the client-server model and with patterns
- Use of objects and object lifecycle services
- Use of object brokers
- Marshalling
Applications (including the use of mobile components)
Architecture of component-based systems
Component-oriented design
Event handling: detection, notification, and response
Middleware
- The object-oriented paradigm within middleware
- Object request brokers
- Transaction processing monitors
- Workflow systems
- State-of-the-art tools

Learning objectives:

1. Explain and apply recognized principles to the building of high-quality software components.

2. Discuss and select an architecture for a component-based system suitable for a given scenario.

3. Identify the kind of event handling implemented in one or more given APIs.

4. Explain the role of objects in middleware systems and the relationship with components.

5. Apply component-oriented approaches to the design of a range of software including those required for concurrency and transactions, reliable communication services, database interaction including services for remote query and database management, secure communication and access.

SE10. Formal methods [elective]

Topics:

Formal methods concepts
Formal specification languages
Executable and nonexecutable specifications
Pre and post assertions
Formal verification

Learning objectives:

1. Apply formal verification techniques to software segments with low complexity.

2. Discuss the role of formal verification techniques in the context of software validation and testing.

3. Explain the potential benefits and drawbacks of using formal specification languages.

4. Create and evaluate pre- and post-assertions for a variety of situations ranging from simple through complex.

5. Using a common formal specification language, formulate the specification of a simple software system and demonstrate the benefits from a quality perspective.

SE11. Software reliability [elective]

Topics:

Software reliability models
Redundancy and fault tolerance
Defect classification
Probabilistic methods of analysis

Learning objectives:

1. Demonstrate the ability to apply multiple methods to develop reliability estimates for a software system.

2. Identify and apply redundancy and fault tolerance for a medium-sized application.

3. Explain the problems that exist in achieving very high levels of reliability.

4. Identify methods that will lead to the realization of a software architecture that achieves a specified reliability level.

SE12. Specialized systems development [elective]

Topics:

Real-time systems
Client-server systems
Distributed systems
Parallel systems
Web-based systems
High-integrity systems

Learning objectives:

1. Identify and discuss different specialized systems.

2. Discuss life cycle and software process issues in the context of software systems designed for a specialized context.

3. Select, with appropriate justification, approaches that will result in the efficient and effective development and maintenance of specialized software systems.

4. Given a specific context and a set of related professional issues, discuss how a software engineer involved in the development of specialized systems should respond to those issues.

5. Outline the central technical issues associated with the implementation of specialized systems development.

Computational Science and Numerical Methods (CN)

CN1. Numerical analysis [elective]
CN2. Operations research [elective]
CN3. Modeling and simulation [elective]
CN4. High-performance computing [elective]

From the earliest days of the discipline, numerical methods and the techniques of scientific computing have constituted a major area of computer science research. As computers increase in their problem-solving power, this area—like much of the discipline—has grown in both breadth and importance. At the end of the millennium, scientific computing stands as an intellectual discipline in its own right, closely related to but nonetheless distinct from computer science.

Although courses in numerical methods and scientific computing are valuable components of an undergraduate program in computer science, the CC2001 Task Force believes that none of the topics in this area represent core knowledge. From our surveys of curricula and interaction with the computer science education community, we are convinced no consensus exists that this material is essential for all CS undergraduates. It remains a vital part of the discipline, but need not be a part of every program.

For those who choose to pursue it, this area offers exposure to many valuable ideas and techniques, including precision of numerical representation, error analysis, numerical techniques, parallel architectures and algorithms, modeling and simulation, and scientific visualization. At the same time, students who take courses in this area have an opportunity to apply these techniques in a wide range of application areas, such as the following:

- Molecular dynamics
- Fluid dynamics
- Celestial mechanics
- Economic forecasting
- Optimization problems
- Structural analysis of materials
- Bioinformatics
- Computational biology
- Geologic modeling
- Computerized tomography

Each of the units in this area corresponds to a full-semester course at most institutions. The level of specification of the topic descriptions and the learning objectives is therefore different from that used in other areas in which the individual units typically require smaller blocks of time.

CN1. Numerical analysis [elective]

Topics:

> Floating-point arithmetic
> Error, stability, convergence
> Taylor's series
> Iterative solutions for finding roots (Newton's Method)
> Curve fitting; function approximation

Numerical differentiation and integration (Simpson's Rule)
Explicit and implicit methods
Differential equations (Euler's Method)
Linear algebra
Finite differences

Learning objectives:

1. Compare and contrast the numerical analysis techniques presented in this unit.

2. Define error, stability, machine precision concepts. and the inexactness of computational approximations.

3. Identify the sources of inexactness in computational approximations.

4. Design, code, test, and debug programs that implement numerical methods.

CN2. Operations research [elective]

Topics:

Linear programming
   – Integer programming
   – The Simplex method
Probablistic modeling
Queueing theory
   – Petri nets
   – Markov models and chains
Optimization
Network analysis and routing algorithms
Prediction and estimation
   – Decision analysis
   – Forecasting
   – Risk management
   – Econometrics, microeconomics
   – Sensitivity analysis
Dynamic programming
Sample applications
Software tools

Learning objectives:

1. Apply the fundamental techniques of operations research.

2. Describe several established techniques for prediction and estimation.

3. Design, code, test, and debug application programs to solve problems in the domain of operations research.

CN3. Modeling and simulation [elective]

Topics:

Random numbers
   – Pseudorandom number generation and testing
   – Monte Carlo methods
   – Introduction to distribution functions
Simulation modeling
   – Discrete-event simulation
   – Continuous simulation

Verification and validation of simulation models
  – Input analysis
  – Output analysis
Queueing theory models
Sample applications

Learning objectives:

1. Discuss the fundamental concepts of computer simulation.

2. Evaluate models for computer simulation.

3. Compare and contrast methods for random number generation.

4. Design, code, test, and debug simulation programs.

CN4. High-performance computing [elective]

Topics:

Introduction to high-performance computing
  – History and importance of computational science
  – Overview of application areas
  – Review of required skills
High-performance computing
  – Processor architectures
  – Memory systems for high performance
  – Input/output devices
  – Pipelining
  – Parallel languages and architectures
Scientific visualization
  – Presentation of results
  – Data formats
  – Visualization tools and packages
Sample problems
  – Ocean and atmosphere models
  – Seismic wave propagation
  – N-body systems (the Barnes-Hut algorithm)
  – Chemical reactions
  – Phase transitions
  – Fluid flow

Learning objectives:

1. Recognize problem areas where computational modeling enhances current research methods.

2. Compare and contrast architectures for scientific and parallel computing, recognizing the strengths and weaknesses of each.

3. Implement simple performance measurements for high-performance systems.

4. Design, code, test, and debug programs using techniques of numerical analysis, computer simulation, and scientific visualization.

Appendix B
Course Descriptions

This appendix to the Computing Curricula 2001 report consists of a set of course descriptions intended to serve as models for institutions offering undergraduate degrees in computer science. Although some institutions will presumably follow these models with little modification, the course designs presented here are intentionally designed to be flexible, allowing individual institutions to customize them to fit their own needs.

In most cases, the courses described here are similar to those already offered at the undergraduate level. The CC2001 Task Force sought to identify and document successful practice rather than to create entirely new models. While we encourage the development of innovative curricular strategies and experimental courses, we recognize that course design requires considerable time and in-class assessment that cannot be done effectively by committee. The model courses in this appendix are therefore best regarded as a common starting point for experimentation. While each course is presented in enough detail to be usable as it stands, institutions and individual faculty are encouraged to adapt and extend these courses as part of the dynamic process of curriculum develoment.

Fundamental concepts

The rationale behind the CC2001 curriculum is outlined in the full report of the task force. The appendices, however, are likely to have wide circulation and will certainly be read by many who do not have time to study the full report. For this reason, the task force has chosen to include in each appendix a summary of the fundamental concepts that are necessary to understand the recommendations. The most important concepts for understanding the course descriptions are as follows:

- *The CS body of knowledge.* The courses described in this appendix are defined in relation to a general taxonomy of that portion of computer science appropriate for an undergraduate curriculum. That taxonomy represents the **body of knowledge** for computer science. The body of knowledge is organized hierarchically into three levels. The **area**—the highest level of the hierarchy—represents a particular disciplinary subfield. Each area is identified by a two-letter abbreviation, such as OS (operating systems) or PL (programming languages). The areas are broken down into smaller divisions called **units,** which represent individual thematic modules within an area. Each unit is identified by adding a numeric suffix to the area name; as an example, OS3 is a unit on *concurrency.* Each unit is further subdivided into a set of **topics**—the hierarchy's lowest level. The complete set of areas, units, and topics is specified in Appendix A.

- *Core and elective units.* Given the expanding scope of the computing discipline, it is impossible to insist that every undergraduate learn all the topics that were at one time considered fundamental to the field. The CC2001 Task Force has therefore sought to define a minimal set of **core** units for which there is a broad consensus that the material is essential to anyone obtaining an undergraduate degree in computer science. Because the core is defined as minimal, the core alone cannot constitute a complete undergraduate curriculum. Every undergraduate program must include additional **elective** units from the body of knowledge, although the CC2001 report does not define what those units must be. These elective units will typically vary by institution, field of study, and the needs of the individual student.

- *Introductory, intermediate, and advanced courses.* The courses in this appendix are divided into three categories according to the level at which they occur in the curriculum. Courses designated as **introductory** are typically offered in the first year of a college or university curriculum. Courses listed as **intermediate** are usually offered in the second or third year and build a foundation for further study in the field. Courses designated as **advanced** tend to be taken in later years and focus on those topics that require significant preparation in the earlier coursework. While these distinctions are easy to understand in their own right, it is important to recognize that there is no necessary relationship between the notions of *core* and *elective*—which apply to units in the body of knowlege—and the level of the course. Although introductory and intermediate courses will certainly concentrate on core material, it is perfectly reasonable to include some elective material even in the earliest courses. Similarly, advanced courses will include some core material. These designations are independent and should not be confused.

- *Hours.* To give readers a sense of the time required to cover a particular unit, the CC2001 Task Force had to identify some metric that would provide at least a comparative assessment of time. Choosing such a metric proved difficult, because there is no standard measure that is recognized throughout the world. For consistency with the earlier curriculum reports, the task force has chosen to express time in **hours,** corresponding to the in-class time required to present the material in a traditional lecture-oriented format. Note that this time does not include the instructor's preparation time or the time students spend outside of class. As a general guideline, the time required outside of class is approximately three times the in-class time. Thus, a unit that is listed as requiring 3 hours will typically entail a total of 12 hours (3 in class and 9 outside). It is also important to keep in mind that the time associated with each unit represents the *minimum* number of hours required for adequate coverage, and that it is always appropriate to spend more time than the listed minimum.

Organization and format of the course descriptions

As described in the preceding section, the courses presented in this appendix are organized into three levels: introductory, intermediate, and advanced. The point of this division is to provide natural boundaries for defining implementation strategies. Chapter 7, for example, defines six distinct instantiations of the introductory curriculum; Chapter 8 outlines four thematic approaches to the intermediate courses, along with a set of hybrid strategies that combine elements from these approaches. The implementation strategies and their relationship in the curriculum are shown in Figure B-1.

In general, it should be possible to use any of the introductory approaches and follow it up with any of the intermediate approaches, although doing so may require transition material to ensure that all core units are covered. The strategies and tactics required to ensure a successful transition are described in Chapters 6 to 8.

Figure B-1. Course levels and implementation strategies

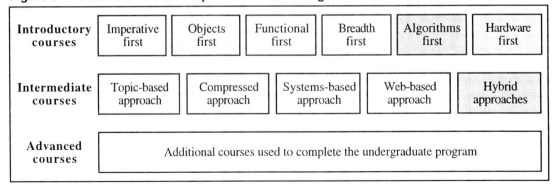

Figure B-2. Course numbering scheme

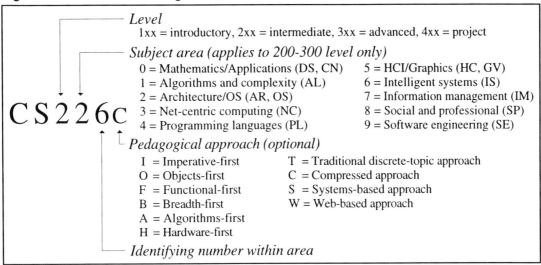

The names of the individual pedagogical approaches have been chosen so that each begins with a unique letter. This fact makes it possible to assign course numbers in a way that simultaneously encodes the level, area, and pedagogical approach, as illustrated in Figure B-2. In the example shown, the subscript at the end of CS226$_C$ indicates that this intermediate-level course is part of the compressed approach.

The format of each individual course description is shown in Figure B-3. The parts of the template that vary from course to course appear in boxes.

Figure B-3. Components of a course description

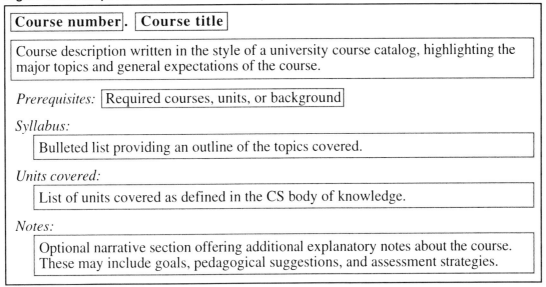

B.1 Introductory tracks

In the course descriptions that follow, the introductory tracks are arranged in the order in which they are presented in Chapter 8.

B.1.1 Imperative-first

The imperative-first approach offers two separate implementations: one that covers the material in three courses (CS101I-102I-103I) and one that uses a more traditional two-course sequence (CS111I-112I).

CS101I. Programming Fundamentals

Introduces the fundamental concepts of procedural programming. Topics include data types, control structures, functions, arrays, files, and the mechanics of running, testing, and debugging. The course also offers an introduction to the historical and social context of computing and an overview of computer science as a discipline.

Prerequisites: No programming or computer science experience is required. Students should have sufficient facility with high-school mathematics to solve simple linear equations and to appreciate the use of mathematical notation and formalism.

Syllabus:

- Computing applications: Word processing; spreadsheets; editors; files and directories

- Fundamental programming constructs: Syntax and semantics of a higher-level language; variables, types, expressions, and assignment; simple I/O; conditional and iterative control structures; functions and parameter passing; structured decomposition

- Algorithms and problem solving: Problem-solving strategies; the role of algorithms in the problem-solving process; implementation strategies for algorithms; debugging strategies; the concept and properties of algorithms

- Fundamental data structures: Primitive types; arrays; records; strings and string processing

- Machine level representation of data: Bits, bytes, and words; numeric data representation and number bases; representation of character data

- Overview of operating systems: The role and purpose of operating systems; simple file management

- Introduction to net-centric computing: Background and history of networking and the Internet; demonstration and use of networking software including e-mail, telnet, and FTP

- Human-computer interaction: Introduction to design issues

- Software development methodology: Fundamental design concepts and principles; structured design; testing and debugging strategies; test-case design; programming environments; testing and debugging tools

- Social context of computing: History of computing and computers; evolution of ideas and machines; social impact of computers and the Internet; professionalism, codes of ethics, and responsible conduct; copyrights, intellectual property, and software piracy

Units covered:

PF1	Fundamental programming constructs	10 hours (9 core + 1)
PF2	Algorithms and problem solving	3 core hours (of 6)
PF3	Fundamental data structures	2 core hours (of 14)
AR2	Machine level representation of data	1 core hour (of 3)
AR3	Assembly level machine organization	2 core hours (of 9)

OS1	Overview of operating systems	1 core hour (of 2)
NC1	Introduction to net-centric computing	1 core hour (of 2)
PL3	Introduction to language translation	1 core hour (of 2)
PL4	Declarations and types	3 core hours
PL5	Abstraction mechanisms	3 core hours
HC1	Foundations of human-computer interaction	1 core hour (of 6)
GV1	Fundamental techniques in graphics	1 core hour (of 2)
SP1	History of computing	1 core hour
SP2	Social context of computing	1 core hour (of 3)
SP4	Professional and ethical responsibilities	1 core hour (of 3)
SP6	Intellectual property	1 core hour (of 3)
SE1	Software design	3 core hours (of 8)
SE3	Software tools and environments	2 core hours (of 3)
SE4	Software processes	1 core hour (of 2)
	Elective topics	1 hour

Notes:

This course is part of an alternative implementation of the imperative-first introductory track that covers the fundamental programming concepts in three semesters rather than two. In terms of the curriculum, students should be able to move on to more advanced courses after taking either the sequence CS101I-102I-103I or the two-semester sequence sequence CS111I-112I, which covers the same material in a more concentrated fashion. Although covering programming fundamentals in two semesters has long been standard in computer science education, more and more programming topics can legitimately be identified as fundamental, making it more difficult to provide a complete introduction to this material in a single year. The CC2001 Task Force anticipates that three-semester introductory sequences will become increasingly common over the next decade and encourages departments and individual faculty to experiment with models along these lines.

CS102ı. The Object-Oriented Paradigm

Introduces the concepts of object-oriented programming to students with a background in the procedural paradigm. The course begins with a review of control structures and data types with emphasis on structured data types and array processing. It then moves on to introduce the object-oriented programming paradigm, focusing on the definition and use of classes along with the fundamentals of object-oriented design. Other topics include an overview of programming language principles, simple analysis of algorithms, basic searching and sorting techniques, and an introduction to software engineering issues.

Prerequisites: CS101ı

Syllabus:

- Review of control structures, functions, and primitive data types

- Object-oriented programming: Object-oriented design; encapsulation and information-hiding; separation of behavior and implementation; classes, subclasses, and inheritance; polymorphism; class hierarchies

- Fundamental computing algorithms: simple searching and sorting algorithms (linear and binary search, selection and insertion sort)

- Fundamentals of event-driven programming

- Introduction to computer graphics: Using a simple graphics API

- Overview of programming languages: History of programming languages; brief survey of programming paradigms

- Virtual machines: The concept of a virtual machine; hierarchy of virtual machines; intermediate languages

- Introduction to language translation: Comparison of interpreters and compilers; language translation phases; machine-dependent and machine-independent aspects of translation

- Introduction to database systems: History and motivation for database systems; use of a database query language

- Software evolution: Software maintenance; characteristics of maintainable software; reengineering; legacy systems; software reuse

Units covered:

PF1	Fundamental programming constructs	3 core hours (of 9)
PF2	Algorithms and problem-solving	6 core hours
PF3	Fundamental data structures	5 core hours (of 14)
PF5	Event-driven programming	1 core hour (of 4)
AL3	Fundamental computing algorithms	3 core hours (of 12)
AR2	Machine level representation of data	2 core hours (of 3)
PL1	Overview of programming languages	1 core hour (of 2)
PL2	Virtual machines	1 core hour
PL3	Introduction to language translation	1 core hour (of 2)
PL6	Object-oriented programming	6 core hours (of 10)
HC1	Foundations of human-computer interaction	1 core hour (of 6)
HC2	Building a simple graphical user interface	2 core hours
IM2	Database systems	1 core hour (of 3)
SE1	Software design	1 core hour (of 8)
SE2	Using APIs	2 core hours (of 5)
SE5	Software requirements and specifications	1 core hour (of 4)

SE6	Software validation	1 core hour (of 3)
SE7	Software evolution	1 core hour (of 3)
	Elective topics	1 hour

Notes:

This course represents the second semester of an imperative-first introductory track that covers the fundamental programming concepts in three semesters rather than two. The rationale for including the three-course sequence CS101I-102I-103I as an alternative to the more traditional two-semester sequence CS111I-112I is summarized in the notes for CS101I and discussed in Chapter 7 of the main report.

CS103i. Data Structures and Algorithms

Builds on the foundation provided by the CS101i-102i sequence to introduce the fundamental concepts of data structures and the algorithms that proceed from them. Topics include recursion, the underlying philosophy of object-oriented programming, fundamental data structures (including stacks, queues, linked lists, hash tables, trees, and graphs), the basics of algorithmic analysis, and an introduction to the principles of language translation.

Prerequisites: CS102i; discrete mathematics at the level of CS105 is also desirable.

Syllabus:

- Review of elementary programming concepts
- Fundamental data structures: Stacks; queues; linked lists; hash tables; trees; graphs
- Object-oriented programming: Object-oriented design; encapsulation and information hiding; classes; separation of behavior and implementation; class hierarchies; inheritance; polymorphism
- Fundamental computing algorithms: O(N log N) sorting algorithms; hash tables, including collision-avoidance strategies; binary search trees; representations of graphs; depth- and breadth-first traversals
- Recursion: The concept of recursion; recursive mathematical functions; simple recursive procedures; divide-and-conquer strategies; recursive backtracking; implementation of recursion
- Basic algorithmic analysis: Asymptotic analysis of upper and average complexity bounds; identifying differences among best, average, and worst case behaviors; big "O," little "o," omega, and theta notation; standard complexity classes; empirical measurements of performance; time and space tradeoffs in algorithms; using recurrence relations to analyze recursive algorithms
- Algorithmic strategies: Brute-force algorithms; greedy algorithms; divide-and-conquer; backtracking; branch-and-bound; heuristics; pattern matching and string/text algorithms; numerical approximation algorithms
- Overview of programming languages: Programming paradigms
- Software engineering: Software validation; testing fundamentals, including test-plan creation and test-case generation; object-oriented testing

Units covered:

DS5	Graphs and trees	2 core hours (of 4)
PF3	Fundamental data structures	12 core hours (of 14)
PF4	Recursion	5 core hours
AL1	Basic algorithmic analysis	2 core hours (of 4)
AL2	Algorithmic strategies	3 core hours (of 6)
AL3	Fundamental computing algorithms	5 core hours (of 12)
AL5	Basic computability	1 core hour (of 6)
PL1	Overview of programming languages	1 core hour (of 2)
PL6	Object-oriented programming	8 core hours (of 10)
SE6	Software validation	1 core hour (of 3)

Notes:

This course represents the third and final semester of an imperative-first introductory track that covers the fundamental programming concepts in three semesters rather than two. The rationale for including the three-course sequence CS101i-102i-103i as an alternative to the more traditional two-semester sequence CS111i-112i is summarized in the notes for CS101i and discussed in Chapter 7 of the main report.

CS111ɪ. Introduction to Programming

Introduces the fundamental techniques of programming as a foundation for more advanced study of computer science. Considerable attention is devoted to developing effective software engineering practice, emphasizing such principles as design, decomposition, encapsulation, procedural abstraction, testing, and software reuse. Topics include standard programming constructs, problem-solving strategies, the concept of an algorithm, and fundamental data structures (strings, arrays, and records) along with an introduction to machine representation, graphics, and networking.

Prerequisites: No programming or computer science experience is required. Students should have sufficient facility with high-school mathematics to solve simple linear equations and to appreciate the use of mathematical notation and formalism.

Syllabus:

- Background: History of computing, overview of programming languages and the compilation process
- Fundamental programming constructs: Syntax and semantics of a higher-level language; variables, types, expressions, and assignment; simple I/O; conditional and iterative control structures; functions and parameter passing; structured decomposition
- Algorithms and problem solving: Problem-solving strategies; the concept of an algorithm; properties of algorithms; implementation strategies; sequential and binary search algorithms; quadratic sorting algorithms (selection, insertion)
- Basic computability theory: Tractable and intractable problems; the existence of noncomputable functions
- Graphics: Using a graphics API
- Principles of encapsulation: Encapsulation and information-hiding; separation of behavior and implementation
- Fundamental data structures: Primitive types; arrays; records; strings and string processing; pointers and references; static, stack, and heap allocation; runtime storage management
- Machine level representation of data: Bits, bytes, and words; binary representation of integers; representation of character data; representation of records and arrays
- Assembly level machine organization: Basic organization of the von Neumann machine; instruction fetch, decode, and execution; assembly language programming for a simulated machine
- Software development methodology: Fundamental design concepts and principles; structured design; testing and debugging strategies; test-case design; programming environments; testing and debugging tools

Units covered:

PF1	Fundamental programming constructs	9 core hours
PF2	Algorithms and problem solving	3 core hours (of 6)
PF3	Fundamental data structures	6 core hours (of 14)
AL3	Fundamental computing algorithms	2 core hours (of 12)
AL5	Basic computability	1 core hour (of 6)
AR2	Machine level representation of data	1 core hour (of 3)
AR3	Assembly level machine organization	2 core hours (of 9)
PL1	Overview of programming languages	1 core hour (of 2)
PL4	Declarations and types	1 core hour (of 3)
PL5	Abstraction mechanisms	2 core hours (of 3)
PL6	Object-oriented programming	3 core hours (of 10)

GV1	Fundamental techniques in graphics	2 core hours
SP1	History of computing	1 core hour
SE1	Software design	2 core hours (of 8)
SE3	Software tools and environments	1 core hour (of 3)
SE5	Software requirements and specifications	1 core hour (of 4)
SE6	Software validation	1 core hour (of 3)
	Elective topics	1 hour

Notes:

This course introduces the fundamental concepts of programming, emphasizing the traditional procedural or imperative paradigm. Most modern programming languages are suitable as a foundation for the programming assignments in this course, including those that support the object-oriented paradigm; indeed, introductory courses that use object-oriented languages often begin by emphasizing the procedural aspects of those languages. What sets this course apart from the objects-first implementation in CS110 is the ordering and emphasis of topics. In this course, the discussion of control statements precedes the discussion of classes, subclasses, and inheritance; in the objects-first version, this ordering is reversed.

Just as the procedural aspects of programming can be taught in an object-oriented language, some of the fundamental principles of object-oriented programming can be included even in the context of a traditional imperative language. The syllabus topic entitled "Principles of encapsulation" makes sense in either domain, but would be approached differently depending on the language. In either case, this presentation would encompass some of the ideas in the PL6 unit on object-oriented programming.

CS112I. Data Abstraction

Continues the introduction of programming begun in CS111I, with a particular focus on the ideas of data abstraction and object-oriented programming. Topics include recursion, programming paradigms, principles of language design, virtual machines, object-oriented programming, fundamental data structures, and an introduction to language translation.

Prerequisites: CS111I; discrete mathematics at the level of CS105 is also desirable.

Syllabus:

- Review of elementary programming

- Recursion: The concept of recursion; recursive specification of mathematical functions (such as factorial and Fibonacci); simple recursive procedures (Towers of Hanoi, permutations, fractal patterns); divide-and-conquer strategies; recursive backtracking; implementation of recursion

- Introduction to computational complexity: Asymptotic analysis of upper and average complexity bounds; big-O notation; standard complexity classes; empirical measurements of performance

- Fundamental computing algorithms: O(N log N) sorting algorithms (Quicksort, heapsort, mergesort); hashing, including collision-avoidance strategies; binary search trees

- Programming languages: History of programming languages; brief survey of programming paradigms (procedural, object-oriented, functional)

- Fundamental issues in language design: General principles of language design, design goals, typing regimes, data structure models, control structure models, abstraction mechanisms

- Virtual machines: The concept of a virtual machine, hierarchy of virtual machines, intermediate languages

- Object-oriented programming: Object-oriented design; encapsulation and information-hiding; separation of behavior and implementation; classes, subclasses, and inheritance; polymorphism; class hierarchies; collection classes and iteration protocols; fundamental design patterns

- Fundamental data structures: Linked structures; implementation strategies for stacks, queues, hash tables, graphs, and trees; strategies for choosing data structures

- Introduction to language translation: Comparison of interpreters and compilers; language translation phases (lexical analysis, parsing, code generation, optimization); machine-dependent and machine-independent aspects of translation

Units covered:

DS5	Graphs and trees	2 core hours (of 4)
PF3	Fundamental data structures	6 core hours (of 14)
PF4	Recursion	5 core hours
AL1	Basic algorithmic analysis	2 core hours (of 4)
AL3	Fundamental computing algorithms	4 core hours (of 12)
PL1	Overview of programming languages	1 core hour (of 2)
PL2	Virtual machines	1 core hour
PL3	Introduction to language translation	2 core hours
PL4	Declarations and types	2 core hours (of 3)
PL5	Abstraction mechanisms	1 core hour (of 3)
PL6	Object-oriented programming	7 core hours (of 10)
SE1	Software design	2 core hours (of 8)
SE2	Using APIs	2 core hours (of 5)

SE3	Software tools and environments	2 core hours (of 3)
	Elective topics	1 hour

Notes:

As noted in the description of the CS111I prerequisite, there is no guarantee that students coming into this course will have used an object-oriented language. In any event, the courses in the imperative-first track assume that the introductory course—even if it happens to use an object-oriented language—concentrates on the imperative components of that language rather than any object-oriented mechanisms. (For an object-oriented implementation of the introductory curriculum, see the CS111o/CS112o sequence.) One of the main goals of CS112I is to introduce the object-oriented paradigm and give students experience using it. The other major topics are recursion, data structures, and the core units in the Programming Languages area (PL), which fit appropriately into this course.

B.1.2 Objects-first

Like the imperative-first approach, the objects-first strategy is also divided into a three-course (CS1010-1020-1030) and a two-course implementation (CS1110-1120).

CS1010. Introduction to Object-Oriented Programming

Introduces the fundamental concepts of programming from an object-oriented perspective. Topics include simple data types, control structures, an introduction to array and string data structures and algorithms, as well as debugging techniques and the social implications of computing. The course emphasizes good software engineering principles and developing fundamental programming skills in the context of a language that supports the object-oriented paradigm.

Prerequisites: No programming or computer science experience is required. Students should have sufficient facility with high-school mathematics to solve simple linear equations and to appreciate the use of mathematical notation and formalism.

Syllabus:

- Introduction to the history of computer science
- Ethics and responsibility of computer professionals
- Introduction to computer systems and environments
- Introduction to object-oriented paradigm: Abstraction; objects; classes; methods; parameter passing; encapsulation; inheritance; polymorphism
- Fundamental programming constructs: Basic syntax and semantics of a higher-level language; variables, types, expressions, and assignment; simple I/O; conditional and iterative control structures; structured decomposition
- Fundamental data structures: Primitive types; arrays; records; strings and string processing
- Introduction to programming languages
- Algorithms and problem solving: Problem-solving strategies; the role of algorithms in the problem-solving process; implementation strategies for algorithms; debugging strategies; the concept and properties of algorithms

Units covered:

PF1	Fundamental programming constructs	9 core hours
PF2	Algorithms and problem solving	3 core hours (of 6)
PF3	Fundamental data structures	3 core hours (of 14)
AL3	Fundamental computing algorithms	1 core hour (of 12)
AL5	Basic computability	1 core hour (of 6)
AR2	Machine level representation of data	2 core hours (of 3)
PL1	Overview of programming languages	2 core hours
PL4	Declarations and types	2 core hours (of 3)
PL6	Object-oriented programming	7 core hours (of 10)
PL8	Language translation systems	1 hour
SP1	History of computing	1 core hour
SP4	Professional and ethical responsibilities	1 core hour (of 3)
SP5	Risks and liabilities of computer-based systems	1 core hour (of 2)
SE3	Software tools and environments	1 core hour (of 3)
SE6	Software validation	1 core hour (of 3)
	Elective topics	4 hours

Notes:

This course is part of an alternative implementation of the objects-first introductory track that covers the fundamental programming concepts in three semesters rather than two. In terms of the curriculum, students should be able to move on to more advanced courses after taking either the sequence CS101o-102o-103o or the two-semester sequence sequence CS111o-112o, which covers the same material in a more concentrated fashion. Although covering programming fundamentals in two semesters has long been standard in computer science education, more and more programming topics can legitimately be identified as fundamental, making it more difficult to provide a complete introduction to this material in a single year. The CC2001 Task Force anticipates that three-semester introductory sequences will become increasingly common over the next decade and encourages departments and individual faculty to experiment with models along these lines.

What differentiates this course from the imperative-first implementation in CS101i-102i-103i is the early emphasis on objects. In this course, the discussion of classes, subclasses, and inheritance typically precedes even such basic concepts as conditional and iterative control statements.

CS102o. Objects and Data Abstraction

Continues the introduction from CS101o to the methodology of programming from an object-oriented perspective. Through the study of object design, this course also introduces the basics of human-computer interfaces, graphics, and the social implications of computing, with an emphasis on software engineering.

Prerequisites: CS101o

Syllabus:

- Review of object-oriented programming: Object-oriented methodology, object-oriented design; software tools
- Principles of object-oriented programming: Inheritance; class hierarchies; polymorphism; abstract and interface classes; container/collection classes and iterators
- Object-oriented design: Concept of design patterns and the use of APIs; modeling tools such as class diagrams, CRC cards, and UML use cases
- Virtual machines: The concept of a virtual machine; hierarchy of virtual machines; intermediate languages
- Fundamental computing algorithms: Searching; sorting; introduction to recursive algorithms
- Fundamental data structures: Built-in, programmer-created, and dynamic data structures
- Event-driven programming: Event-handling methods; event propagation; exception handling
- Foundations of human-computer interaction: Human-centered development and evaluation; principles of good design and good designers; engineering tradeoffs; introduction to usability testing
- Fundamental techniques in graphics: Hierarchy of graphics software; using a graphics API; simple color models; homogeneous coordinates; affine transformations; viewing transformation; clipping
- Software engineering issues: Tools; processes; requirements; design and testing; design for reuse; risks and liabilities of computer-based systems

Units covered:

PF3	Fundamental data structures	3 core hours (of 14)
PF4	Recursion	2 core hours (of 5)
PF5	Event-driven programming	2 core hours (of 4)
SE2	Using APIs	2 core hours (of 5)
AL1	Basic algorithmic analysis	1 core hour (of 4)
AL3	Fundamental computing algorithms	2 core hours (of 12)
AR2	Machine level representation of data	1 core hour (of 3)
PL2	Virtual machines	1 core hour
PL4	Declarations and types	1 core hour (of 3)
PL5	Abstraction mechanisms	3 core hours
PL6	Object-oriented programming	7 core hours (of 10)
HC1	Foundations of human-computer interaction	1 core hour (of 6)
GV1	Fundamental techniques in graphics	2 core hours
SE1	Software design	3 core hours (of 8)
SE3	Software tools and environments	1 core hour (of 3)
SE5	Software requirements and specifications	1 core hour (of 4)
SE6	Software validation	1 core hour (of 3)
SE7	Software evolution	1 core hour (of 3)
	Elective topics	5 hours

Notes:

This course represents the second semester of an objects-first introductory track that covers the fundamental programming concepts in three semesters rather than two. The rationale for including the three-course sequence CS101o-102o-103o as an alternative to the more traditional two-semester sequence CS111o-112o is summarized in the notes for CS101o and discussed in Chapter 7 of the main report.

CS103o. Algorithms and Data Structures

Builds on the introduction to object-oriented programming begun in CS101o and CS102o with an emphasis on algorithms, data structures, and software engineering.

Prerequisites: CS102o

Syllabus:

- Review of object-oriented design
- Review of basic algorithm design
- Review of professional and ethical issues
- Algorithms and problem-solving: Classic techniques for algorithm design; problem-solving in the object-oriented paradigm; application of algorithm design techniques to a medium-sized project, with an emphasis on formal methods of testing
- Basic algorithmic analysis: Asymptotic analysis of upper and average complexity bounds; identifying differences among best, average, and worst-case behaviors; big "O" notation; standard complexity classes; empirical measurements of performance; time and space tradeoffs in algorithms
- Recursion: The concept of recursion; recursive mathematical functions; simple recursive procedures; divide-and-conquer strategies; recursive backtracking; implementation of recursion; recursion on trees and graphs
- Fundamental computing algorithms: Hash tables; binary search trees; representations of graphs; depth- and breadth-first traversals; shortest-path algorithms; transitive closure; minimum spanning tree; topological sort
- Fundamental data structures: Pointers and references; linked structures; implementation strategies for stacks, queues, and hash tables; implementation strategies for graphs and trees; strategies for choosing the right data structure
- Software engineering: Software project management; building a medium-sized system, in teams, with algorithmic efficiency in mind

Units covered:

PF2	Algorithms and problem solving	3 core hours (of 6)
PF3	Fundamental data structures	11 core hours (of 14)
PF4	Recursion	6 hours (5 core + 1)
AL1	Basic algorithmic analysis	3 core hours (of 4)
AL2	Algorithmic strategies	6 core hours
AL3	Fundamental computing algorithms	5 core hours (of 12)
SE1	Software design	1 core hour (of 8)
SE8	Software project management	1 core hour (of 3)
	Elective topics	4 hours

Notes:

This course represents the third and final semester of an objects-first introductory track that covers the fundamental programming concepts in three semesters rather than two. The rationale for including the three-course sequence CS101o-102o-103o as an alternative to the more traditional two-semester sequence CS111o-112o is summarized in the notes for CS101o and discussed in Chapter 7 of the main report.

CS111o. Object-Oriented Programming

Introduces the fundamental concepts programming from an object-oriented perspective. Through the study of object design, this course also introduces the basics of human-computer interfaces, graphics, and the social implications of computing, along with significant coverage of software engineering.

Prerequisites: No programming or computer science experience is required. Students should have sufficient facility with high-school mathematics to solve simple linear equations and to appreciate the use of mathematical notation and formalism.

Syllabus:

- Background: History of computing, overview of programming languages and the compilation process
- Introduction to object-oriented programming: Using an object-oriented language; classes and objects; syntax of class definitions; methods; members
- Simple data: variables, types, and expressions; assignment
- Message passing: Simple methods; parameter passing
- Subclassing and inheritance
- Control structures: Iteration; conditionals
- Algorithms: Problem-solving strategies; the concept of an algorithm; properties of algorithms; implementation strategies
- Simple data structures: Arrays; strings
- Collection classes and iteration protocols
- Using APIs: Class libraries; packages for graphics and GUI applications
- Object-oriented design: Fundamental design concepts and principles; introduction to design patterns; object-oriented analysis and design; design for reuse
- Software engineering issues: Tools; processes; requirements; design and testing; risks and liabilities of computer-based systems

Units covered:

PF1	Fundamental programming constructs	7 core hours (of 9)
PF2	Algorithms and problem-solving	2 core hours (of 6)
PF3	Fundamental data structures	3 core hours (of 14)
PF4	Recursion	2 core hours (of 5)
AL3	Fundamental computing algorithms	3 core hours (of 12)
AL5	Basic computability	1 core hour (of 6)
PL4	Declarations and types	2 core hours (of 3)
PL5	Abstraction mechanisms	1 core hour (of 3)
PL6	Object-oriented programming	8 core hours (of 10)
GV1	Fundamental techniques in graphics	2 core hours
SP1	History of computing	1 core hour
SP5	Risks and liabilities of computer-based systems	1 core hour (of 2)
SE1	Software design	2 core hours (of 8)
SE2	Using APIs	1 core hour (of 5)
SE3	Software tools and environments	2 core hours (of 3)
	Elective topics	2 hours

Notes:

This course introduces the fundamental concepts of programming, starting from the very beginning with the object-oriented paradigm. What differentiates this course from the imperative-first implementation in CS111r is the early emphasis on objects. In this course, the discussion of classes, subclasses, and inheritance typically precedes even such basic concepts as conditional and iterative control statements.

To illustrate how this emphasis on objects affects the design of this course, it helps to consider a common sample application—a simple numeric calculator—that might reasonably fit into either an imperative-first or objects-first implementation of an introductory course. Under the imperative paradigm, such a program would typically be organized as a loop that repeatedly requested commands from the user and then used a conditional dispatch operation—typically implemented as a **switch** statement in C-based languages—to execute the appropriate code for each operation. An object-oriented approach to the same problem would typically have no explicit loops or conditionals. Instead, the buttons on the calculator would all be part of an object hierarchy. The buttons for the digits, for example, would all be instances of a digit button class whose common action would be to append the appropriate digit to the end of the displayed value; the individual instances of the digit buttons would differ only in the value of the local member variable representing the digit to which that button corresponds. Similarly, the operator buttons would all be part of a separate class hierarchy containing an **operate** method to perform an arithmetic operation. The plus button would implement one definition for **operate**; the minus button would implement another. The use of the object-oriented paradigm makes it possible for students to solve this sort of problem far earlier in the course, since the number and complexity of the necessary control structures are significantly reduced.

Most courses that adopt an objects-first approach will do so in an environment that supports a rich collection of application programmer interfaces, or APIs. These APIs can be an enormous help to students, because they enable the creation of much more exciting programs at an early level, thereby heightening student motivation. At the same time, the scale of most API packages can be intimidating to many students, since there are so many classes and methods from which to choose. To mitigate the effects of this conceptual overload, faculty should not hesitate to simplify the problem domain by creating restricted class libraries for introductory use.

CS112o. Object-Oriented Design and Methodology

Continues the introduction to object-oriented programming begun in CS110, with an emphasis on algorithms, data structures, software engineering, and the social context of computing.

Prerequisites: CS110

Syllabus:

* Review of object oriented design, and programming, including review of tools
* Review of simple algorithm design, with concern for ethical and social responsibility (for example, the need for testing)
* Classic techniques for algorithm design and implementation and their place in an object-oriented design
* Abstraction and encapsulation through classic data structures: Introduction to (use, not implementation of) classic data structures (list, stack, and queue) and their relation to algorithm design
* Introduction to basic algorithmic analysis
* Application of algorithm design techniques to a medium-sized project, with an emphasis on formal methods of testing
* Recursion: Recursion as a design technique; implementation of recursion and its relation to iteration; introduction to trees and graphs
* Introduction to distributed algorithms
* Software engineering: Building a medium-sized system, in teams, with algorithmic efficiency in mind

Units covered:

PF1	Fundamental programming constructs	2 core hours (of 9)
PF2	Algorithms and problem solving	2 core hours (of 6)
PF3	Fundamental data structures	8 core hours (of 14)
PF4	Recursion	3 core hours (of 5)
PF5	Event-driven programming	2 core hours (of 4)
AL1	Basic algorithmic analysis	2 core hours (of 4)
AL2	Algorithmic strategies	2 core hours (of 6)
AL3	Fundamental computing algorithms	3 core hours (of 12)
PL1	Overview of programming languages	2 core hours
PL2	Virtual machines	1 core hour
PL4	Declarations and types	1 core hour (of 3)
PL5	Abstraction mechanisms	2 core hours (of 3)
PL6	Object-oriented programming	4 core hours (of 10)
HC1	Foundations of human-computer interaction	1 core hour (of 6)
SE1	Software design	2 core hours (of 8)
SE2	Using APIs	1 core hour (of 5)
SE5	Software requirements and specifications	1 core hour (of 4)
SE6	Software validation	1 core hour (of 3)

Notes:

This course builds on the foundation established by CS110 to complete a full year of introductory programming. Because the first course has included more material on the mechanics of object-oriented programming than is typical in an imperative-first introduction, CS112o can devote more time to issues of design and software engineering along with the traditional coverage of data structures and algorithms.

B.1.3 Functional-first

The functional-first approach exists only in the two-semester form. If the approach proves popular, it may be appropriate to consider a three-semester implementation.

CS111F. Introduction to Functional Programming

Introduces the basic concepts of programming in the context of a functional language that emphasizes algorithmic strategies over syntactic detail.

Prerequisites: none

Syllabus:

- Overview of the history of computing

- Procedural abstraction: Simple functions; parameters and results; composition; conditional expressions

- Recursion: The concept of recursion; recursive mathematical functions; simple recursive procedures

- Data abstraction: List structure; hierarchical data; symbolic data; the importance of data abstraction

- Algorithms and problem-solving: Problem-solving strategies; the role of algorithms in the problem-solving process; implementation strategies for algorithms; debugging strategies; the concept and properties of algorithms

- Algorithmic strategies: Brute-force algorithms; greedy algorithms; divide-and-conquer; backtracking; numerical approximation algorithms

- Basic computability theory: Tractable and intractable problems; the existence of noncomputable functions

- Basic computational complexity: Asymptotic analysis of upper and average complexity bounds; big-O notation; standard complexity classes; empirical measurements of performance

- Overview of programming languages: History of programming languages; brief survey of programming paradigms; the role of language translation in the programming process

- Evaluation strategies: Representing computation state; streams; lazy evaluation; nondeterminism; the construction of an interpreter

- Machine level representation of data: Bits, bytes, and words; numeric data representation and number bases; signed and twos-complement representations; representation of nonnumeric data

Units covered:

DS5	Graphs and trees	3 core hours (of 4)
PF1	Fundamental programming constructs	3 core hours (of 9)
PF2	Algorithms and problem solving	2 core hours (of 6)
PF3	Fundamental data structures	6 core hours (of 14)
PF4	Recursion	5 core hours
OS3	Concurrency	2 core hours (of 6)
AL1	Basic algorithmic analysis	2 core hours (of 4)
AL2	Algorithmic strategies	2 core hours (of 6)
AL3	Fundamental computing algorithms	4 core hours (of 12)
AL5	Basic computability	1 core hour (of 6)
PL1	Overview of programming languages	1 core hour (of 2)
PL4	Declarations and types	1 core hour (of 3)

189

PL5	Abstraction mechanisms	1 core hour (of 3)
PL7	Functional programming	4 hours (of 7)
SP1	History of computing	1 core hour
SE1	Software design	1 core hour (of 8)
SE3	Software tools and environments	1 core hour (of 3)

CS112F. Objects and Algorithms

Extends the foundation developed in CS111F to encompass object-oriented programming and design.

Prerequisites: CS111F

Syllabus:

- Fundamental programming constructs: Basic syntax and semantics of a higher-level language; variables, types, expressions, and assignment; simple I/O; conditional and iterative control structures; functions and parameter passing; structured decomposition
- Object-oriented programming: Object-oriented design; encapsulation and information-hiding; separation of behavior and implementation; classes, subclasses, and inheritance; polymorphism; class hierarchies; collection classes and iteration protocols; fundamental design patterns
- Fundamental data structures: Primitive types; arrays; records; strings and string processing; pointers and references; linked structures; strategies for choosing the right data structure
- Event-driven and concurrent programming: Event-handling methods; event propagation; managing concurrency in event handling; exception handling
- Using APIs: API programming; class browsers and related tools; programming by example; debugging in the API environment
- Algorithmic strategies: Brute-force algorithms; greedy algorithms; divide-and-conquer; backtracking; heuristics
- Fundamental computing algorithms: Simple numerical algorithms; sequential and binary search algorithms; sorting algorithms
- Virtual machines: The concept of a virtual machine; hierarchy of virtual machines; intermediate languages; security issues arising from running code on an alien machine
- Fundamental techniques in graphics: Hierarchy of graphics software; using a graphics API
- Software development methodology: Fundamental design concepts and principles; structured design; testing and debugging strategies; test-case design; programming environments; testing and debugging tools

Units covered:

PF1	Fundamental programming constructs	6 core hours (of 9)
PF2	Algorithms and problem solving	1 core hour (of 6)
PF3	Fundamental data structures	5 core hours (of 14)
PF5	Event-driven programming	2 core hours (of 4)
AL2	Algorithmic strategies	2 core hours (of 6)
AL3	Fundamental computing algorithms	2 core hours (of 12)
PL1	Overview of programming languages	1 core hour (of 2)
PL2	Virtual machines	1 core hour
PL4	Declarations and types	2 core hours (of 3)
PL5	Abstraction mechanisms	2 core hours (of 3)
PL6	Object-oriented programming	8 core hours (of 10)
SE1	Software design	3 core hours (of 8)
SE2	Using APIs	2 core hours (of 5)
SE3	Software tools and environments	1 core hour (of 3)
SE5	Software requirements and specifications	1 core hour (of 4)
SE6	Software validation	1 core hour (of 3)

B.1.4 Breadth-first

As outlined in Chapter 8, we propose two implementations of a breadth-first approach. The first is simply to include an overview course (CS100B) before a more conventional programming sequence. The second is to expand the introductory curriculum into a three-semester sequence (CS101B-102B-103B) to provide time for the additional topics.

CS100B. Preview of Computer Science

Offers a broad overview of computer science designed to provide students with an appreciation for and an understanding of the many different aspects of computer science. Topics include discrete mathematics, an introduction to programming languages, algorithmic problem solving, analysis of algorithmic complexity, basic concepts in hardware, operating systems, networks, graphics, and an overview of the social context of computing. No background in computer science is assumed or expected. The course is intended for both students who expect to major or minor in computer science as well as for those not planning on taking additional course work.

Prerequisites: none

Syllabus:

- Mathematical preliminaries: Sets, functions, logic, proofs
- Algorithms: Definition, design, and implementation; introduction to classical algorithms (sorting, searching, and pattern matching)
- Algorithmic analysis: Efficiency; asymptotic analysis; computational complexity; big-O notation; polynomial vs. exponential growth; computability
- Hardware realizations of algorithms: Data representation; the von Neumann model of computation; the fetch/decode/execute cycle; basic machine organization
- Programming fundamentals: Overview of programming fundamentals and object-oriented design principles; brief introduction to a programming language that supports the object-oriented paradigm
- Operating systems and virtual machines: Historical evolution of operating systems; responsibilties of an operating system; basic components of an operating system
- Networking and computer graphics: Brief introduction to some of the basic concepts in networking and computer graphics
- Social and professional issues: Social context of computing; responsibilities of computing professionals

Units covered:

DS1	Functions, relations, and sets	2 core hours (of 6)
DS2	Basic logic	2 core hours (of 10)
PF1	Fundamental programming constructs	5 core hours (of 9)
PF2	Algorithms and problem solving	3 core hours (of 6)
AL1	Basic algorithmic analysis	4 core hours
AL3	Fundamental computing algorithms	4 core hours (of 12)
AR6	Functional organization	4 core hours (of 7)
OS1	Overview of operating systems	2 core hours
OS2	Operating system principles	1 core hour (of 2)
NC1	Introduction to net-centric computing	2 core hours
NC2	Communication and networking	1 core hour (of 7)
PL6	Object-oriented programming	4 core hours (of 10)
GV1	Fundamental techniques in graphics	2 core hours
GV2	Graphic systems	1 core hour
SP2	Social context of computing	3 core hours

Notes:

It is, of course, impossible to cover all of computer science within a single course. The exact list of topics and their ordering will therefore vary based on the interests and background of the instructor. At a minimum, an initial breadth-first course should include a solid introduction to algorithms, some basic concepts in hardware and computer organization, an exposure to abstraction and the virtual environments created by software, a brief introduction to programming and software development, and a treatment of the social, ethical, and professional issues that arise in the field. Beyond that, each instructor should feel free to choose the specific topics covered, particularly in terms of the treatment of modern computing applications. The sample syllabus includes about six hours of material on networking and computer graphics, both important and rapidly growing areas. It would, however, be appropriate to expand these topics or supplement them with material on other important issues such as databases, artificial intelligence, and distributed systems.

There are two important considerations in the design of a breadth-first introduction to computer science. The first is to treat discrete mathematics not as a separate and unrelated subject, but as a fully integrated component of the course. By doing so, students will better understand and appreciate the importance of discrete mathematics to our discipline. For example, Boolean logic could be introduced during a discussion of programming language operators, counting methods could be presented during a discussion of the efficiency of iterative algorithms, while recurrence relations are a natural way to study the performance of recursive algorithms. The goal is for students to be introduced to mathematical concepts within the context of their use in solving important computing problems.

The second point is that the many disparate topics typically found in a breadth-first course must be tied together into an integrated whole. Students must not see the course as a collection of interesting but unrelated topics in a "if this is Tuesday it must be computer organization" style. They should instead develop an appreciation for the important relationships among the major subfields of computer science. This goal can be achieved by demonstrating how each of the course topics utilizes earlier ideas and builds on them to produce newer and more powerful abstractions. This type of "spiral" approach, which reinforces, emphasizes, and builds on previous concepts, is an important aspect to the success of such a course.

CS101B. Introduction to Computer Science

Presents a broad overview of computer science that integrates programming with discrete mathematics, hardware fundamentals, algorithms, and computability.

Prerequisites: No programming or computer science experience is required. Students should have sufficient facility with high-school mathematics to solve simple linear equations and to appreciate the use of mathematical notation and formalism.

Syllabus:

- Discrete mathematics: Functions, relations, and sets; basic logic; proof techniques; basics of counting; discrete probability

- Fundamental programming constructs: Basic syntax and semantics of a higher-level language; variables, types, expressions, and assignment; simple I/O; conditional and iterative control structures; functions and parameter passing; structured decomposition

- Algorithms and problem-solving: Problem-solving strategies; the role of algorithms in the problem-solving process; the concept and properties of algorithms

- Fundamental data structures: Primitive types; arrays; strings and string processing

- Recursion: The concept of recursion; recursive mathematical functions; divide-and-conquer strategies

- Basic algorithmic analysis: Big "O" notation; standard complexity classes

- Fundamental computing algorithms: Simple numerical algorithms; sequential and binary search algorithms; quadratic and O(n log n) sorting algorithms

- Basic computability: Finite-state machines; Turing machines; tractable and intractable problems; uncomputable functions; the halting problem; implications of uncomputability

- Overview of programming languages: History of programming languages

- Digital logic and digital systems: Overview and history of computer architecture; fundamental building blocks; logic expressions

- History of computing

- Introduction to the social implications of computing

Units covered:

DS1	Functions, relations, and sets	4 core hours (of 6)
DS2	Basic logic	5 core hours (of 10)
DS3	Proof techniques	4 core hours (of 12)
DS4	Basics of counting	3 core hours (of 5)
DS6	Discrete probability	4 core hours (of 6)
PF1	Fundamental programming constructs	3 core hours (of 9)
PF2	Algorithms and problem solving	2 core hours (of 6)
PF3	Fundamental data structures	2 core hours (of 14)
PF4	Recursion	2 core hours (of 5)
AL1	Basic algorithmic analysis	1 core hour (of 4)
AL3	Fundamental computing algorithms	2 core hours (of 12)
AL5	Basic computability	1 core hour (of 6)
AR1	Digital logic and digital systems	2 core hours (of 6)
PL1	Overview of programming languages	1 core hour (of 2)
PL3	Introduction to language translation	1 core hour (of 2)
PL4	Declarations and types	1 core hour (of 3)
SP1	History of computing	1 core hour
SP2	Social context of computing	1 core hour (of 3)

Notes:

This course is the first of a three-semester sequence (CS101B-102B-103B) that seeks to offer a broad, integrated introduction to computer science, along the lines advocated by the 1989 "Computing as a Discipline" report [Denning89] and *Computing Curricula 1991* [Tucker91]. Each of the three courses in the sequence includes theory along with programming, and a range of additional topics are introduced in each course in the sequence.

As we note in Chapter 7, the breadth-first model has not enjoyed the success that its proponents had envisioned. We believe, however, that part of the problem may have come from trying to fit all these topics into too small a space. Given the expansion of prorgamming-related material that must be covered in the introductory sequence, there simply isn't time to cover the broader concepts of the discipline at any depth in the confines of the traditional two-semester sequence. As a result, most breadth-first courses that exist today seem to be lead-ins to a more traditional programming sequence. This model, which has several successful implementations, is outlined in the syllabus for CS100B.

In the last few years, however, the two-semester introductory sequence has become cramped even for the programming material. As a result, several institutions are moving toward a three-semester introductory sequence. We endorse these efforts in section 7.7.3 and offer a sample implementation in CS100B. The interesting question that this move toward three-semester sequences brings up is whether the additional time makes a breadth-first approach more viable.

The material presented in the CS101B-102B-103B sequence is quite similar to that offered in any of the traditional two-semester introductions and the CS115 discrete structures class. The difference is the ordering of the material. In the breadth-first sequence, mathematics is distributed throughout all three semesters and is more directly coupled to the topics that use it. In this way, students will have a greater opportunity to appreciate the connections between theory and practice.

A major danger of all breadth-first approaches lies in the fact that students tend to be far more attracted by the programming material, which they see as exciting and empowering, than they are to the more theoretical material. In this treatment, we have taken care to include more programming in the first course than has sometimes been true of breadth-first introductions. In the count of units, a third of the material in CS101B is directly related to programming and much of the rest can be presented so as to emphasize its practical importance.

We recognize that this approach has not been tested and that it may therefore suffer from the same modes of failure that plagued the earlier breadth-first attempts. We believe, however, that the expansion to three semesters may help to address these problems. After all, three-semester sequences—a breadth-first preliminary course followed by a two-semester programming sequence—do exist and seem to be reasonably successful. The advantage of the more integrated design is that students will be exposed to more programming in the first course and more theory in the courses that follow.

CS102B. Algorithms and Programming Techniques

Provides an introduction to programming that builds on a broad introduction to the computer science discipline.

Prerequisites: CS101B

Syllabus:

- Discrete mathematics: Basic logic; proof techniques

- Algorithms and problem solving: Implementation strategies for algorithms; debugging strategies

- Fundamental programming constructs: Declaration models; garbage collection; abstraction mechanisms; modules

- Fundamental data structures: Arrays; records; strings and string processing; data representation in memory; static, stack, and heap allocation; runtime storage management; pointers and references

- Object-oriented programming: Encapsulation and information-hiding; separation of behavior and implementation; classes and subclasses; inheritance; polymorphism; class hierarchies

- Fundamental computing algorithms: Simple numerical algorithms; hash tables

- Overview of programming languages: Brief survey of programming paradigms

- Virtual machines: The concept of a virtual machine; hierarchy of virtual machines; intermediate languages

- Machine level representation of data: Bits, bytes, and words; numeric data representation and number bases; fixed- and floating-point systems; signed and twos-complement representations; representation of nonnumeric data; representation of records and arrays

- Assembly level machine organization: Basic organization of the von Neumann machine; control unit; instruction fetch, decode, and execution

- Introduction to net-centric computing: Background and history of networking and the Internet; network architectures

- Building a simple graphical user interface: Principles of graphical user interfaces; GUI toolkits

- Software engineering: Software design; software tools and environments; requirements and specifications; software validation; testing and debugging strategies

Units covered:

DS2	Basic logic	5 core hours (of 10)
DS3	Proof techniques	2 core hours (of 12)
PF1	Fundamental programming constructs	5 core hours (of 9)
PF2	Algorithms and problem solving	1 core hour (of 6)
PF3	Fundamental data structures	3 core hours (of 14)
PF4	Recursion	1 core hour (of 5)
PF5	Event-driven programming	1 core hour (of 4)
AL3	Fundamental computing algorithms	1 core hour (of 12)
AR1	Digital logic and digital systems	1 core hour (of 6)
AR2	Machine level representation of data	1 core hour (of 3)
AR3	Assembly level machine organization	1 core hour (of 9)
NC1	Introduction to net-centric computing	1 core hour (of 2)
PL1	Overview of programming languages	1 core hour (of 2)
PL2	Virtual machines	1 core hour

PL4	Declarations and types	2 core hours (of 3)
PL5	Abstraction mechanisms	2 core hours (of 3)
PL6	Object-oriented programming	3 core hours (of 10)
HC1	Foundations of human-computer interaction	1 core hour (of 6)
HC2	Building a simple graphical user interface	2 core hours
SE1	Software design	2 core hours (of 8)
SE3	Software tools and environments	1 core hour (of 3)
SE5	Software requirements and specifications	1 core hour (of 4)
SE6	Software validation	1 core hour (of 3)

Notes:

This course is the second of a three-semester sequence (CS101B-102B-103B) that seeks to offer a broad, integrated introduction to computer science. The rationale for the design of the sequence and suggestions for its implementation are given in the notes to CS101B.

CS103B. Principles of Object-Oriented Design

Offers students the opportunity to extend their understanding of object-oriented programming by focusing on data structures, the interactions of algorithms and programming, and the principles of object-oriented design.

Prerequisites: CS103B

Syllabus:

- Discrete mathematics: functions, relations, and sets; proof techniques; solving recurrence relations; mathematical properties of graphs and trees; discrete probability

- Fundamental programming constructs: Iterators and iteration models; recursion in data structures

- Fundamental data structures: Implementation strategies for stacks, queues, hash tables, graphs, and trees; strategies for choosing the right data structure

- Using APIs: API programming; class browsers and related tools; programming by example; debugging in the API environment; introduction to component-based computing

- Algorithmic analysis: Asymptotic analysis of upper and average complexity bounds; identifying differences among best, average, and worst case behaviors; little "o," omega, and theta notation; empirical measurements of performance; time and space tradeoffs in algorithms; using recurrence relations to analyze recursive algorithms

- Fundamental computing algorithms: Binary search trees; representations of graphs; depth- and breadth-first traversals; shortest-path algorithms; transitive closure; minimum spanning tree; topological sort

- Introduction to language translation: Comparison of interpreters and compilers; language translation phases; machine-dependent and machine-independent aspects of translation; parsing strategies

- Object-oriented programming: Object-oriented design; encapsulation and information-hiding; separation of behavior and implementation; collection classes and iteration protocols; internal representations of objects and method tables

- Overview of operating systems: Role and purpose of the operating system; history of operating system development; functionality of a typical operating system

- Fundamental issues in intelligent systems: History of artificial intelligence; philosophical questions; fundamental definitions; philosophical questions; modeling the world; the role of heuristics

- Software engineering: Software design; object-oriented analysis and design; design for reuse; design patterns; programming environments; testing tools

Units covered:

DS1	Functions, relations, and sets	2 core hours (of 6)
DS3	Proof techniques	3 core hours (of 12)
DS4	Basics of counting	2 core hours (of 5)
DS5	Graphs and trees	2 core hours (of 4)
DS6	Discrete probability	2 core hours (of 6)
PF1	Fundamental programming constructs	1 core hour (of 9)
PF3	Fundamental data structures	6 core hours (of 14)
PF4	Recursion	2 core hours (of 5)
AL1	Basic algorithmic analysis	2 core hours (of 4)
AL3	Fundamental computing algorithms	3 core hours (of 12)
OS1	Overview of operating systems	1 core hour (of 2)
PL3	Introduction to language translation	1 core hour (of 2)

PL5	Abstraction mechanisms	1 core hour (of 3)
PL6	Object-oriented programming	5 core hours (of 10)
IS1	Fundamental issues in intelligent systems	1 core hour
IM1	Information models and systems	1 core hour (of 3)
SE1	Software design	2 core hours (of 8)
SE2	Using APIs	2 core hours (of 5)
SE3	Software tools and environments	1 core hour (of 3)

Notes:

This course is the third of a three-semester sequence (CS101B-102B-103B) that seeks to offer a broad, integrated introduction to computer science. The rationale for the design of the sequence and suggestions for its implementation are given in the notes to CS101B.

B.1.5 Algorithms-first

The algorithms-first approach exists only in the two-semester form. If the approach proves popular, it may be appropriate to consider a three-semester implementation.

CS111A. Introduction to Algorithms and Applications

Offers a two-part survey of computing applications and algorithmic principles. The first part introduces the range of algorithmic concepts and constructs, independent of any particular programming language, together with a wide range of application software. The second part begins the transfer of the conceptual foundation to an executable programming context.

Prerequisites: none

Syllabus:

- Background: History of technology and human thought, including technology as a catalyst of paradigmatic change
- Introduction to algorithms: Problem-solving strategies; basic data types; decisions and control; abstraction via functions
- Introduction to recursion
- Abstraction techniques: dynamic data, procedures, compound data types
- Iteration and arrays
- Introduction to computational complexity
- Introduction to object-oriented programming: classes and methods; inheritance; polymorphism
- Fundamental computing algorithms
- The limits of computing

Units covered:

PF1	Fundamental programming constructs	9 core hours
PF2	Algorithms and problem solving	3 core hours (of 6)
PF3	Fundamental data structures	6 core hours (of 14)
PF4	Recursion	3 core hours (of 5)
AL1	Basic algorithmic analysis	2 core hours (of 4)
AL2	Algorithmic strategies	2 core hours (of 6)
AL3	Fundamental computing algorithms	2 core hours (of 12)
AL5	Basic computability	1 core hour (of 6)
AL6	The complexity classes P and NP	1 hour
PL1	Overview of programming languages	1 core hour (of 2)
PL5	Abstraction mechanisms	2 core hours (of 3)
PL6	Object-oriented programming	4 core hours (of 10)
SP1	History of computing	1 core hour
SE1	Software design	2 core hours (of 8)
SE5	Software requirements and specifications	1 core hour (of 4)

Notes:

This course has a three-part agenda:

1. It introduces key algorithmic concepts and constructs apart from any particular programming language and without executable performance requirements. Students learn to construct and analyze algorithms in the context of a pseudocode that is executable only "by hand and mind." This permits students to distinguish between

essential concepts/constructs and the features of any particular programming language. The absence of execution requirements permits comparatively rapid progress through the range of concepts and constructs essential to functional, imperative, and object-oriented paradigms.

2. Concurrent with the first agenda item, it introduces students to essential computing applications in order to (a) provide students with hands-on computing experience to complement the "by hand and mind" approach of the first item, (b) explicate the power of, and need for, abstraction in contexts other than traditional programming contexts, and (c) provide students with a foundation in powerful abstraction-based approaches to using such applications.

3. Subsequent to the first two agenda items, once students have experience in reasoned algorithmic development, tracing, and analysis, the course's lecture and project agendas merge, providing an introduction to applying these concepts and constructs in the context of a modern, production-quality programming environment.

The lecture-and-homework agenda emphasizes abstraction, algorithm construction and algorithm analysis in the context of a nonexecutable pseudocode. The lab-and-project agenda emphasizes the development of both application-use and programming skills, with a focus on abstraction as a key component in the successful use of applications and programming languages. The goal is to provide students with a broad foundation that explicates essential algorithmic constructs and their effective use in a language-independent way, thus preparing students for a fast-paced "Introduction to Programming" in any of a variety of programming languages and paradigms.

CS112A. Programming Methodology

Builds on the foundation provided by CS111A to provide students with immersion in programming experience and associated techniques, with a focus on the object-oriented paradigm. Emphasis on effective software engineering practices, including incremental development, systematic testing, and hypothesis-driven debugging of software artifacts.

Prerequisites: CS111A

Syllabus:

- Review of elementary programming and data structures
- Debugging strategies, methods, and aids
- Review of object-oriented programming: encapsulation via objects; inheritance; polymorphism
- Object-oriented design
- Review of stacks and queues
- Exceptions and exception handling
- Search techniques: DFS, BFS, Dijkstra's
- Spanning trees: Primm's, Kruskal's
- Self-balancing trees
- Graphs
- Heaps
- Hashing techniques
- Graphics
- Graphical user interfaces
- Game trees
- Cryptography

Units covered:

PF3	Fundamental data structures	5 core hours (of 14)
PF4	Recursion	2 core hours (of 5)
PF5	Event-driven programming	3 core hours (of 4)
AL2	Algorithmic strategies	2 core hours (of 6)
AL3	Fundamental computing algorithms	4 core hours (of 12)
AL9	Cryptographic algorithms	2 hours
PL1	Overview of programming languages	1 core hour (of 2)
PL2	Virtual machines	1 core hour
PL3	Introduction to language translation	2 core hours
PL4	Declarations and types	3 core hours
PL5	Abstraction mechanisms	1 core hour (of 3)
PL6	Object-oriented programming	4 core hours (of 10)
GV1	Fundamental techniques in graphics	2 core hours
SE1	Software design	2 core hours (of 8)
SE2	Using APIs	2 core hours (of 5)
SE3	Software tools and environments	2 core hours (of 3)
SE6	Software validation	1 core hour (of 3)
SE7	Software evolution	1 core hour (of 3)

Notes:

As specified in the description of CS111A, students in that course are exposed to the complete range of algorithmic concepts and constructs. This liberates the teaching-and-learning agenda of the current course to focus on effective programming skills, including systematic approaches to design, implementation, testing and debugging. It also permits students to proceed more rapidly through this agenda than might otherwise be possible, as they enter the course with a broad and appropriate conceptual foundation.

Transfer students who have had only a single CS course other than CS111A are likely to have difficulty in this course, as they will not likely have an adequate foundation. Except in exceptional circumstances, they should be counseled to obtain a remedial foundation in CS111A material prior to taking this course. Transfer students who have succeeded in alternate versions of both CS111 and CS112 are likely to succeed in this course and to appreciate its orientation to effective programming skills.

B.1.6 Hardware-first

The hardware-first approach exists only in the two-semester form. If the approach proves popular, it may be appropriate to consider a three-semester implementation.

CS111H. Introduction to the Computer

Offers a bottom-up introduction to the computer, beginning with bits and moving up the conceptual hierarchy to higher-level languages.

Prerequisites: none

Syllabus:

- Introduction: Brief history of computing; the components of a computing system
- Machine level representation of data: Bits, bytes, and words; numeric data representation and number bases; signed and twos-complement representations; fundamental operations on bits; representation of nonnumeric data
- Digital logic: Switching circuits; gates; memory
- Assembly level machine organization: Basic organization of the von Neumann machine; control unit; instruction fetch, decode, and execution; instruction sets and types; assembly/machine language programming; instruction formats
- Algorithms and problem-solving: Problem-solving strategies; the role of algorithms in the problem-solving process; implementation strategies for algorithms; debugging strategies; the concept and properties of algorithms
- Input and output: simple I/O; files
- Overview of programming languages: History of programming languages; brief survey of programming paradigms; the role of language translation in the programming process
- Fundamental programming constructs: Basic syntax and semantics of a higher-level language; variables, types, expressions, and assignment; simple I/O; conditional and iterative control structures; functions and parameter passing; structured decomposition
- Fundamental data structures: Primitive types; arrays; records; strings and string processing; data representation in memory; static, stack, and heap allocation; runtime storage management; pointers and references; linked structures
- Recursion: The concept of recursion; recursive mathematical functions; simple recursive procedures; implementation of recursion
- Software development methodology: Fundamental design concepts and principles; structured design; testing and debugging strategies; test-case design; programming environments; testing and debugging tools

Units covered:

PF1	Fundamental programming constructs	5 core hours (of 9)
PF2	Algorithms and problem solving	2 core hours (of 6)
PF3	Fundamental data structures	5 core hours (of 14)
PF4	Recursion	5 core hours
AL2	Algorithmic strategies	2 core hours (of 6)
AL3	Fundamental computing algorithms	2 core hours (of 12)
AL5	Basic computability	1 core hour (of 6)
AR1	Digital logic and digital systems	3 core hours (of 6)
AR2	Machine level representation of data	2 core hours (of 3)
AR3	Assembly level machine organization	2 core hours (of 9)
AR4	Memory system organization and architecture	2 core hours (of 5)

PL1	Overview of programming languages	1 core hour (of 2)
PL4	Declarations and types	1 core hour (of 3)
PL5	Abstraction mechanisms	2 core hours (of 3)
SP1	History of computing	1 core hour
SE1	Software design	2 core hours (of 8)
SE3	Software tools and environments	1 core hour (of 3)
SE6	Software validation	1 core hour (of 3)

CS112H. Object-Oriented Programming Techniques

Extends the foundation developed in CS111H to encompass object-oriented programming and algorithmic analysis.

Prerequisites: CS111H

Syllabus:

- Review of programming concepts

- Algorithms and problem-solving: Problem-solving strategies; the role of algorithms in the problem-solving process; implementation strategies for algorithms

- Object-oriented programming: Object-oriented design; encapsulation and information-hiding; separation of behavior and implementation; classes, subclasses, and inheritance; polymorphism; class hierarchies; collection classes and iteration protocols; fundamental design patterns

- Fundamental data structures: Primitive types; arrays; records; strings and string processing; data representation in memory; static, stack, and heap allocation; runtime storage management; pointers and references; linked structures; implementation strategies for stacks, queues, and hash tables; implementation strategies for graphs and trees; strategies for choosing the right data structure

- Event-driven and concurrent programming: Event-handling methods; event propagation; managing concurrency in event handling; exception handling

- Using APIs: API programming; class browsers and related tools; programming by example; debugging in the API environment

- Basic algorithmic analysis: Asymptotic analysis of upper and average complexity bounds; identifying differences among best, average, and worst case behaviors; big "O," little "o," omega, and theta notation; standard complexity classes; empirical measurements of performance; time and space tradeoffs in algorithms; using recurrence relations to analyze recursive algorithms

- Algorithmic strategies: Brute-force algorithms; greedy algorithms; divide-and-conquer; backtracking; heuristics

- Fundamental computing algorithms: Simple numerical algorithms; sequential and binary search algorithms; sorting algorithms

- Overview of programming languages: History of programming languages; brief survey of programming paradigms; the role of language translation in the programming process

- Fundamental issues in language design: General principles of language design; design goals; typing regimes; data structure models; control structure models; abstraction mechanisms

- Virtual machines: The concept of a virtual machine; hierarchy of virtual machines; intermediate languages; security issues arising from running code on an alien machine

- Introduction to language translation: Comparison of interpreters and compilers; language translation phases; machine-dependent and machine-independent aspects of translation; language translation as a software engineering activity

- Basic computability theory: Tractable and intractable problems; the existence of noncomputable functions

- Fundamental techniques in graphics: Hierarchy of graphics software; using a graphics API

- Software design: Fundamental design concepts and principles; software architecture; structured design; object-oriented analysis and design; component-level design; design for reuse
- Software tools and environments: Programming environments; testing tools

Units covered:

PF1	Fundamental programming constructs	4 core hours (of 9)
PF2	Algorithms and problem-solving	1 core hour (of 6)
PF3	Fundamental data structures	6 core hours (of 14)
PF5	Event-driven programming	2 core hours (of 4)
AL1	Basic algorithmic analysis	2 core hours (of 4)
AL2	Algorithmic strategies	2 core hours (of 6)
AL3	Fundamental computing algorithms	4 core hours (of 12)
PL1	Overview of programming languages	1 core hour (of 2)
PL2	Virtual machines	1 core hour
PL4	Declarations and types	2 core hours (of 3)
PL5	Abstraction mechanisms	1 core hour (of 3)
PL6	Object-oriented programming	8 core hours (of 10)
SE1	Software design	2 core hours (of 8)
SE2	Using APIs	2 core hours (of 5)
SE3	Software tools and environments	1 core hour (of 3)
SE5	Software requirements and specifications	1 core hour (of 4)

B.2 Other first-year courses

The courses in this section are arranged in numerical order.

CS105. Discrete Structures I

Introduces the foundations of discrete mathematics as they apply to computer science, focusing on providing a solid theoretical foundation for further work. Topics include functions, relations, sets, simple proof techniques, Boolean algebra, propositional logic, digital logic, elementary number theory, and the fundamentals of counting.

Prerequisites: Mathematical preparation sufficient to take calculus at the college level.

Syllabus:

- Introduction to logic and proofs: Direct proofs; proof by contradiction; mathematical induction
- Fundamental structures: Functions (surjections, injections, inverses, composition); relations (reflexivity, symmetry, transitivity, equivalence relations); sets (Venn diagrams, complements, Cartesian products, power sets); pigeonhole principle; cardinality and countability
- Boolean algebra: Boolean values; standard operations on Boolean values; de Morgan's laws
- Propositional logic: Logical connectives; truth tables; normal forms (conjunctive and disjunctive); validity
- Digital logic: Logic gates, flip-flops, counters; circuit minimization
- Elementary number theory: Factorability; properties of primes; greatest common divisors and least common multiples; Euclid's algorithm; modular arithmetic; the Chinese Remainder Theorem
- Basics of counting: Counting arguments; pigeonhole principle; permutations and combinations; binomial coefficients

Units covered:

DS1	Functions, relations, and sets	9 hours (6 core + 3)
DS2	Basic logic	5 core hours (of 10)
DS3	Proof techniques	4 core hours (of 12)
DS4	Basics of counting	9 hours (5 core + 4)
AR1	Digital logic and digital systems	3 core hours (of 6)
	Elementary number theory	5 hours
	Elective topics	5 hours

Notes:

This implementation of the Discrete Structures area (DS) divides the material into two courses. CS105 covers the first half of the material and is followed by CS106, which completes the core topic coverage. Because the material is stretched over two courses—as opposed to CS115 which covers the material in a single course—many of the units are given more coverage than is strictly required in the core. Similarly, the two-course version includes additional topics, reducing the need to cover these topics in more advanced courses, such as the introductory course in algorithmic analysis (CS210).

Although the principal focus is discrete mathematics, the course is likely to be more successful if it highlights applications whose solutions require proof, logic, and counting. For example, the number theory section could be developed in the context of public-key cryptography, so that students who tend to focus on the applications side of computer science will have an incentive to learn the underlying theoretical material.

CS106. Discrete Structures II

Continues the discussion of discrete mathematics introduced in CS105. Topics in the second course include predicate logic, recurrence relations, graphs, trees, matrices, computational complexity, elementary computability, and discrete probability.

Prerequisites: CS105

Syllabus:

- Review of previous course
- Predicate logic: Universal and existential quantification; modus ponens and modus tollens; limitations of predicate logic
- Recurrence relations: Basic formulas; elementary solution techniques
- Graphs and trees: Fundamental definitions; simple algorithms ; traversal strategies; proof techniques; spanning trees; applications
- Matrices: Basic properties; applications
- Computational complexity: Order analysis; standard complexity classes
- Elementary computability: Countability and uncountability; diagonalization proof to show uncountability of the reals; definition of the P and NP classes; simple demonstration of the halting problem
- Discrete probability: Finite probability spaces; conditional probability, independence, Bayes' rule; random events; random integer variables; mathematical expectation

Units covered:

DS2	Basic logic	7 core hours (of 10)
DS3	Proof techniques	8 core hours (of 12)
DS5	Graphs and trees	4 core hours
DS6	Discrete probability	6 core hours
AL1	Basic algorithmic analysis	2 core hours (of 4)
AL5	Basic computability	3 core hours (of 6)
AL6	The complexity classes P and NP	2 hours
	Matrices	3 hours
	Elective topics	5 hours

Notes:

This implementation of the Discrete Structures area (DS) divides the material into two courses: CS105 and CS106. For programs that wish to accelerate the presentation of this material, there is also CS115, which covers the core topics in a single course. The two-course sequence, however, covers some additional material that is not in the compressed version, primarily in the Algorithms and Complexity area (AL). As a result, the introductory course in algorithmic analysis (CS210) can devote more time to advanced topics if an institution adopts the two-course implementation.

Like CS105, this course introduces mathematical topics in the context of applications that require those concepts as tools. For this course, likely applications include transportation network problems (such as the traveling salesperson problem) and resource allocation.

CS115. Discrete Structures for Computer Science

Offers an intensive introduction to discrete mathematics as it is used in computer science. Topics include functions, relations, sets, propositional and predicate logic, simple circuit logic, proof techniques, elementary combinatorics, and discrete probability.

Prerequisites: Mathematical preparation sufficient to take calculus at the college level.

Syllabus:

- Fundamental structures: Functions (surjections, injections, inverses, composition); relations (reflexivity, symmetry, transitivity, equivalence relations); sets (Venn diagrams, complements, Cartesian products, power sets); pigeonhole principle; cardinality and countability
- Basic logic: Propositional logic; logical connectives; truth tables; normal forms (conjunctive and disjunctive); validity; predicate logic; limitations of predicate logic; universal and existential quantification; modus ponens and modus tollens
- Digital logic: Logic gates, flip-flops, counters; circuit minimization
- Proof techniques: Notions of implication, converse, inverse, contrapositive, negation, and contradiction; the structure of formal proofs; direct proofs; proof by counterexample; proof by contraposition; proof by contradiction; mathematical induction; strong induction; recursive mathematical definitions; well orderings
- Basics of counting: Counting arguments; pigeonhole principle; permutations and combinations; recurrence relations
- Discrete probability: Finite probability spaces; conditional probability, independence, Bayes' rule; random events; random integer variables; mathematical expectation

Units covered:

DS1	Functions, relations, and sets	6 core hours
DS2	Basic logic	10 core hours
DS3	Proof techniques	9 core hours (of 12)
DS4	Basics of counting	5 core hours
DS6	Discrete probability	6 core hours
AR1	Digital logic and digital systems	3 core hours (of 6)
	Elective topics	1 hour

Notes:

This implementation of the Discrete Structures area (DS) compresses the core material into a single course. Although such a strategy is workable, many institutions will prefer to use two courses to cover this material in greater depth. For an implementation that uses the two-course model, see the descriptions of CS105 and CS106.

CS120. Introduction to Computer Organization

Introduces the concept of computers and information systems by presenting the process of computation as a hierarchy of virtual machines, beginning with the hardware and moving upward through various levels of increasingly sophisticated software. This course outlines the facilities provided by each virtual machine, along with the mechanisms and software tools that lead to the realization of the hierarchy.

Prerequisites: none

Syllabus:

- The fundamental elements of digital logic and their use in computer construction

- Register-level description of computer execution and the functional organization of a computer
- Representation of data of different kinds
- The elements of machine- and assembly-language programming
- The role and function of programming languages and their associated libraries
- The role and function of an operating system (including networking and distributed systems)
- Applications including description of the functionality of the relevant software (word processors, databases, browsers, search engines, and so forth)
- Human-computer interaction and its importance for interface software
- Introduction to the World Wide Web: Fundamentals of the Web; browsers; search engines; information retrieval; web-page construction
- Networked information: Information servers; newsgroups; search strategies; information storage and retrieval; underlying principles.
- Intellectual property issues

Units covered:

AR2	Machine level representation of data	1 core hour (of 3)
AR3	Assembly level machine organization	3 core hours (of 9)
AR6	Functional organization	1 core hour (of 7)
OS2	Operating system principles	1 core hour (of 2)
NC1	Introduction to net-centric computing	1 core hour (of 2)
NC2	Communication and networking	4 core hours (of 7)
NC4	The web as an example of client-server computing	2 core hours (of 3)
PL3	Introduction to language translation	1 core hour (of 2)
HC1	Foundations of human-computer interaction	3 core hours (of 6)
HC2	Building a simple graphical user interface	2 core hours
HC3	Human-centered software evaluation	3 hours
HC4	Human-centered software development	3 hours
IS1	Fundamental issues in intelligent systems	1 core hour
IS2	Search and constraint satisfaction	2 core hours (of 5)
IM1	Information models and systems	2 core hours (of 3)
IM2	Database systems	1 core hour (of 3)
SP1	History of computing	1 core hour
SP2	Social context of computing	2 core hours (of 3)
SP4	Professional and ethical responsibilities	1 core hour (of 3)
SP6	Intellectual property	1 core hour (of 3)
	Elective topics	4 hours

Notes:

Computer systems appear to be immensely complex. Yet when viewed as a hierarchy of abstract (or virtual) machines, their construction takes on an elegance and sophistication that illustrates vital aspects of the discipline of computer science. The purpose of this course is to consider the various commonly understood virtual machines, the facilities and mechanisms provided by each virtual machine, and the nature of the mechanisms or software tools that lead to the realization of the different levels in the hierarchy.

In addressing this material, there is a challenge in terms of ensuring that the material is presented in a manner that is interesting and exciting. An up-to-date description of a computer system can help to set expectations and provide motivation for further study.

The treatment should recognize the importance not just of traditional data but also of sound, video, and so forth.

Given the wide range of resources available via the World Wide Web, there is enormous scope for using this module to teach students a range of personal and transferable skills: undergraduate research, presentational skills of various kinds, and so on. At the same time, it is essential that students recognize there are problems in dealing with vast volumes of information.

For their own purposes, students will need to be able to cope with a range of e-mail messages of varying importance, documents or information for different classes, Web site references, software tools, case studies and illustrations, and so on. If properly and carefully structured, these tools can be used to create environments for efficient and effective operation. Thus, the material in this course should be of high value to students. In more general terms, the same principles can be used to create environments with a range of possible uses: learning, desk-top publishing, project management, information retrieval and Web searching, computer graphics and animation, developing computer games, and so on. The principles outlined in this course should provide a framework for these other areas.

CS130. Introduction to the World Wide Web

Introduces students to the world of computer science through the World Wide Web, focusing on the techniques of web-page creation. No programming background is required, although students will learn some programming through scripting languages.

Prerequisites: none

Syllabus:

- Introduction to the Internet: Background and history of networking and the Internet; overview of network architectures
- Communication and networking: Overview of network standards and protocols; circuit switching vs. packet switching
- Introduction to the World Wide Web: Web technologies; the HTML protocol; the format of a Web page; support tools for Web site creation
- Multimedia data technologies: Sound and audio, image and graphics, animation and video; input and output devices; tools to support multimedia development
- Interactivity on the web: Scripting languages; the role of applets
- Human-computer interaction: HCI aspects of Web-page design; graphical user-interface design
- Network management: Overview of the issues of network management; use of passwords and access control mechanisms; domain names and name services; issues for Internet service providers; security issues and firewalls
- Compression and decompression: Analog and digital representations; overview of encoding and decoding algorithms; lossless and lossy compression
- Network security: Fundamentals of cryptography; secret-key algorithms; public-key algorithms; authentication protocols; digital signatures; examples
- Software tools and environments: Web-page development tools
- Intellectual property: Foundations of intellectual property;copyrights, patents, and trade secrets; issues regarding the use of intellectual property on the Web

- Privacy and civil liberties: Ethical and legal basis for privacy protection; freedom of expression in cyberspace; international and intercultural implications

Units covered:

NC1	Introduction to net-centric computing	2 core hours
NC2	Communication and networking	2 core hours (of 7)
NC3	Network security	3 core hours
NC4	The Web as an example of client-server computing	3 core hours
NC5	Building Web applications	3 hours
NC6	Network management	2 hours
NC7	Compression and decompression	3 hours
NC8	Multimedia data technologies	3 hours
HC5	Graphical user-interface design	2 hours
HC7	HCI aspects of multimedia systems	2 hours
SE3	Software tools and environments	2 core hours (of 3)
SP6	Intellectual property	2 core hours (of 3)
SP7	Privacy and civil liberties	2 core hours
	Elective topics	9 hours

B.3 Intermediate courses

Although the courses in this section are typically identified with thematic tracks—topics, compressed, systems, and Web-based—the course numbers are unique. This property makes it useful to list these courses in numerical order. If the same course appears in more than one track, all appropriate suffixes are shown.

CS210{C,S,T,W}. Algorithm Design and Analysis

Introduces formal techniques to support the design and analysis of algorithms, focusing on both the underlying mathematical theory and practical considerations of efficiency. Topics include asymptotic complexity bounds, techniques of analysis, algorithmic strategies, and an introduction to automata theory and its application to language translation.

Prerequisites: introduction to computer science (any implementation of CS103 or CS112), discrete structures (CS106 or CS115)

Syllabus:

- Review of proof techniques

- Basic algorithmic analysis: Asymptotic analysis of upper and average complexity bounds; best, average, and worst case behaviors; big-O, little-o, Ω, and $\emptyset$ notation; standard complexity classes; empirical measurements of performance; time and space tradeoffs in algorithms; using recurrence relations to analyze recursive algorithms

- Fundamental algorithmic strategies: Brute-force; greedy; divide-and-conquer; backtracking; branch-and-bound; heuristics; pattern matching and string/text algorithms; numerical approximation

- Fundamental data structures: Implementation strategies for graphs and trees; performance issues for data structures

- Graph and tree algorithms: Depth- and breadth-first traversals; shortest-path algorithms (Dijkstra's and Floyd's algorithms); transitive closure (Floyd's algorithm); minimum spanning tree (Prim's and Kruskal's algorithms); topological sort

- Automata theory: Finite-state machines; Turing machines; context-free grammars; uncomputable functions; the halting problem; implications of uncomputability

- Introduction to language translation: Comparison of interpreters and compilers; language translation phases; machine-dependent and machine-independent aspects of translation; language translation as a software engineering activity

Units covered:

DS3	Proof techniques	3 core hours (of 12)
DS5	Graphs and trees	4 core hours
PF2	Algorithms and problem solving	3 core hours (of 6)
PF3	Fundamental data structures	3 core hours (of 14)
PL3	Introduction to language translation	2 core hours
AL1	Basic algorithmic analysis	2 core hours (of 4)
AL2	Algorithmic strategies	6 core hours
AL3	Fundamental computing algorithms	6 core hours (of 12)
AL5	Basic computability	6 core hours
AL6	The complexity classes P and NP	2 hours
AL7	Automata theory	2 hours
	Elective topics	1 hour

Notes:

The topic of algorithmic analysis is central to much of computer science. The thrust of this course is to explore and examine a range of algorithms that can be used to solve practical problems. Each algorithm possesses strengths and weaknesses. Moreover, the performance or any particular algorithm typically varies according to the size and nature of the input data. Students need a thorough understanding of the tools of analysis in order to select the right algorithm for the job.

Students are most receptive to the material presented in this course if they understand the connections between theory and practice. To this end, instructors should try to find ways to reinforce the theoretical topics through practical activity. It is also important for instructors to provide compelling demonstrations of the enormous differences in running time that can occur when algorithms have different complexity characteristics. The importance of complexity measures must be made real.

Algorithmic animation can be a powerful tool toward getting students to understand both the algorithms themselves and the associated complexity measures. Tools for creating graphical animations of classical algorithms are widely available on the Web. These tools provide visible evidence of the complexity measures and thus reinforce the theoretical results.

It is also possible to take a more formal approach to this topic that focuses on formal specification of algorithms and proofs of correctness, possibly supported by appropriate specification and verification tools. A more informal approach, however, is likely to appeal to a wider spectrum of students.

Students who complete this course should be able to perform the following tasks:

- Explain the mathematical concepts used in describing the complexity of an algorithm.
- Select and apply algorithms appropriate to a particular situation.
- Employ one from a range of strategies leading to the design of algorithms to serve particular purposes.
- Explain the tradeoffs that exist between a range of algorithms that possess the same functionality.

CS220{C,S,T}. Computer Architecture

Introduces students to the organization and architecture of computer systems, beginning with the standard von Neumann model and then moving forward to more recent archictural concepts.

Prerequisites: introduction to computer science (any implementation of CS103 or CS112), discrete structures (CS106 or CS115)

Syllabus:

- Digital logic: Fundamental building blocks (logic gates, flip-flops, counters, registers, PLA); logic expressions, minimization, sum of product forms; register transfer notation; physical considerations (gate delays, fan-in, fan-out)

- Data representation: Bits, bytes, and words; numeric data representation and number bases; fixed- and floating-point systems; signed and twos-complement representations; representation of nonnumeric data (character codes, graphical data); representation of records and arrays

- Assembly level organization: Basic organization of the von Neumann machine; control unit; instruction fetch, decode, and execution; instruction sets and types (data manipulation, control, I/O); assembly/machine language programming; instruction formats; addressing modes; subroutine call and return mechanisms; I/O and interrupts

- Memory systems: Storage systems and their technology; coding, data compression, and data integrity; memory hierarchy; main memory organization and operations; latency, cycle time, bandwidth, and interleaving; cache memories (address mapping, block size, replacement and store policy); virtual memory (page table, TLB); fault handling and reliability

- Interfacing and communication: I/O fundamentals: handshaking, buffering, programmed I/O, interrupt-driven I/O; interrupt structures: vectored and prioritized, interrupt acknowledgment; external storage, physical organization, and drives; buses: bus protocols, arbitration, direct-memory access (DMA); introduction to networks; multimedia support; raid architectures

- Functional organization: Implementation of simple datapaths; control unit: hardwired realization vs. microprogrammed realization; instruction pipelining; introduction to instruction-level parallelism (ILP)

- Multiprocessor and alternative architectures: Introduction to SIMD, MIMD, VLIW, EPIC; systolic architecture; interconnection networks; shared memory systems; cache coherence; memory models and memory consistency

- Performance enhancements: RISC architecture; branch prediction; prefetching; scalability

- Contemporary architectures: Handheld devices; embedded systems; trends in processor architecture

Units covered:

AR1	Digital logic and digital systems	3 core hours (of 6)
AR2	Machine level representation of data	3 core hours
AR3	Assembly level machine organization	9 core hours
AR4	Memory system organization and architecture	5 core hours
AR5	Interfacing and communication	3 core hours
AR6	Functional organization	7 core hours
AR7	Multiprocessing and alternative architectures	3 core hours
AR8	Performance enhancements	3 hours
	Contemporary architectures	2 hours
	Elective topics	2 hours

Notes:

Differences in the internal structure and organization of a computer lead to significant differences in performance and functionality, giving rise to an extraordinary range of computing devices, from handheld computers to large-scale, high-performance machines. This course addresses the various options involved in designing a computer system, the range of design considerations, and the tradeoffs involved in the design process.

A key issue in relation to this course is motivation. It is important to heighten the motivation of both students and faculty into seeing hardware design as an increasingly interesting, relevant, and challenging area. One approach is to include a significant laboratory component with the course that gives students the opportunity to build their own computer system. In doing so, they will appreciate the underlying issues at a much greater level of detail. In addition, those students will experience a sense of accomplishment in the hardware area similar to what most students describe when they complete a significant software project.

Software tools can play an important role in this course, particularly when funding for a hardware laboratory is not available. These tools include, for example, instruction set simulators, software that will simulate cache performance, benchmark systems that will evaluate performance, and so on.

Students who complete this course should be able to perform the following tasks:

• Write and debug simple programs using assembly code.

• Explain the principles underlying the design and development of computer systems for a variety of purposes.

• Trace the influences of important computing developments (such as compiler technology, networking, the Web, multimedia, safety, security) on the architecture of computer systems.

• Outline the architectural features of a modern computer system.

CS221w. Architecture and Operating Systems

Presents a combined introduction to the concepts of architecture and operating systems.

Prerequisites: introduction to computer science (any implementation of CS103 or CS112), discrete structures (CS106 or CS115)

Syllabus:

- Digital logic and digital systems: Fundamental building blocks; logic expressions, minimization, sum of product forms; register transfer notation; physical considerations

- Machine level representation of data: Bits, bytes, and words; numeric data representation and number bases; fixed- and floating-point systems; signed and twos-complement representations; representation of nonnumeric data; representation of records and arrays

- Assembly level machine organization: Basic organization of the von Neumann machine; control unit; instruction fetch, decode, and execution; instruction sets and types; assembly/machine language programming; instruction formats; addressing modes; subroutine call and return mechanisms; I/O and interrupts

- Memory system organization and architecture: Storage systems and their technology; coding, data compression, and data integrity; memory hierarchy; main memory organization and operations; latency, cycle time, bandwidth, and interleaving; cache memories; virtual memory; fault handling and reliability

- Functional organization: Implementation of simple datapaths; control unit; instruction pipelining; introduction to instruction-level parallelism

- Overview of operating systems: Role and purpose of the operating system; history of operating system development; functionality of a typical operating system; mechanisms to support client-server models, handheld devices; design issues; influences of security, networking, multimedia, windows

- Operating system principles: Structuring methods; abstractions, processes, and resources; concepts of application program interfaces; applications needs and the evolution of hardware/software techniques; device organization; interrupts; concept of user/system state and protection, transition to kernel mode

- Concurrency: dispatching and context switching; the role of interrupts; concurrent execution; the "mutual exclusion" problem and some solutions

- Scheduling and dispatch: Preemptive and nonpreemptive scheduling; schedulers and policies; processes and threads

- Memory management: Review of physical memory and memory management hardware; overlays, swapping, and partitions; paging and segmentation; placement and replacement policies; working sets and thrashing; caching

Units covered:

AR1	Digital logic and digital systems	3 core hours (of 6)
AR2	Machine level representation of data	3 core hours
AR3	Assembly level machine organization	9 core hours
AR4	Memory system organization and architecture	5 core hours
AR6	Functional organization	7 core hours
OS1	Overview of operating systems	2 core hours
OS2	Operating system principles	2 core hours
OS3	Concurrency	2 core hours (of 6)
OS4	Scheduling and dispatch	2 core hours (of 3)
OS5	Memory management	5 core hours

CS222w. Architectures for Networking and Communication

Presents those aspects of computer architecture that are central to communications and networking.

Prerequisites: CS221w

Syllabus:

- Distributed algorithms: Consensus and election; termination detection; fault tolerance; stabilization

- Interfacing and communication: I/O fundamentals; interrupt structures; external storage, physical organization, and drives; buses; introduction to networks; multimedia support; RAID architectures

- Multiprocessing and alternative architectures: Introduction to SIMD, MIMD, VLIW, EPIC; systolic architecture; interconnection networks; shared memory systems; cache coherence; memory models and memory consistency

- Architecture for networks and distributed systems: Introduction to LANs and WANs; layered protocol design, ISO/OSI, IEEE 802; impact of architectural issues on distributed algorithms; network computing; distributed multimedia

- Concurrency: States and state diagrams; structures; dispatching and context switching; the role of interrupts; concurrent execution; the "mutual exclusion" problem and some solutions; deadlock; models and mechanisms; producer-consumer problems and synchronization; multiprocessor issues

- Scheduling and dispatch: Review of processes and scheduling; deadlines and real-time issues

- Real-time and embedded systems: Process and task scheduling; memory/disk management requirements in a real-time environment; failures, risks, and recovery; special concerns in real-time systems

- Fault tolerance: Fundamental concepts; spatial and temporal redundancy; methods used to implement fault tolerance; examples of reliable systems

- System performance evaluation: Why system performance needs to be evaluated; what is to be evaluated; policies for caching, paging, scheduling, memory management, security, and so forth; evaluation models; how to collect evaluation data

- Scripting: Scripting and the role of scripting languages; basic system commands; creating scripts, parameter passing; executing a script; influences of scripting on programming

Units covered:

AL4	Distributed algorithms	3 core hours
AR5	Interfacing and communication	3 core hours
AR7	Multiprocessing and alternative architectures	3 core hours
AR9	Architecture for networks and distributed systems	5 hours
OS3	Concurrency	4 core hours (of 6)
OS4	Scheduling and dispatch	2 core hours (of 3)
OS9	Real-time and embedded systems	5 hours
OS10	Fault tolerance	5 hours
OS11	System performance evaluation	4 hours
OS12	Scripting	3 hours
	Elective topics	3 hours

CS225{S,T}. Operating Systems

Introduces the fundamentals of operating systems design and implementation. Topics include an overview of the components of an operating system, mutual exclusion and synchronization, implementation of processes, scheduling algorithms, memory management, and file systems.

Prerequisites: CS220

Syllabus:

- Overview: Role and purpose of operating systems; history of operating system development; functionality of a typical operating system; design issues (efficiency, robustness, flexibility, portability, security, compatibility)

- Basic principles: Structuring methods; abstractions, processes, and resources; design of application programming interfaces (APIs); device organization; interrupts; user/system state transitions

- Concurrency: The idea of concurrent execution; states and state diagrams; implementation structures (ready lists, process control blocks, and so forth); dispatching and context switching; interrupt handling in a concurrent environment

- Mutual exclusion: Definition of the "mutual exclusion" problem; deadlock detection and prevention; solution strategies; models and mechanisms (semaphores, monitors, condition variables, rendezvous); producer-consumer problems; synchronization; multiprocessor issues

- Scheduling: Preemptive and nonpreemptive scheduling; scheduling policies; processes and threads; real-time issues

- Memory management: Review of physical memory and memory management hardware; overlays, swapping, and partitions; paging and segmentation; page placement and replacement policies; working sets and thrashing; caching

- Device management: Characteristics of serial and parallel devices; abstracting device differences; buffering strategies; direct memory access; recovery from failures

- File systems: Fundamental concepts (data, metadata, operations, organization, buffering, sequential vs. nonsequential files); content and structure of directories; file system techniques (partitioning, mounting and unmounting, virtual file systems); memory-mapped files; special-purpose file systems; naming, searching, and access; backup strategies

- Security and protection: Overview of system security; policy/mechanism separation; security methods and devices; protection, access, and authentication; models of protection; memory protection; encryption; recovery management

Units covered:

AL4	Distributed algorithms	3 core hours
OS1	Overview of operating systems	2 core hours
OS2	Operating system principles	2 core hours
OS3	Concurrency	6 core hours
OS4	Scheduling and dispatch	3 core hours
OS5	Memory management	5 core hours
OS6	Device management	4 hours
OS7	Security and protection	4 hours
OS8	File systems	5 hours
OS11	System performance evaluation	2 hours
	Elective topics	4 hours

CS226{C,S}. Operating Systems and Networking

Introduces the fundamentals of operating systems together with the basics of networking and communications.

Prerequisites: introduction to computer science (any implementation of CS103 or CS112), discrete structures (CS106 or CS115)

Syllabus:

- Introduction to event-driven programming

- Using APIs: API programming; class browsers and related tools; programming by example; debugging in the API environment

- Overview of operating systems: Role and purpose of the operating system; history of operating system development; functionality of a typical operating system

- Operating system principles: Structuring methods; abstractions, processes, and resources; concepts of application program interfaces; device organization; interrupts; concepts of user/system state and protection

- Introduction to concurrency: Synchronization principles; the "mutual exclusion" problem and some solutions; deadlock avoidance

- Introduction to concurrency: States and state diagrams; structures; dispatching and context switching; the role of interrupts; concurrent execution; the "mutual exclusion" problem and some solutions; deadlock; models and mechanisms; producer-consumer problems and synchronization

- Scheduling and dispatch: Preemptive and nonpreemptive scheduling; schedulers and policies; processes and threads; deadlines and real-time issues

- Memory management: Review of physical memory and memory management hardware; overlays, swapping, and partitions; paging and segmentation; placement and replacement policies; working sets and thrashing; caching

- Introduction to distributed algorithms: Consensus and election; fault tolerance

- Introduction to net-centric computing: Background and history of networking and the Internet; network architectures; the range of specializations within net-centric computing

- Introduction to networking and communications: Network architectures; issues associated with distributed computing; simple network protocols; APIs for network operations

- Introduction to the World Wide Web: Web technologies; characteristics of Web servers; nature of the client-server relationship; Web protocols; support tools for Web site creation and Web management

- Network security: Fundamentals of cryptography; secret-key algorithms; public-key algorithms; authentication protocols; digital signatures; examples

Units covered:

PF5	Event-driven programming	2 core hours (of 4)
AL4	Distributed algorithms	3 core hours
OS1	Overview of operating systems	2 core hours
OS2	Operating system principles	2 core hours
OS3	Concurrency	6 core hours
OS4	Scheduling and dispatch	3 core hours
OS5	Memory management	5 core hours
NC1	Introduction to net-centric computing	2 core hours
NC2	Communication and networking	7 core hours
NC3	Network security	3 core hours
NC4	The web as an example of client-server computing	3 core hours
PL6	Object-oriented programming	2 core hours (of 10)

Notes:

Because this course includes a range of topics, CS226 is an example of a "crosscutting" approach to designing a core. In a more traditional implementation of the core, an institution might offer one course in operating systems and another in networks. There is, however, a good deal of interplay between these topics. It therefore makes sense to design a course that looks at these pieces of system software together, particularly since the web is extremely appealing to students. Combining the operating system topics with the discussion of networking helps motivate students and stimulates their thinking about both the effect of the web on operating systems and the more general principles involved.

The issue of motivation is paramount in the design of the course. The area of operating systems is often regarded as difficult for both students and faculty, but nonetheless contains many ideas of relevance to all computer scientists. Faculty must ask themselves how they can make operating systems relevant to undergraduates. This consideration must drive the choice of approach to learning and teaching. To this end, students must see these issues as related to the systems that they use. As an example, students might be asked to consider the impact on the operating system of such developments as networking, multimedia, security, and handheld devices. Similarly, one could also ask about the impact of other developments, such as the following:

- Playing music on a CD at the same time as using the computer

- Downloading TV pictures onto a window

- Docking systems or devices such as digital cameras and handheld computers

- Client-server architectures

In pursuing any course on operating systems, students need to be made aware of the wider relevance of many of the ideas. It is therefore useful to highlight the following connections:

- The cache idea, while relevant at the hardware level, shows up again in the context of the web and downloading material from web sites.

- The concepts that arise in the discussion of virtual memory come up again in the development of virtual environments.

- The material on concurrency is relevant in the wider context of concurrent and parallel programming.

- The material on resource allocation and scheduling features as a major component of operations research.

- Much of the course material is relevant to the design and construction of real-time and dependable systems.

Students are likely to take a greater interest in operating systems if they see themselves as working in the context of a real system rather than some highly simplified and more abstract simulation. In this regard, the open-source movement has made an important contribution to pedagogy in the operating systems area, because the source code for several well-known operating systems is now available free of charge. These public-domain resources make it easier to illustrate aspects of operating systems and can often provide useful examples of how different systems implement particular features. It is worth observing that many of the students are likely to be fired up with the idea of installing Linux (for example) on their own machines.

Students who complete this course should be able to perform the following tasks:

- Summarize the principles underlying the design and construction of a typical operating system, giving particular recognition to the wider applicability of the ideas and the influences from such developments as high-level languages, networking, multimedia, and security concerns.

- Use the facilities of the operating system to achieve a range of simple tasks, including enhancing the functionality by integrating new software components.

- Identify the security issues associated with distributed Web applications and be able to suggest mechanisms leading to a resolution of these problems.

CS230{T,W}. Net-centric Computing

Introduces the structure, implementation, and theoretical underpinnings of computer networking and the applications that have been enabled by that technology.

Prerequisites: CS222w or CS225t

Syllabus:

- Communication and networking: Network standards and standardization bodies; the ISO 7-layer reference model in general and its instantiation in TCP/IP; circuit switching and packet switching; streams and datagrams; physical layer networking concepts; data link layer concepts; Internetworking and routing; transport layer services

- The Web as an example of client-server computing: Web technologies; characteristics of Web servers; role of client computers; nature of the client-server relationship; Web protocols; support tools for Web site creation and Web management; developing Internet information servers; publishing information and applications

- Building Web applications: Protocols at the application layer; principles of Web engineering; database-driven Web sites; remote procedure calls; lightweight distributed objects; the role of middleware; support tools; security issues in distributed object systems; enterprise-wide Web-based applications

- Network management: Review of the issues of network management; issues for Internet service providers; security issues and firewalls; quality of service issues

- Compression and decompression: Review of basic data compression; audio compression and decompression; image compression and decompression; video compression and decompression; performance issues

- Multimedia data technologies: Review of multimedia technologies; multimedia standards; capacity planning and performance issues; input and output devices; MIDI keyboards, synthesizers; storage standards; multimedia servers and file systems; tools to support multimedia development

- Wireless and mobile computing: Overview of the history, evolution, and compatibility of wireless standards; the special problems of wireless and mobile computing; wireless local area networks and satellite-based networks; wireless local loops ; mobile Internet protocol; mobile aware adaption; extending the client-server model to accommodate mobility; mobile data access; the software packages to support mobile and wireless computing; the role of middleware and support tools; performance issues; emerging technologies

Units covered:

PF5	Event-driven programming	2 core hours (of 4)
NC1	Introduction to net-centric computing	2 core hours
NC2	Communication and networking	7 core hours
NC3	Network security	3 core hours
NC4	The Web as an example of client-server computing	3 core hours
NC5	Building Web applications	8 hours
NC6	Network management	2 hours
NC7	Compression and decompression	3 hours
NC8	Multimedia data technologies	3 hours
NC9	Wireless and mobile computing	4 hours
PL6	Object-oriented programming	2 core hours (of 10)
	Elective topics	1 hour

CS240s. Programming Language Translation

Introduces the theory and practice of programming language translation. Topics include compiler design, lexical analysis, parsing, symbol tables, declaration and storage management, code generation, and optimation techniques.

Prerequisites: CS210, CS220

Syllabus:

- Overview of programming languages: History of programming languages; brief survey of programming paradigms; the role of language translation in the programming process

- Fundamental issues in language design: General principles of language design; design goals; typing regimes; data structure models; control structure models; abstraction mechanisms

- Virtual machines: The concept of a virtual machine; hierarchy of virtual machines; intermediate languages

- Introduction to language translation: Comparison of interpreters and compilers; language translation phases; machine-dependent and machine-independent aspects of translation; language translation as a software engineering activity

- Lexical analysis: Application of regular expressions in lexical scanners; hand-coded vs. automatically generated scanners; formal definition of tokens; implementation of finite-state automata

- Syntactic analysis: Formal definition of grammars; BNF and EBNF; bottom-up vs. top-down parsing; tabular vs. recursive-descent parsers; error handling; automatic generation of tabular parsers; symbol table management; the use of tools in support of the translation process

- Models of execution control: Order of evaluation of subexpressions; exceptions and exception handling; runtime systems

- Declaration, modularity, and storage management: Declaration models; parameterization mechanisms; type parameterization; mechanisms for sharing and restricting visibility of declarations; garbage collection

- Type systems: Data type as set of values with set of operations; data types; type-checking models; semantic models of user-defined types; parametric polymorphism; subtype polymorphism; type-checking algorithms

- Interpretation: Iterative vs. recursive interpretation; iterative interpretation of intermediate code; recursive interpretation of a parse tree

- Code generation: Intermediate and object code; intermediate representations; implementation of code generators; code generation by tree walking; context-sensitive translation; register use

- Optimization: Machine-independent optimization; data-flow analysis; loop optimizations; machine-dependent optimization

Units covered:

PL1	Overview of programming languages	2 core hours
PL2	Virtual machines	1 core hour
PL3	Introduction to language translation	2 core hours
PL8	Language translation systems	15 hours
PL9	Type systems	4 hours
	Elective topics	16 hours

Notes:

This course has two distinct but interrelated goals. First, it explores the theory of language translation. Second, it shows how to apply this theory to build compilers and interpreters as well as compiler generators. It covers the building of translators both from scratch and using compiler generators. In the process, the course also identifies and explores the main issues of the design of translators.

As is the case in many computer science courses with a significant theoretical component, visualization tools can improve the quality of lectures and serve as animated lecture notes. The most useful kind of algorithm animations are those that show in a synchronized way both an operational view and a conceptual view of the algorithm steps.

The construction of a compiler/interpreter is a necessary component of this course, so students can obtain the necessary skills. Compiler programming projects, however, are often problematic for the following reasons:

- The size of a compiler implementation is usually much larger than that of the projects students have undertaken in earlier courses.
- Most compiler generators are tabular, which makes the resulting compiler more difficult to debug.

The severity of these problems can be reduced by using declarative scanners and parser generators that produce recursive-descent parsers.

CS250w. Human-Computer Interaction

Presents a comprehensive introduction to the principles and techniques of human-computer interaction.

Prerequisites: introduction to computer science (any implementation of CS103 or CS112), discrete structures (CS106 or CS115)

Syllabus:

- Foundations of human-computer interaction: Motivation; contexts for HCI; human-centered development and evaluation; human performance models; human performance models; accommodating human diversity; principles of good design and good designers; engineering tradeoffs; introduction to usability testing

- Human-centered software evaluation: Setting goals for evaluation; evaluation without users; evaluation with users

- Human-centered software development: Approaches, characteristics, and overview of process; functionality and usability; specifying interaction and presentation; prototyping techniques and tools

- Graphical user-interface design: Choosing interaction styles and interaction techniques; HCI aspects of common widgets; HCI aspects of screen design; handling human failure; beyond simple screen design; multimodal interaction; 3D interaction and virtual reality

- Graphical user-interface programming: Dialogue independence and levels of analysis; widget classes; event management and user interaction; geometry management; GUI builders and UI programming environments; cross-platform design

- HCI aspects of multimedia systems: Categorization and architectures of information; information retrieval and human performance; HCI design of multimedia information systems; speech recognition and natural language processing; information appliances and mobile computing

- HCI aspects of collaboration and communication: Groupware to support specialized tasks; asynchronous group communication; synchronous group communication; online communities; software characters and intelligent agents

Units covered:

PF5	Event-driven programming	2 core hours (of 4)
HC1	Foundations of human-computer interaction	6 core hours
HC2	Building a simple graphical user interface	2 core hours
HC3	Human-centered software evaluation	5 hours
HC4	Human-centered software development	5 hours
HC5	Graphical user-interface design	6 hours
HC6	Graphical user-interface programming	3 hours
HC7	HCI aspects of multimedia systems	5 hours
HC8	HCI aspects of collaboration and communication	3 hours
PL6	Object-oriented programming	2 core hours (of 10)
	Elective topics	1 hour

CS255{s,w}. Computer Graphics

Offers an introduction to computer graphics, which has become an increasingly important area within computer science. Computer graphics, particularly in association with the multimedia aspects of the World Wide Web, have opened up exciting new possibilities for the design of human-computer interfaces. The purpose of this course is to investigate the principles, techniques, and tools that have enabled these advances.

Prerequisites: introduction to computer science (any implementation of CS103 or CS112), discrete structures (CS106 or CS115), linear algebra

Syllabus:

• Graphic systems: Raster and vector graphics systems; video display devices; physical and logical input devices; issues facing the developer of graphical systems

• Fundamental techniques in graphics: Hierarchy of graphics software; using a graphics API; simple color models; homogeneous coordinates; affine transformations; viewing transformation; clipping

• Graphical algorithms: Line-generation algorithms; structure and use of fonts; parametric polynomial curves and surfaces; polygonal representation of 3D objects; parametric polynomial curves and surfaces; introduction to ray tracing; image synthesis, sampling techniques, and anti-aliasing; image enhancement

• Principles of human-computer interaction: Human-centered software development and evaluation

• Graphical user-interface design: Choosing interaction styles and interaction techniques; HCI aspects of interface design; dynamics of color; structuring a view for effective understanding

• Graphical user-interface programming: Graphical widgets; event management and user interaction; GUI builders and programming environments

• Computer animation: Key-frame animation; camera animation; scripting system; animation of articulated structures; motion capture; procedural animation; deformation

• Multimedia techniques: Sound, video, and graphics; design of multimedia systems; tools for multimedia development; virtual reality

Units covered:

AL10	Geometric algorithms	2 hours
HC2	Building a simple graphical user interface	2 core hours
HC3	Human-centered software evaluation	2 hours
HC4	Human-centered software development	2 hours
HC5	Graphical user-interface design	5 hours
HC6	Graphical user-interface programming	5 hours
GV1	Fundamental techniques in graphics	2 core hours
GV2	Graphic systems	1 core hour
GV3	Graphic communication	2 hours
GV4	Geometric modeling	3 hours
GV5	Basic rendering	3 hours
GV8	Computer animation	2 hours
GV10	Virtual reality	2 hours
IM13	Multimedia information and systems	4 hours
SE2	Using APIs	2 core hours (of 5)
	Elective topics	1 hour

Notes:

Computer graphics is extremely exciting to students and can serve as an excellent motivator for students, particularly to the extent that the course structure offers students the opportunity to create graphical systems. Although implementation must be a central component of this course, it is equally important to emphasize the mathematical underpinnings of the area, thereby reinforcing the relationship between theory and practice.

Software tools play a particularly critical role in this course. While it is useful for students to learn basic principles at an abstract level, it is also essential for them to have exposure to sophisticated graphical libraries, which will vastly extend their ability to construct interesting applications. In addition to programmer-oriented graphical APIs, it may make sense to include other packages—multimedia tools, modeling languages, virtual reality—in this course as well.

Students who complete this course should be able to perform the following tasks:

- Offer a meaningful critique of graphical and multimedia interfaces that incorporates an understanding of the principles of HCI design.
- Apply the principles that underpin the design of graphics and multimedia systems.
- Describe the range of tools that can be used to support the development of graphical and multimedia systems.
- Use existing graphics and multimedia packages to develop appropriate graphical applications.

CS260{S,T}. Artificial Intelligence

Introduces students to the fundamental concepts and techniques of artificial intelligence (AI).

Prerequisites: introduction to computer science (any implementation of CS103 or CS112), discrete structures (CS106 or CS115)

Syllabus:

- Fundamental issues in intelligent systems: History of artificial intelligence; philosophical questions; fundamental definitions; philosophical questions; modeling the world; the role of heuristics
- Search and constraint satisfaction: Problem spaces; brute-force search; best-first search; two-player games; constraint satisfaction
- Knowledge representation and reasoning: Review of propositional and predicate logic; resolution and theorem proving; nonmonotonic inference; probabilistic reasoning; Bayes' theorem
- Advanced search: Genetic algorithms; simulated annealing; local search
- Advanced knowledge representation and reasoning: Structured representation; nonmonotonic reasoning; reasoning on action and change; temporal and spatial reasoning; uncertainty; knowledge representation for diagnosis, qualitative representation
- Agents: Definition of agents; successful applications and state-of-the-art agent-based systems; software agents, personal assistants, and information access; multiagent systems
- Machine learning and neural networks: Definition and examples of machine learning; supervised learning; unsupervised learning; reinforcement learning; introduction to neural networks
- AI planning systems: Definition and examples of planning systems; planning as search; operator-based planning; propositional planning

Units covered:

IS1	Fundamental issues in intelligent systems	1 core hour
IS2	Search and constraint satisfaction	5 core hours
IS3	Knowledge representation and reasoning	4 core hours
IS4	Advanced search	6 hours
IS5	Advanced knowledge representation and reasoning	5 hours
IS6	Agents	3 hours
IS8	Machine learning and neural networks	5 hours
IS9	AI planning systems	5 hours
	Elective topics	6 hours

CS261w. AI and Information

Introduces the basics of artificial intelligence and information management.

Prerequisites: introduction to computer science (any implementation of CS103 or CS112), discrete structures (CS106 or CS115)

Syllabus:

- Fundamental issues in intelligent systems: History of artificial intelligence; philosophical questions; fundamental definitions; philosophical questions; modeling the world; the role of heuristics

- Search and constraint satisfaction: Problem spaces; brute-force search; best-first search; two-player games; constraint satisfaction

- Knowledge representation and reasoning: Review of propositional and predicate logic; resolution and theorem proving; nonmonotonic inference; probabilistic reasoning; bayes theorem

- Advanced search: Genetic algorithms; simulated annealing; local search

- Machine learning and neural networks: Definition and examples of machine learning; supervised learning; learning decision trees; learning neural networks; learning belief networks; the nearest neighbor algorithm; learning theory; the problem of overfitting; unsupervised learning; reinforcement learning

- Information models and systems: History and motivation for information systems; information storage and retrieval; information management applications; information capture and representation; analysis and indexing; search, retrieval, linking, navigation; information privacy, integrity, security, and preservation; scalability, efficiency, and effectiveness

- Database systems: History and motivation for database systems; components of database systems; DBMS functions; database architecture and data independence

- Data modeling: Data modeling; conceptual models; object-oriented model; relational data model

- Relational databases: Mapping conceptual schema to a relational schema; entity and referential integrity; relational algebra and relational calculus

- Database query languages: Overview of database languages; SQL; query optimization; QBE and 4th-generation environments; embedding nonprocedural queries in a procedural language; introduction to Object Query Language

Units covered:

IS1	Fundamental issues in intelligent systems	1 core hour
IS2	Search and constraint satisfaction	5 core hours
IS3	Knowledge representation and reasoning	4 core hours
IS4	Advanced search	3 hours
IS8	Machine learning and neural networks	3 hours
IM1	Information models and systems	3 core hours
IM2	Database systems	3 core hours
IM3	Data modeling	4 core hours
IM4	Relational databases	3 hours
IM5	Database query languages	3 hours
SP6	Intellectual property	1 core hour (of 3)
	Elective topics	7 hours

CS262C. Information and Knowledge Management

Uses the idea of information as a unifying theme to investigate a range of issues in computer science, including database systems, artificial intelligence, human-computer interaction, multimedia system, and data communication.

Prerequisites: introduction to computer science (any implementation of CS103 or CS112), discrete structures (CS106 or CS115)

Syllabus:

- Information models and systems: History and motivation for information systems; information storage and retrieval; information management applications; information capture and representation; analysis and indexing; search, retrieval, linking, navigation; information privacy, integrity, security, and preservation; scalability, efficiency, and effectiveness

- Database systems: History and motivation for database systems; components of database systems; DBMS functions; database architecture and data independence; use of a database query language

- Data modeling: Data modeling; conceptual models; object-oriented model; relational data model

- Relational databases: Mapping conceptual schema to a relational schema; entity and referential integrity; relational algebra and relational calculus

- Search and constraint satisfaction: Problem spaces; brute-force search; best-first search; two-player games; constraint satisfaction

- Knowledge representation and reasoning: Review of propositional and predicate logic; resolution and theorem proving; nonmonotonic inference; probabilistic reasoning; bayes theorem

- Foundations of human-computer interaction: Motivation; contexts for HCI; human-centered development and evaluation; human performance models; human performance models; accommodating human diversity; principles of good design and good designers; engineering tradeoffs; introduction to usability testing

- Fundamental issues in intelligent systems: History of artificial intelligence; philosophical questions; fundamental definitions; philosophical questions; modeling the world; the role of heuristics

- Cryptographic algorithms: Historical overview of cryptography; private-key cryptography and the key-exchange problem; public-key cryptography; digital signatures; security protocols

- Introduction to compression and decompression: Encoding and decoding algorithms; lossless and lossy compression

- Multimedia information and systems

- Intellectual property: Foundations of intellectual property; copyrights, patents, and trade secrets; software piracy; software patents; transnational issues concerning intellectual property

- Privacy and civil liberties: Ethical and legal basis for privacy protection; privacy implications of massive database systems; technological strategies for privacy protection; freedom of expression in cyberspace; international and intercultural implications

Units covered:

AL9	Cryptographic algorithms	3 hours
NC7	Compression and decompression	2 hours
HC1	Foundations of human-computer interaction	4 core hours (of 6)
IS1	Fundamental issues in intelligent systems	1 core hour
IS2	Search and constraint satisfaction	5 core hours
IS3	Knowledge representation and reasoning	4 core hours
IM1	Information models and systems	3 core hours
IM2	Database systems	3 core hours
IM3	Data modeling	4 core hours
IM4	Relational databases	4 hours
IM13	Multimedia information and systems	2 hours
SP6	Intellectual property	3 core hours
SP7	Privacy and civil liberties	2 core hours

Notes:

Given that it addresses a mix of topics from such areas as databases, artificial intelligence, and human-computer interaction, it is unlikely that courses like CS262c appear in existing curricula. We believe, however, that courses of this sort, which take a unifying theme and use that to provide structure to an otherwise diverse set of topics, provide a useful way to develop a "crosscutting core" that focuses on broad themes rather than specific artifacts. In this case, the broad theme is that of the management, representation, and manipulation of information. It addresses, for example, the entire area of storing, retrieving, encoding, and managing information, whether for database use, intelligent systems use, telecommunications, or graphics. It also addresses the social and ethical issues related to information management, such as the ownership of intellectual property and individual privacy rights.

More than the other courses in the compressed approach, CS262c has room for a range of interesting topics outside the core. This implementation, for example, includes such topics as cryptography, compression, and multimedia, all of which fit the theme of information management. Depending on the particular strengths of the faculty and the interests of the students, other topics could be incorporated as well.

CS270T. Databases

Introduces the concepts and techniques of database systems.

Prerequisites: introduction to computer science (any implementation of CS103 or CS112), discrete structures (CS106 or CS115)

Syllabus:

- Information models and systems: History and motivation for information systems; information storage and retrieval; information management applications; information capture and representation; analysis and indexing; search, retrieval, linking, navigation; information privacy, integrity, security, and preservation; scalability, efficiency, and effectiveness

- Database systems: History and motivation for database systems; components of database systems; DBMS functions; database architecture and data independence

- Data modeling: Data modeling; conceptual models; object-oriented model; relational data model

- Relational databases: Mapping conceptual schema to a relational schema; entity and referential integrity; relational algebra and relational calculus

- Database query languages: Overview of database languages; SQL; query optimization; 4th-generation environments; embedding non-procedural queries in a procedural language; introduction to Object Query Language

- Relational database design: Database design; functional dependency; normal forms; multivalued dependency; join dependency; representation theory

- Transaction processing: Transactions; failure and recovery; concurrency control

- Distributed databases: Distributed data storage; distributed query processing; distributed transaction model; concurrency control; homogeneous and heterogeneous solutions; client-server

- Physical database design: Storage and file structure; indexed files; hashed files; signature files; b-trees; files with dense index; files with variable length records; database efficiency and tuning

Units covered:

HC1	Foundations of human-computer interaction	2 core hours (of 6)
IM1	Information models and systems	3 core hours
IM2	Database systems	3 core hours
IM3	Data modeling	4 core hours
IM4	Relational databases	5 hours
IM5	Database query languages	4 hours
IM6	Relational database design	4 hours
IM7	Transaction processing	3 hours
IM8	Distributed databases	3 hours
IM9	Physical database design	3 hours
SP6	Intellectual property	3 core hours
SP7	Privacy and civil liberties	2 core hours
	Elective topics	1 hour

CS271s. Information Management

The task of organizing large volumes of information of potentially different kinds is a daunting one. Typically, resolution of the associated problems depends on the use of an underlying database technology, often involving networking. This course addresses both the technical and social issues involved.

Prerequisites: introduction to computer science (any implementation of CS103 or CS112), discrete structures (CS106 or CS115), CS120

Syllabus:

- Overview of information management: History and motivation for information systems; common problems of information management; the business perspective

- Social issues in information technology: Intellectual property; computer crime; privacy; security and civil liberties; the need for a legal and ethical framework; guidelines for computer use

- Introduction to database systems: History and motivation for database systems; components of database systems; DBMS functions; database architecture and data independence; use of a database query language; the relational model

- Building databases: Underlying methodology; database query languages; particular database issues

- Information systems to serve particular purposes: Intranets and extranets; the information retrieval problem

- Design and development of information systems: Database design; relational database design; life-cycle issues

- Security and control issues: Overview of problems and standard solutions; database integrity; transactions; the role of encryption

- Evaluation of information systems

Units covered:

IM1	Information models and systems	2 core hours (of 3)
IM2	Database systems	2 core hours (of 3)
IM3	Data modeling	4 core hours
IM4	Relational databases	5 hours
IM5	Database query languages	5 hours
IM6	Relational database design	2 hours
IM7	Transaction processing	3 hours
IM11	Information storage and retrieval	2 hours
IM13	Multimedia information and systems	2 hours
IM14	Digital libraries	2 hours
SP2	Social context of computing	1 core hour (of 3)
SP3	Methods and tools of analysis	2 core hours
SP4	Professional and ethical responsibilities	2 core hours (of 3)
SP5	Risks and liabilities of computer-based systems	1 core hour (of 2)
SP6	Intellectual property	2 core hours (of 3)
SP7	Privacy and civil liberties	2 core hours
	Elective topics	1 hour

Notes:

The material for this class builds on the work of earlier classes, in particular CS140s. The focus of the course is on the decisions that need to be made about how best to manage complex information and how to store it in a manner that ensures ease of retrieval, with a simple and natural conceptual framework.

With the development of any information system, there will be imperatives of various kinds. One important one is the business or commercial perspective. Accordingly, this course can be used as a vehicle for introducing students to the world of business and commerce and to the imperatives—including the ethical ones—that operate in this environment. But ultimately there will be an underlying life-cycle model with a requirements phase, a specification phase, a design phase, a development phase, as well as validation and verification phases. Ideas from human-computer interaction and networking will also be relevant. Students need to be exposed to these ideas to convey the notion of a disciplined and considered approach to the development of these systems.

At some level, all information systems depend on database technology. Many other issues, however, also come into play including human factors and the dynamics of the World Wide Web. Examples of good practice can be made available by exposing students to suitable Web sites and to suitable digital libraries.

Students typically respond positively and responsibly to instances of computer disasters and malpractice. Such illustrations and case studies can be used as a vehicle to engender an appreciation of the importance of a study of social and ethical issues. Indeed, it is vital to have an approach which ensures that students understand the importance and relevance of this topic.

In the wider environment of the university, ideas from this course can be reinforced by appealing to other sets of rules to which students must adhere. These systems of rules provide living examples of the discipline that must be practiced within laboratories and the management practices that should be associated with the running of computer systems by support staff.

Students who complete this course should be able to perform the following tasks:

- Describe the different business and other imperatives (including legal and ethical) that influence the development of information systems, and this includes the requirements of remote access.
- Apply the basic principles of database technology.
- Explain the potential of distributed information management systems and the problems such systems entail.
- Identify common security and control mechanisms associated with information management and be able to apply these mechanisms effectively.
- Justify the need for codes of conduct and a legal framework for computer use.
- Give examples of several computing applications that raise sensitive legal and ethical concerns.

CS280T. Social and Professional Issues

Introduces students to the social and professional issues that arise in the context of computing.

Prerequisites: introduction to computer science (any implementation of CS103 or CS112)

Syllabus:

- History of computing: Prehistory—the world before 1946; history of computer hardware, software, networking; pioneers of computing

- Social context of computing: Introduction to the social implications of computing; social implications of networked communication; growth of, control of, and access to the Internet; gender-related issues; international issues

- Methods and tools of analysis: Making and evaluating ethical arguments; identifying and evaluating ethical choices; understanding the social context of design; identifying assumptions and values

- Professional and ethical responsibilities: Community values and the laws by which we live; the nature of professionalism; various forms of professional credentialing and the advantages and disadvantages; the role of the professional in public policy; maintaining awareness of consequences; ethical dissent and whistle-blowing; codes of ethics, conduct, and practice; dealing with harassment and discrimination; "Acceptable use" policies for computing in the workplace

- Risks and liabilities of computer-based systems: Historical examples of software risks; implications of software complexity; risk assessment and management

- Intellectual property: Foundations of intellectual property; copyrights, patents, and trade secrets; software piracy; software patents; transnational issues concerning intellectual property

- Privacy and civil liberties: Ethical and legal basis for privacy protection; privacy implications of massive database systems; technological strategies for privacy protection; freedom of expression in cyberspace; international and intercultural implications

- Computer crime: History and examples of computer crime; "Cracking" and its effects; viruses, worms, and Trojan horses; crime prevention strategies

- Economic issues in computing: Monopolies and their economic implications; effect of skilled labor supply and demand on the quality of computing products; pricing strategies in the computing domain; differences in access to computing resources and the possible effects thereof

- Philosophical frameworks: Philosophical frameworks, particularly utilitarianism and deontological theories; problems of ethical relativism; scientific ethics in historical perspective; differences in scientific and philosophical approaches

Units covered:

SP1	History of computing	1 core hour
SP2	Social context of computing	3 core hours
SP3	Methods and tools of analysis	2 core hours
SP4	Professional and ethical responsibilities	3 core hours
SP5	Risks and liabilities of computer-based systems	2 core hours
SP6	Intellectual property	3 core hours
SP7	Privacy and civil liberties	2 core hours
SP8	Computer crime	3 hours
SP9	Economic issues in computing	2 hours
SP10	Philosophical frameworks	2 hours
	Elective topics	17 hours

Notes:

A computer science program can incorporate social and professional issues into the curriculum in many different ways. In many ways, the ideal approach is to include discussion of this material in a wide variety of courses so that students have the chance to consider these issues in the context of each technical area. Unfortunately, this strategy sometimes fails to have the desired effect. Unless faculty members commit to give this material serious consideration, social and professional issues are often given low priority in the context of other courses, to the sometimes wind up being left out altogether in the press to cover more traditional material.

To ensure that students have a real opportunity to study this material, many departments choose to devote an entire course to social and professional issues. Programs that adopt this strategy must make sure that they make the material relevant to students by discussing these issues in the context of concrete examples that arise in computer science.

CS290T. Software Development

Provides an intensive, implementation-oriented introduction to the software-development techniques used to create medium-scale interactive applications, focusing on the use of large object-oriented libraries to create well-designed graphical user interfaces. Topics include event-driven programming, computer graphics, human-computer interaction (HCI), and graphical user interfaces.

Prerequisites: introduction to computer science (any implementation of CS103 or CS112), discrete structures (CS106 or CS115)

Syllabus:

- Event-driven programming: Event-handling methods; event propagation; managing concurrency in event handling; exception handling

- Using application programmer interfaces (APIs): API programming; class browsers and related tools; programming by example; debugging in the api environment; component-based computing

- Computer graphics: Raster and vector graphics systems; video display devices; physical and logical input devices; issues facing the developer of graphical systems

- Introduction to human-computer interaction (HCI): Motivation and context; human-centered development and evaluation; human performance models; accommodating human diversity; principles of good design and good designers; engineering tradeoffs; introduction to usability testing

- Human-centered software evaluation: Setting goals for evaluation; evaluation strategies

- Human-centered software development: Approaches, characteristics, and overview of process; prototyping techniques and tools

- Graphical user interfaces (GUIs): Graphical APIs; choosing interaction styles and interaction techniques; HCI aspects of graphical design (layout, color, fonts, labeling); geometry management; programming environments for creating GUIs

- Software development techniques: Object-oriented analysis and design; component-level design; software requirements and specifications; prototyping; characteristics of maintainable software; software reuse; team management; project scheduling

Units covered:

PF5	Event-driven programming	4 core hours
HC1	Foundations of human-computer interaction	6 core hours
HC2	Building a simple graphical user interface	2 core hours
HC3	Human-centered software evaluation	1 hour
HC4	Human-centered software development	1 hour
HC5	Graphical user-interface design	3 hours
HC6	Graphical user-interface programming	3 hours
GV1	Fundamental techniques in graphics	2 core hours
GV2	Graphic systems	1 core hour
SE1	Software design	2 core hours (of 8)
SE2	Using APIs	3 core hours (of 5)
SE3	Software tools and environments	2 core hours (of 3)
SE5	Software requirements and specifications	2 core hours (of 4)
SE6	Software validation	1 core hour (of 3)
SE7	Software evolution	2 core hours (of 3)
SE8	Software project management	2 core hours (of 3)
	Elective topics	3 hours

CS291s. Software Development and Systems Programming

Extends the ides of software design and development from the introductory programming sequence to encompass the problems encountered in large-scale programs. Topics include software engineering techniques for programming in the large, advanced issues in object-oriented prorgamming, design patterns, client-server computing, and principles of interface design.

Prerequisites: introduction to computer science (any implementation of CS103 or CS112), CS210s

Syllabus:

- Large-system engineering: Separate compilation; design issues; verification and validation; integrating components; documentation

- Advanced issues in object-oriented programming: Modularity; storage management; parallelism; event-centered programming; common design patterns; software reuse

- Client-server computing: Software support needed for client and server implementation; varieties of server structures; strategies for client-server design; tools for client-server system development; middleware

- The Web as an example of client-server computing: Web technologies; characteristics of Web servers; role of client computers; the applet concept; Web protocols; support tools for Web site creation and Web management; publishing information and applications; performance issues

- Introduction to human-computer interaction (HCI): Human-centered software design and evaluation; relevant psychological and cognitive background theory; user modeling; teachability and learnability concerns

- Principles of HCI design: Building interactive systems; guidelines for interface design; illustrations of good and bad examples of interface design; tools and classes that support interface design; metrics

- Graphical user-interface design: Choosing interaction styles and interaction techniques; HCI aspects of common widgets; HCI aspects of screen design; special problems associated with color, sound, video, and multimedia

Units covered:

PF3	Fundamental data structures	6 core hours (of 14)
PF5	Event-driven programming	4 core hours
NC4	The Web as an example of client-server computing	2 core hours (of 3)
HC1	Foundations of human-computer interaction	3 core hours (of 6)
HC3	Human-centered software evaluation	2 hours
HC4	Human-centered software development	2 hours
HC5	Graphical user-interface design	2 hours
HC6	Graphical user-interface programming	2 hours
PL6	Object-oriented programming	4 core hours (of 10)
SE1	Software design	2 core hours (of 8)
SP5	Risks and liabilities of computer-based systems	1 core hour (of 2)
SE2	Using APIs	3 core hours (of 5)
SE4	Software processes	1 core hour (of 2)
SE5	Software requirements and specifications	2 core hours (of 4)
SE6	Software validation	2 core hours (of 3)
SE7	Software evolution	1 core hour (of 3)
SE8	Software project management	1 core hour (of 3)

Notes:

An important stage in the education of a good software developer consists of making the transition from programming-in-the-small to programming-in-the-large. The purpose of this course is to bridge that gap by enabling students to develop large programs in well defined stages. In the process, this course explores the requirements at each stage of the development along with various issues of quality control. In the practical component of the course, students learn to appreciate the range of facilities that a typical object-oriented language offers and to apply sound approaches to software design in the large-system environment.

Moving from programming-in-the-small to programming-in-the-large, however, is not straightforward. Students need to be provided with a range of reasonable illustrations and examples for them to attempt. In the syllabus presented here, those illustrations are drawn from net-centric computing and user-interface design. Other possibilities, however, exist as well. For example, courses designed to introduce programming-in-the-large might be based on e-commerce, groupware, or other kinds of sophisticated application servers. In every case, it is important to emphasize the importance of complexity management by showing how large tasks can be broken down into smaller tasks that can often be addressed through the selection of appropriate algorithms. In this way, students see the relevance of earlier course work, including the study of algorithms and complexity.

With the transition to larger systems, the quality of the user interface becomes increasingly vital, because the interface has a significant bearing on the usability of software. This course therefore includes a study of the basic principles of human-computer interaction (HCI). While human-computer interaction can be seen as a subject in its own right or interpreted as an aspect of software engineering, there is merit in taking the former view, since the basic ideas will be relevant in many contexts. An understanding of these same principles provides essential insight into the design and development of other software systems including Web sites, multimedia systems, and so forth.

A useful starting point in the study of HCI consists of having students evaluate interfaces of various kinds, making sure that they are exposed to both good and bad practice. Ultimately, however, the students must demonstrate their understanding of the principles by designing an interface of some sophistication. An important aspect of the practical component of HCI lies in exposing students to state-of-the-art software that supports such development, including special-purpose tools and class libraries to support interface development. The laboratory aspect of this course can also benefit from the use of design languages and associated tools.

Students who complete this course should be able to perform the following tasks:

- Apply guidelines for the design of application software and user interfaces.
- Apply the principles of program design (involving the design and development of a range of objects) to the construction of a significant piece of software, justifying the design decisions made at each stage and addressing the relevant quality issues.
- Identify the basic techniques that result in efficient and effective ways of building large software systems and be able to use those techniques in practice.
- Discuss the power and potential of net-centric computing, including both the technical issues involved and the range of software needed to exploit this technology.
- Apply the principles associated with the design and development to a range of Web applications.

- Outline the theories that underpin the design and development of human-computer interfaces.
- Assess in a systematic fashion the quality of the interfaces in a range of software systems.

CS292{C,W}. Software Development and Professional Practice

Combines a range of topics integral to the design, implementation, and testing of a medium-scale software system with the practical experience of implementing such a project as a member of a programmer team. In addition to material on software engineering, this course treats also includes material on professionalism and ethical responsibilities in software development and human-computer interaction.

Prerequisites: CS226c and CS262c, or CS221w and CS250w

Syllabus:

- Event-driven programming: Event-handling methods; event propagation; exception handling

- Foundations of human-computer interaction: Human-centered development and evaluation; human performance models; accommodating human diversity; principles of good design and good designers; engineering tradeoffs; introduction to usability testing

- Using APIs: API programming; class browsers and related tools; programming by example; debugging in the API environment; introduction to component-based computing

- Building a simple graphical user interface: Principles of graphical user interfaces; GUI toolkits

- Graphic systems: Raster and vector graphics systems; video display devices; physical and logical input devices; issues facing the developer of graphical systems

- Software processes: Software life-cycle and process models; process assessment models; software process metrics

- Software requirements and specifications: Requirements elicitation; requirements analysis modeling techniques; functional and nonfunctional requirements; prototyping; basic concepts of formal specification techniques

- Software design: Fundamental design concepts and principles; design patterns; software architecture; structured design; object-oriented analysis and design; component-level design; design for reuse

- Software validation: Validation planning; testing fundamentals, including test plan creation and test case generation; black-box and white-box testing techniques; unit, integration, validation, and system testing; object-oriented testing; inspections

- Software evolution: Software maintenance; characteristics of maintainable software; reengineering; legacy systems; software reuse

- Software project management: Team management; project scheduling; software measurement and estimation techniques; risk analysis; software quality assurance; software configuration management; project management tools

- Social context of computing: Introduction to the social implications of computing; social implications of networked communication; growth of, control of, and access to the Internet; gender-related issues; international issues

- Methods and tools of analysis: Making and evaluating ethical arguments; identifying and evaluating ethical choices; understanding the social context of design; identifying assumptions and values

- Professional and ethical responsibilities: Community values and the laws by which we live; the nature of professionalism; various forms of professional credentialing and the advantages and disadvantages; the role of the professional in public policy; maintaining awareness of consequences; ethical dissent and whistle-blowing; codes of ethics, conduct, and practice; dealing with harassment and discrimination; "Acceptable use" policies for computing in the workplace

- Risks and liabilities of computer-based systems: Historical examples of software risks; implications of software complexity; risk assessment and management

Units covered:

PF5	Event-driven programming	2 core hours (of 4)
HC1	Foundations of human-computer interaction	2 core hours (of 6)
HC2	Building a simple graphical user interface	2 core hours
GV1	Fundamental techniques in graphics	2 core hours
GV2	Graphic systems	1 core hour
SP2	Social context of computing	3 core hours
SP3	Methods and tools of analysis	2 core hours
SP4	Professional and ethical responsibilities	3 core hours
SP5	Risks and liabilities of computer-based systems	2 core hours
SE1	Software design	4 core hours (of 8)
SE2	Using APIs	3 core hours (of 5)
SE3	Software tools and environments	1 core hour (of 3)
SE4	Software processes	2 core hours
SE5	Software requirements and specifications	3 core hours (of 4)
SE6	Software validation	2 core hours (of 3)
SE7	Software evolution	3 core hours
SE8	Software project management	3 core hours

B.4 Advanced courses

The CC2001 Task Force has decided not to include in the printed report full descriptions of the advanced courses unless those courses are part of one of the curricular tracks described in Chapter 8. Instead, we plan to create Web pages for these courses, which will be accessible from the CC2001 Web page. A list of the advanced courses we propose appears in Figure B-4.

Figure B-4. Advanced courses by area

Discrete Structures (DS)
CS301. Combinatorics
CS302. Probability and Statistics
CS303. Coding and Information Theory

Computational Science (CN)
CS304. Computational Science
CS305. Numerical Analysis
CS306. Operations Research
CS307. Simulation and Modeling
CS308. Scientific Computing
CS309. Computational Biology

Algorithms and Complexity (AL)
CS310. Advanced Algorithmic Analysis
CS311. Automata and Language Theory
CS312. Cryptography
CS313. Geometric Algorithms
CS314. Parallel Algorithms

Architecture and Organization (AR)
CS320. Advanced Computer Architecture
CS321. Parallel Architectures
CS322. System on a Chip
CS323. VLSI Development
CS324. Device Development

Operating Systems (OS)
CS325. Advanced Operating Systems
CS326. Concurrent and Distributed Systems
CS327. Dependable Computing
CS328. Fault Tolerance
CS329. Real-Time Systems

Net-Centric Computing (NC)
CS330. Advanced Computer Networks
CS331. Distributed Systems
CS332. Wireless and Mobile Computing
CS333. Cluster Computing
CS334. Data Compression
CS335. Network Management
CS336. Network Security
CS337. Enterprise Networking
CS338. Programming for the World Wide Web

Programming Languages (PL)
CS340. Compiler Construction
CS341. Programming Language Design
CS342. Programming Language Semantics
CS343. Programming Paradigms
CS344. Functional Programming
CS345. Logic Programming
CS346. Scripting Languages

Human-Computer Interaction (HC)
CS350. Human-Centered Design and Evaluation
CS351. Graphical User Interfaces
CS352. Multimedia Systems Development
CS353. Interactive Systems Development
CS354. Computer-Supported Cooperative Work

Graphics and Visual Computing (GV)
CS355. Advanced Computer Graphics
CS356. Computer Animation
CS357. Visualization
CS358. Virtual Reality
CS359. Genetic Algorithms

Intelligent Systems (IS)
CS360. Intelligent Systems
CS361. Automated Reasoning
CS362. Knowledge-Based Systems
CS363. Machine Learning
CS364. Planning Systems
CS365. Natural Language Processing
CS366. Agents
CS367. Robotics
CS368. Symbolic Computation
CS369. Genetic Algorithms

Information Management (IM)
CS370. Advanced Database Systems
CS371. Database Design
CS372. Transaction Processing
CS373. Distributed and Object Databases
CS374. Data Mining
CS375. Data Warehousing
CS376. Multimedia Information Systems
CS377. Digital Libraries

Social and Professional Issues (SP)
CS380. Professional Practice
CS381. Social Context of Computing
CS382. Computers and Ethics
CS383. Computing Economics
CS384. Computer Law
CS385. Intellectual Property
CS386. Privacy and Civil Liberties

Software Engineering (SE)
CS390. Advanced Software Development
CS391. Software Engineering
CS392. Software Design
CS393. Software Engineering and Formal Specification
CS394. Empirical Software Engineering
CS395. Software Process Improvement
CS396. Component-Based Computing
CS397. Programming Environments
CS398. Safety-Critical Systems

B.5 Project courses

As we discuss in section 9.3, we believe that it is critical for all undergraduates to complete a significant team project as part of their undergraduate program. In some cases, this experience may be integrated into existing courses, such as those in software engineering. In other cases, however, it is appropriate to offer standalone project courses that allow students to integrate the many concepts and skills they have learned as undergraduates in the context of a significant project.

The curriculum descriptions in this report refer to two different implementations of a project course. The first is

CS490. Capstone Project

which provides a one-semester capstone experience. The second is the two-semester sequence

CS491. Capstone Project I
CS492. Capstone Project II

which makes it possible for students to complete a much more ambitious project over the course of a full year.

The design of these courses will vary greatly from institution to institution. In some programs, the project course may include lectures, particularly if the earlier courses do not cover the full set of required units in the core. In any event, we expect that any project course will provide coverage of some of the material from the body of knowledge, as illustrated in the following table:

HC1	Foundations of human-computer interaction	2 core hours (of 6)
HC5	Graphical user-interface design	2 hours
HC6	Graphical user-interface programming	2 hours
SE1	Software design	4 core hours (of 8)
SE2	Using APIs	3 core hours (of 5)
SE3	Software tools and environments	3 core hours
SE4	Software processes	2 core hours
SE5	Software requirements and specifications	2 core hours (of 4)
SE6	Software validation	3 core hours
SE7	Software evolution	2 core hours (of 3)
SE8	Software project management	3 core hours
	Team management	2 hours
	Communications skills	2 hours

Regardless of whether these topics are covered in lecture or are simply acquired in the completion of the work, the focus of the course must remain on the project, which gives students the chance to reinforce through practice the concepts they have learned earlier in a more theoretical way.

ASSOCIATION FOR COMPUTING MACHINERY (ACM)
1515 Broadway, New York, NY 10036 USA
http://www.acm.org; 1.800.342.6626 (USA and Canada) or +212.626.0500 (Global)

Mission: ACM is an international scientific and educational organization dedicated to advancing the art, science, engineering and application of information technology. It serves both professional and public interests by fostering an open interchange of information and by promoting the highest professional and ethical standards. Founded in 1947, the Association for Computing Machinery is the largest and oldest educational and scientific society for computing professionals in the world. It keeps its members up to date on new trends, directions and developments in computing and emerging technologies.

Activities: ACM carries out its mission through conferences, publications educational programs, public awareness activities and special interest groups. It sponsors nearly 100 conferences annually, including conferences on Computers, Freedom and Privacy (CFP); Computer Graphics (SIGGRAPH); and Object-Oriented Programming Systems, Languages and Applications (OOPSLA).

Organization Structure: ACM's more than 75,000 members come from industry, academia and government institutions around the world. Through its membership, volunteers serve on various ACM boards, committees and task forces that comprise ACM's governing structure.

Principals: Executive Director and Chief Executive Officer, Dr. John R. White, was manager of the Computer Science Laboratory at Xerox PARC (Palo Alto Research Center). President, Dr. Stephen R. Bourne, entrepreneur in residence of El Dorado Ventures, designed the UNIX Command Language known as the "Bourne Shell." He has held senior engineering management positions at leading computer systems and networking companies including Sun Microsystems, Digital Equipment, Silicon Graphics, and Cisco Systems. Vice President Maria Klawe is dean of science and computer science professor at the University of British Columbia. Dr. David Wise, computer science professor at Indiana University, is Secretary/Treasurer.

Publications: ACM publishes, distributes and archives more than two dozen publications that provide original research and first-hand perspectives from the world's leading thinkers in computing and information technologies. *Communications of the ACM*, our flagship publication, includes as contributors some of the most knowledgeable and respected people in the field. Other publications include *Crossroads*, the ACM student magazine; *interactions*, for human and computer interaction; and *Intelligence*, covering trends in artificial intelligence. ACM's newest publications, which are web-based (www.acm.org), include *ACM TECHNews*, a news digest for busy IT professionals; *Ubiquity*, a magazine and forum for critical and in-depth analysis on IT issues; and *e-Learn*, an on-line magazine on distance learning.

ACM Portal: The ACM Portal is the gateway to the ACM Digital Library and the ACM Guide. The ACM Digital Library is a comprehensive collection of more than 20 ACM publications online, including a 40+-year archive of journals, magazines and ACM conference proceedings. The ACM Guide provides access to vast bibliographic sources from computing books, journals, proceedings and theses. Researchers are able to execute elaborate queries across both full text in the Digital Library and bibliographic citations in the Guide. The ACM Portal also enables users to create their own carrel within the library, to organize, store and share articles of interest, and to build bibliographies for future reference.

Special Interest Groups: ACM's 34 Special Interest Groups (SIGs) address the varied needs of today's IT professionals, including computer graphics, human interfaces, artificial intelligence, data mining, mobile communications, programming language and networking. Each SIG organizes itself around specific activities that best serve its practitioner and research-based constituencies. Many SIGs sponsor leading conferences and workshops, produce newsletters and other publications, and support e-mail forums for information exchange.

Annual Awards: Among the honors that ACM bestows each year are the A.M. Turing Award (called the "Nobel Prize of Computing," by *Wired* magazine); the Grace Murray Hopper Award for young computer professionals; the Paris Kanellakis Theory and Practice Award; Karl V. Karlstrom Outstanding Educator Award; and the Allen Newell Award honoring contributions that bridge computer science and other disciplines.

IEEE COMPUTER SOCIETY

Publications Office, 10662 Los Vaqueros Circle, Los Alamitos, CA 90720 USA
http://computer.org Phone: +1 714 821 8380 Fax +1 714 821 4641

Mission: The IEEE Computer Society is dedicated to advancing the theory, practice, and application of computer and information processing technology. With nearly 100,000 members, it is the world's leading organization of computing professionals. Founded in 1946, it is the largest technical society within the IEEE.

Activities: The Computer Society fulfills its mission through conferences, publications, technical committees, standards working groups, and local and student chapters. It sponsors or co-sponsors over 140 conferences, symposia, and workshops annually on topics ranging from computer animation to virtual reality.

Organization Structure: The Computer Society's nearly 100,000 members come from industry, academia, and government institutions around the world. Through its membership, volunteers serve on various boards and committees that comprise the society's structure.

Principals: Executive Director, Dr. David W. Hennage, has more than 30 years experience managing and leading associations in the engineering, scientific, and education fields. President, Dr. Willis K. King, has been involved in Computer Society activities for more than 20 years. Dr. King has been a faculty member in the Department of Computer Science at the University of Houston since 1969.

Publications: The IEEE Computer Society publishes, distributes, and archives more than 20 periodicals that provide peer-reviewed articles and research papers for all areas of computing, including: artificial intelligence, computer hardware, graphics, networking, IT, software development, multimedia, and more. Award-winning *Computer* magazine is part of the basic membership package. Published monthly, *Computer* keeps members informed of the latest technology news, industry trends, and professional issues.

Digital Library: The Computer Society's Digital Library is a comprehensive online collection of 18 society periodicals, and over 850 conference proceedings. The periodicals archive is from 1988 forward, and the conference proceedings archive is from 1995 forward. With over 68,000 articles and papers, the Digital Library is a valuable research tool for computing professionals everywhere.

Technical Committees: The society's Technical committees (TCs) are global networks of professionals with common interests in specific areas of computing, who meet through electronic dialogue or at conferences, and range in size from 500 to 10,000 members. There are 41 TCs that specialize in such areas as computer architecture, operating systems, the Internet, software engineering, and security to name a few. Most TCs publish and distribute newsletters free to members.

Distance Learning Campus: The Computer Society offers its members 100 online training courses through its Distance Learning program. Subjects covered include Java, project management, Cisco, HTML, Unix, CompTIA, and Windows network security to name a few. All courses are vendor-certified, and many focus on helping members prepare for certification exams. This service requires a minimum 56K Internet connection, and is free to members.

Standards Working Groups: The IEEE Computer Society is a leader in developing broadly accepted, technically excellent standards on the computing industry. There are over 200 working groups related to the society's 11 Standards Committees. Members are invited to participate in standards development, and thousands do using their professional expertise to gain stature, serve the public interest, and keep their employers informed.

Awards: To recognize members for their outstanding achievements, the society sponsors an active and prestigious awards program. The awards honor technical achievements as well as service to the profession and the society.

Press Operating Committee

Chair
Mark J. Christensen
Independent Consultant

Editor-in-Chief
Mike Williams
Department of Computer Science, University of Calgary

Board Members

Roger U. Fujii, *Vice President, Logicon Technology Solutions*
Richard Thayer, *Professor Emeritus, California State University, Sacramento*
Sallie Sheppard, *Professor Emeritus, Texas A&M University*
Deborah Plummer, *Group Managing Editor, Press*

IEEE Computer Society Executive Staff
David Hennage, *Executive Director*
Angela Burgess, *Publisher*

IEEE Computer Society Publications

The world-renowned IEEE Computer Society publishes, promotes, and distributes a wide variety of authoritative computer science and engineering texts. These books are available from most retail outlets. Visit the CS Store at *http://computer.org* for a list of products.

IEEE Computer Society Proceedings

The IEEE Computer Society also produces and actively promotes the proceedings of more than 160 acclaimed international conferences each year in multimedia formats that include hard and softcover books, CD-ROMs, videos, and on-line publications.

For information on the IEEE Computer Society proceedings, please e-mail to csbooks@computer.org or write to Proceedings, IEEE Computer Society, P.O. Box 3014, 10662 Los Vaqueros Circle, Los Alamitos, CA 90720-1314. Telephone +1-714-821-8380. Fax +1-714-761-1784.

Additional information regarding the Computer Society, conferences and proceedings, CD-ROMs, videos, and books can also be accessed from our web site at *http://computer.org/cspress*

Revised October 29, 2001